T5-BPY-903

INDIVIDUALISM AND COMMUNITY

The State in Marx and Early Anarchism

JEFFREY H. BARKER

CONTRIBUTIONS IN POLITICAL SCIENCE, NUMBER 143

GREENWOOD PRESS
NEW YORK • WESTPORT, CONNECTICUT • LONDON

Library of Congress Cataloging-in-Publication Data

Barker, Jeffrey H., 1957-
  Individualism and community.

  (Contributions in political science, ISSN 0147-1066 ;
no. 143)
  Bibliography: p.
  Includes index.
  1. Communist state—History—19th century.
2. Marx, Karl, 1818-1883.   3. Anarchism and anarchists—
History—19th century.   I. Title.   II. Series.
JC474.B346   1986   321.9'2   85-17707
ISBN 0-313-24706-4 (lib. bdg. : alk. paper)

Copyright © 1986 by Jeffrey H. Barker

All rights reserved. No portion of this book may be
reproduced, by any process or technique, without the
express written consent of the publisher.

Library of Congress Catalog Card Number: 85-17707
ISBN: 0-313-24706-4
ISSN: 0147-1066

First published in 1986

Greenwood Press, Inc.
88 Post Road West
Westport, Connecticut 06881

Printed in the United States of America

The paper used in this book complies with the
Permanent Paper Standard issued by the National
Information Standards Organization (Z39.48-1984).

10 9 8 7 6 5 4 3 2 1

INDIVIDUALISM AND COMMUNITY

Recent Titles in
Contributions in Political Science
Series Editor: Bernard K. Johnpoll

JC
474
.B346
1986

Copyright Acknowledgments

Grateful acknowledgment is given for permission to reprint the following:

Excerpts from *The Economic and Philosophic Manuscripts of 1844* by Karl Marx, edited and introduced by Dirk J. Struik, translated by Martin Milligan. © 1964. Reprinted by permission of International Publishers Co., Inc., New York.

Excerpts from *The Poverty of Philosophy: Response to "The Philosophy of Poverty" of M. Proudhon* by Karl Marx. © 1973. Reprinted by permission of International Publishers Co., Inc., New York.

Excerpts from *Critique of the Gotha Programme* by Karl Marx, edited and translation revised by C.P. Dutt. © 1973. Reprinted by permission of International Publishers Co., Inc., New York.

Excerpts from *Marx-Engels Collected Works,* volumes I, III, IV, XI by Karl Marx and Friedrich Engels. © 1975. Reprinted by permission of International Publishers Co., Inc., New York.

Excerpts from *Anarchism and Anarcho-Syndicalism: Selected Writings by Marx, Engels, Lenin* by Karl Marx, Friedrich Engels, and V.I. Lenin. © 1972. Reprinted by permission of International Publishers Co., Inc., New York.

Excerpts from *The Ego and His Own* by Max Stirner [pseud.], translated by Steven T. Byington. © 1963. Reprinted by permission of Libertarian Book Club, Inc., New York, an anarchist publisher.

Excerpts from *What is Property? An Inquiry into the Principle of Right and Government* by Pierre-Joseph Proudhon, translated by Benjamin Tucker, with a new introduction by George Woodcock. © 1970. Reprinted by permission of Dover Publications, Inc., New York.

Excerpts from *Hegel's Philosophy of Right* by G.W.F. Hegel, translated and notes by T.M. Knox. © 1967. Reprinted by permission of Oxford University Press, Oxford.

Excerpts from *Karl Marx and the Anarchists* by Paul Thomas. © 1980. Reprinted by permission of Routledge & Kegan Paul PLC, London.

Excerpts from *Critique of Hegel's "Philosophy of Right"* by Karl Marx, translated by Annette Jolin, edited and introduced by Joseph O'Malley. © 1970. Reprinted by permission of Cambridge University Press, New York.

Excerpts from *Selected Writings of Pierre-Joseph Proudhon* edited by L.S. Edwards and translated by Elizabeth Fraser. © 1969. Reprinted by permission of Doubleday & Company, Inc., New York, for publication in the United States of America. Reprinted by permission of Macmillan, London and Basingstoke, for publication in the world exclusive of the United States of America.

275156

CONTENTS

PREFACE

Why another book on Karl Marx? Why any book on anarchism, especially on relatively obscure nineteenth-century anarchists? These are legitimate questions for any reader encountering the massive scholarship in the area of Marxian thought. The importance of the study of Marx is accepted as given in this book. Questions concerning any particular study of Marx must be answered in terms of the object of the study. In the case of this work, the final answer to these questions is the book itself; the initial answer is that this book attends to an important and seldom explored area of Marxian thought: the crucial historical and philosophical link between Marx and the early nineteenth-century anarchists, especially between Marx and Max Stirner (1806-1856) and Pierre-Joseph Proudhon (1809-1865).

The importance of the link between Marx and the early anarchists is ignored or minimized in much political and philosophical debate, whether the source is identified as "pro" or "anti-" Marx. For many of those opposing Marx, the early anarchists are often seen as curiosities of political history, espousing a vague and vaguely sinister doctrine but ideologically useful and perhaps even virtuous in their opposition to Marx's alleged totalitarian tendencies. For many of those supporting Marx, the early anarchists were and are a minor irritation, a movement of adolescent tendencies dotted with (at best) utopian socialists and (at worst) latent petty bourgeois apologists. For both supporters and detractors of Marx, the influence of the early anarchists on the development of Marx's thought specifically and socialism more generally has been held to be minimal. One of the aims of this work is to show the need to reach beyond this understanding of Marx's development, to recognize the importance of early anarchist thought in shaping Marx's problematic and his responses to the political realities of his time. In the course of defining this important link between Marx and the early anarchists, a clearer and more sympathetic image of the approaches and results of the anarchists emerges.

Still, in exploring the basis of the Marx-early anarchist relationship, certain fundamental incompatibilities come to light. These conflicts are centered around the status, role, and causal efficacy of the modern political state. Exploring these issues reveals basic and irreconcilable methodological and philosophical conflicts between Marx's thought and anarchism in general.

Importantly, the significance of the Marx-early anarchist link is also disputed within the group of philosophers and political theorists sympathetic to Marx's project or at least to his critical method. Those interpreters of Marx who classify his explanatory model as that of an "economic determinist" are quick to condemn the early anarchists for their failure to recognize political relations and the oppressive quality of political life in modern society as the (determined) effect of economic relations within capitalist society. In revolutionary struggle, the relations and relative strengths of the classes within capitalist society determine the outcome of the revolution, not the morality or personal transformation of individuals within the revolution or society in general, as the early anarchists would have it. Thus, according to this view, the anarchists were wrong because they focused only on the sphere of moral and political relations; they should have focused exclusively on economic relations. On this interpretation, Marx the mature and scientific economist superseded Marx the immature, Hegel tainted political philosopher. The mistake of the early anarchists was to ignore or downgrade the importance of economic relations; in Marx's sense, the anarchists remained within the realm of moral and political ideology.

This has always seemed to me to be a one-sided and misleading view of Marx and his project. Although Marx did view the early anarchists as ideological (in the pejorative sense), the conflict between the two is distorted when it is cast in terms of a conflict between "scientific," exclusively economic explanations, and "prescientific," moral and political explanations. Marx's historical and materialist method, refined over the course of his career, was neither unidirectional nor unicausal in its explanations. One of the aims of this work is to show the subtlety of Marx's critical method, a subtlety nurtured in Hegelian beginnings and developed in large part in response to the challenges of the early anarchists.

One of the central themes of this work is . . . the distinct starting-points of Marx and the early anarchists, a distinction in methodology, explanation, and basic philosophical assumptions. Marx began within the Hegelian framework and, while rejecting Hegel's formulation of his method and the specific results thus obtained, retained a distinctly Hegelian framework of historical methodology and explanation intrinsically foreign to the early anarchists. Marx's theory is one stressing the reciprocal interplay of political structures (and relations) and economic structures (and relations). Marx makes this clear in his major works, both early and late; the detailed descriptions of this interplay in volume I of *Capital*, for example, become just so many historical "facts" without the accompanying understanding that political, social, and cultural struggles play a reciprocal role in defining the economic relations of society. Thus, Marx without political philosophy is as one-sided as were the anarchists in ignoring or minimizing the reciprocity of the economic and political. It was the early anarchists who helped Marx define the parameters and complexity of this reciprocity. For that reason alone the link between the early anarchists and Marx deserves careful attention.

The present study begins with an examination of the origins of Marx's view of the state in his study and critique of G.W.F. Hegel (1770-1831), focusing on Hegel's influence on Marx and Marx's critique of Hegel, noting at the same time the Hegelian framework retained by Marx and the non-Hegelian framework of the early anarchists. In the second chapter I explore Marx's view of the state in light of his auto-emancipation from Hegel's specific methodological formulations and results. A special focus of this chapter will be the importance of the concepts of "alienation" and "human emancipation" in the development of Marx's view. In chapter five I conclude with an evaluation of this conceptual and practical conflict, critically evaluating the assumptions underlying the conflict. The result of this evaluation is the conclusion that Marxian and anarchist views of the state and society are fundamentally incompatible.

Many people contributed to the completion of this work. If I do not mention them by name, they should be assured that it is for the sake of brevity and not for lack of appreciation. I would like to thank, first, the members of my dissertation committee at Purdue University, Calvin O. Schrag, T. Kermit Scott, and William L. McBride, under whose guidance an earlier version of this work took form. The members of my committee were both supportive and critical. I thank them for both. Particular thanks go to my dissertation director, critic, and friend William L. McBride, whose help was (and is) matched only by his patience. His interpretations of Marx and guidance were essential throughout this project. Of course, any remaining errors or misinterpretations are my responsibility.

Secondly, I would like to thank my former colleagues in the Philosophy Department at Purdue University and my present colleagues and students at Albright College. Their comments on previous versions of sections of this work proved quite valuable.

The editors at Greenwood Press, especially James T. Sabin, have been helpful and patient. I owe their anonymous readers a great deal in making this a more concise and readable work. My typist, Donna Clothier, has been diligent and accurate.

Finally, I would like to express my gratitude to my family and friends, whose support was essential from beginning to end. I am in special debt to Jan Barker, whose contributions went beyond proofreading chapter drafts. As my first editor, her lucid criticisms prevented many mistakes and unclarities. For this, and for her patience and support, I thank her.

ABBREVIATIONS

The following abbreviations are used in the notes sections for works frequently cited in the text. Each work is given a full citation at its first occurrence in the notes.

CBO   John Carroll, *Break-out from the Crystal Palace, The Anarcho-Psychological Critique; Stirner, Nietzsche, Dostoevsky*. London: Routledge and Kegan Paul, 1974.

HOF   Robert L. Hoffman, *Revolutionary Justice: The Social and Political Theory of P.-J. Proudhon*. Urbana, Ill.: University of Illinois Press, 1972.

PR   G.W.F. Hegel, *Philosophy of Right*, trans. with notes by T.M. Knox. London: Oxford University Press, 1967.

MECW   Karl Marx and Friedrich Engels, *Marx-Engels Collected Works*. New York: International Publishers, 1975- .

JOM   Karl Marx, *Critique of Hegel's "Philosophy of Right,"* trans. Annette Jolin and Joseph O'Malley. London: Cambridge University Press, 1970.

EPM   Karl Marx, *The Economic and Philosophic Manuscripts of 1844*, with an introduction by Dirk J. Struik, trans. Martin Milligan. New York: International Publishers, 1964.

CGP   Karl Marx, *Critique of the Gotha Programme*, ed. C.P. Dutt. New York: International Publishers, 1973.

SWP   Pierre-Joseph Proudhon, *Selected Writings of Pierre-Joseph Proudhon*, trans. Elizabeth Fraser, ed. Stewart Edwards. New York: Anchor Books, 1969.

Abbreviations

SEC   Pierre-Joseph Proudhon, *System of Economic Contradictions or the Philosophy of Misery*, 2 vols. Volume I trans. Benjamin R. Tucker. New York: Arno Press, 1972; reprint of edition of 1888.

WIP   Pierre-Joseph Proudhon, *What Is Property? An Inquiry Into the Principle of Right and Government*, trans. Benjamin R. Tucker, with a new introduction by George Woodcock. New York: Dover Publications, 1970.

S-EGO   Max Stirner, *The Ego and His Own*, ed. John Carrol. New York: Harper Torchbook, 1974.

C-EGO   Max Stirner, *The Ego and His Own*, trans. Steven T. Byington, ed. James J. Martin. New York: Libertarian Book Club, 1963.

TKM   Paul Thomas, *Karl Marx and the Anarchists*. London: Routledge and Kegan Paul, 1980.

INDIVIDUALISM AND COMMUNITY

1
HEGEL AND MARX

The various issues on which Karl Marx and the classical anarchists disagreed are difficult to bring together in one account unless one realizes that the starting-points of the two sides are fundamentally different. That is, the intellectual framework in which Marx formulated his conceptions of the state is of a radically different type from that of most anarchist theorists, and the historical understanding of this radical difference is essential to an adequate, single comprehension of the Marxian-anarchist debate on the state. The intellectual key to these differing starting-points lies in Marx's Hegelian heritage. It is to this heritage that we must first turn.

It is a commonplace--but an important commonplace--to note that Marx's early views of the state were profoundly influenced by his exposure to the philosophy of G. W. F. Hegel. Though Marx's conception of the state underwent a significant change in his later years, he never completely separated himself from the original Hegelian influences and goals. The most clearly stated and concise source of these Hegelian influences is found in the *Philosophy of Right*, though there are important sections of the *Jenaer Realphilosophie* and the *Philosophy of History* that need to be considered as well. It is important to draw upon these sources in the course of a critical exposition of the Hegelian position on the state and on the crucial distinction in Hegel between civil society and the state. An understanding of these two aspects of the Hegelian starting-point will illuminate both the Marxian critique of Hegel's account and the still-Hegelian framework in which Marx developed his own theory. This in turn will clarify the Marxian-anarchist debate, as it will become evident that classical anarchism originates in a distinctly non-Hegelian framework.

CIVIL SOCIETY AND THE STATE IN HEGEL

In *The Myth of Sisyphus*, Albert Camus quotes Johann von Goethe: "My field . . . is time."[1] Time, as the measure of the development of history is (in another context) ultimately Hegel's field. The central task of Hegel's philosophical project is to show the ultimate intelligibility of the world, as evidenced in the progress of reason through time. Hence it is possible, indeed philosophical, to discern the movement of reason in history and thus the ultimate rationality of the universe and of human history. History for Hegel is the unfolding of spirit in the world-- the dialectical progress of reason. This philosophical starting-point is crucial to all of Hegel's work but especially to his view of the state and the social conditions of given societies in history. Hegel expressed this central theme of his philosophy in his inaugural speech at the University of Berlin:

> What is great and divine in life, is so through the *idea*; the aim of philosophy is to comprehend it in its true form and universality.
>
> The first condition of *philosophical studies* is the *courage of truth*, the *belief in the power of the spirit*; man should honor himself *and consider himself worthy of the highest*. He cannot exaggerate the greatness and power of spirit; the opaque essence of the universe *has no power* which can withstand the force of cognition. . . .[2]

As will be seen, Hegel's pursuit of spirit in the history of the world necessitates the view that every existent in the course of history contains or imperfectly exemplifies reason; thus the concept of the state exists, albeit imperfectly, in history. There is for Hegel the core of the rational essence of the state in ex-

isting states--the history of states is the history of the progress of reason. Hence, the actuality of the state, the rational
kernel of the concept, is for Hegel an immanent truth. The state
is; the task for Hegel is to explore the contours of its actuality, its rational nature, through the study of the rational core
of existing and previously existing states. In his Berlin inaugural address Hegel clearly states his position: philosophy, especially the vital part of philosophy dealing with the varieties
of human organization, is based on the discerning of the rational
progress of spirit in the world.

Hegel's position was made clear again in the *Philosophy of
Right*. There he stated the famous, often quoted and often misin-
terpreted dictum, "What is rational is actual and what is actual
is rational."[3] Not a defense of existing theories or institutions
per se, the dictum expresses Hegel's conviction that the scientific, that is, philosophical method approaches "the state as
something inherently rational."[4] Existing states are not inherently rational; they embody reason imperfectly.

It was just as important for Hegel to maintain that a philosophical examination of the inherent rationality of the state must
examine existing states. There are two reasons for this. First, as
has been stated, existing states, insofar as they are states, do
exemplify the rationality inherent in the concept, no matter how
imperfectly. Secondly, Hegel was loathe to predict or prescribe
social or political forms; for him, the task must be to examine
what is.

"To comprehend what is, this is the task of philosophy, because what is, is reason. Whatever happens, every individual is a
child of his time; so philosophy too is its own time apprehended
in thoughts. It is just as absurd to fancy that a philosophy can
transcend its contemporary world as it is to fancy that an individual can overleap his own age. . . ."[5]

Hegel's own work, as a child of his time, became a legacy to
Marx. His examination of the science of the state, its essential
rationality, and the core of his legacy to Marx rest on the distinction and relations between civil society (*bürgerliche
Gesellschaft*) and the state.

In the *Philosophy of Right*, Hegel set out both to counter the romantic nationalism of his time[6] and to found the truths of Right, to found freedom in the integration and sublimation of the particular and the universal in the state. The vehicle for this project is Hegel's historical-philosophical description, separated into analyses of abstract right, morality, and ethical life. For an examination of the Hegelian legacy to Marx and the ensuing debate between Marx and the nineteenth century anarchists, the most significant aspect of Hegel's work is the description of civil society and the state in the third part of the *Philosophy of Right*, the section concerned with ethical life.

The movement from abstract right to morality is the movement from the philosophy of the abstract will as personality, as a unit that has a formal capacity for rights, to the philosophy of moral agency, where the subject of abstract rights recognizes the universal laws of morality as well as the particular abstract rights. Morality, however, is not the final stage in Hegel's analysis. From this recognition he moves to ethical life, where the development of family, civil society, and the state is traced.

The transition from the immediate, felt unity of the family to the particularity and separation of civil society involves the particularity of the concrete (not, in the Hegelian sense, "individual") person, man as a unit with abstract right, plus the added dimension of a subject who pursues his own ends. These ends are not necessarily the individual ends of each man, as Max Stirner would have it, but rather the ends shared by individuals as human beings. The pursuit of these ends and the ends themselves are mediated by civil society, by the recognition of the necessity of a regulatory social fabric, a medium of interchange and economic interdependence among the members of the society. This represents, in the Hegelian scheme, the move in ethical life from particularity to universality, at the same time dialectically encompassing the particularity of the members.

Hegel gives an illuminating account of the role of the idea at this stage:

> The Idea in this its stage of division imparts to each of its
> moments a characteristic embodiment: to particularity it

gives the right to develop and launch forth in all directions; and to universality the right to prove itself not only
the ground and necessary form of particularity, but also the
authority standing over it and its final end. It is the
system of ethical order, split into its extremes and lost,
which constitutes the Idea's abstract moment, its moment of
reality.   Here the Idea is present only as a relative totality and as the inner necessity behind this outward appearance.[7]

There are three moments of this stage. They include (a) the interchange of need and need satisfaction (the System of Needs), (b)
the "actuality of the universal principle of freedom contained
therein--the protection of property through the Administration of
Justice," and (c) the enforcement of a and b and caring "for particular interests as a common interest"[8] (Police and the Corporation).

Hegel divided the System of Needs into three main subdivisions: (a)the Kind of Need and Satisfaction (typical of civil
society), (b)the Kind of Work (typical of civil society), and (c)
Capital (and class divisions).[9] Each of these three subdivisions
delineates the economic structure of civil society, where for the
most part every member is concerned with the pursuit of his own
ends. Hegel's analysis, as will be seen, is acute and unintention-
ally prophetic. Marx was to accept many of Hegel's conclusions
within these sections, while at the same time rejecting the place
of these aspects of civil society within society as a whole. The
anarchists, on the other hand, usually remain within the analytical framework of the System of Needs in their critiques of existing societies, though not by their own design.

Hegel does not want to state that in civil society the kind
of end-need pursued by the members is individual need. He writes:
"In abstract right, what we had before us was the person; in the
sphere of morality, the subject; in the family, the family member;
in civil society as a whole, the burgher or *bourgeois*. Here at
the standpoint of needs . . . what we have before us is the composite idea which we call *man*."[10] In speaking of the composite
idea of man, of man as such, Hegel reiterates the point that needs

are common to people in general, and it is these more general
needs which take precedence in civil society. Man separates
himself from animals by multiplying and particularizing his needs
and means of satisfaction, needs which nonetheless are common to
man *qua* man. A very important part of this process is the refinement of needs and need satisfaction where, looked at as a whole,
civil society continually refines its considered needs by multiplying needs in general. This process will be of major significance to Hegel's discussion of poverty and social justice in the
latter sections of "civil society" and so is of major significance
in understanding Marx's early social problematic. Marx was concerned very early in his career with the process of impoverishment, a concern that led to a rejection of traditional liberal
solutions for poverty. This bears directly on Marx's later
rejection of the state as a device for solving social problems.
Hegel's framework, and especially the dearth of genuine solutions
found by Hegel, profoundly affected Marx's position.

The needs of civil society and the means necessary to satisfy
them are not simply the more general needs of men; they are, when
abstracted and seen as an interdependent web of socio-economic
interchange, made "concrete, i.e., social."[11] The link between
the members of the society is concrete in the sense that each is
bound to the other in an interdependent society. For Hegel, this
is different from the substantive connection of family members.
In the family the members are brought together into an immediate
whole, while in civil society the group-connection is mediated by
the continuation of the members in their roles as separate parts
of the society.

The work typical of civil society is just the way in which
members acquire the means to satisfy their needs. Hegel's insight
into the nature of this work, however, is at once both disturbingly modern and an implicit critique of "natural man" theories. For,
in civil society, Hegel makes it clear that man cannot satisfy his
needs with what is given to him in nature, as his needs are beyond
that of a "natural man." One class (the agricultural) is primarily concerned with the immediate products of the soil. However,
the work in civil society gives value to the means of production,

making these the subject of needs. Thus, "man in what he consumes is mainly concerned with the products of men."[12] The process of need-multiplication and refinement complicates and elaborates civil society so that man is unable to survive on what is given in nature. Each man is, rather, inevitably dependent on other men to assist him in satisfying his needs.

There are clear parallels here with the Marxian and later Marxist analyses of the artifical manipulation of needs. The more subtle comparison that will be the subject of much discussion in connection with Stirner and Pierre-Joseph Proudhon is that of Hegel's discussion with the ideas of early utopian and anarchist thinkers. Hegel clearly rejects on philosophical, that is rational, grounds the utopian notion that it is even possible, let alone better, for man to return to a vaguely defined "natural state." If, as Hegel claimed, his analysis was a reading of the face of reason in history, then such a backward looking claim or hope is neither positive nor negative--it simply does not make sense. Yet, this yearning for a simpler, more pastoral existence characterizes much of the anarchist thinking in the nineteenth century. Michael Bakunin is a notable exception here, though even he at times celebrated the virtues of the isolated rural commune. Marx did not share this preoccupation with rural simplicity, as he accepted the basic, historical Hegelian methodology.

The continuous or near continuous process of multiplying and refining needs and the means to satisfy these needs brings in its train, for Hegel as for Marx, the division of labor. This ever more particularizing division of labor is, at the same time, for Hegel the "universal and objective element in work,"[13] as the specialization produced increases the web of interdependence and relative weakness among the workers. As Shlomo Avineri comments: "The dialectics of civil society create a universal dependence of man on man. No man is an island any more, and each finds himself irretrievably interwoven into the texture of production, exchange and consumption. . . ."[14]

The results of this process include the increasing production of consumer goods while capital is at the same time increasingly isolated in fewer and fewer hands. The poverty that results

concerns Hegel at this point and later in his discussion of class
divisions. An important point to be made here is that, along with
all other significant aspects of civil society, poverty is not
merely the byproduct of economic relations. It is in fact a necessary component of civil society, inherent in the form of organization. As such Hegel separates his social theory from most marketplace theories (including, as Avineri notes, that of Adam
Smith[15]), for Hegel sees poverty, as the working out of reason in
civil society, as inevitable, while the Smithian model sees
poverty as the byproduct and marginal concern of a well-ordered
marketplace. This is not to say that Hegel supported the development of poverty. Much of Hegel's writings on the state and society
are attempts to reconcile the development of poverty in civil
society with the development of the rational state. Clearly, Hegel
was quite uncomfortable with the fact of this unfortunate but inevitable poverty.

The development of the System of Needs is the development of
a web of interdependence which in its expansion dialectically
mediates the particular through the universal. Hegel represents
the particular by the division of labor, such as the pursuit of
interests, while the universal is represented by the need for an
assembly and interchange of labor-products, such as the benefit of
other members of society by the efforts of each. The result of
this dialectical mediation is the creation or recognition of what
Hegel terms the "universal permanent capital,"[16] in which all, to
a greater or lesser extent, partake.

> The compulsion which brings this [mediation] about is rooted
> in the complex interdependence of each on all, and it now
> presents itself to each as the universal permanent capital
> . . . which gives each the opportunity, by the exercise of
> his education and skill, to draw a share from it and so be
> assured of his livelihood, while what he thus earns by means
> of his work maintains and increases the general capital.[17]

At first Hegel seems to be describing a system where all can
enjoy the fruits of civil society simply by using the requisite
education and skill. Hegel recognizes, however, that other circumstances of an "accidental" nature can intervene to prevent the

individual member from sharing in the capital. There is, then, a
natural, accidental inequality, one caused by inherited social
position, or physical disability. This inequality is not opposed
by Hegel, however. Though physical accident or economic placement
may hinder an individual's attempt to gain equality, this too is
inherent in the system and follows from the concept.

> Men are made unequal by nature, where inequality is in its
> element, and in civil society the right of particularity is
> so far from annulling this natural inequality that it pro-
> duces it out of mind and raises it to an inequality of skill
> and resources, and even to one of moral and intellectual
> attainment. *To oppose to this right a demand for equality is*
> *a folly of the Understanding which takes as real and rational*
> *its abstract equality and its "ought-to-be."*[18]

Given this natural and developed (a curious distinction perhaps,
for Hegel) inequality, a system develops where three classes are
formed according to need, means, abilities, and position. These
three classes, (1)the substantial, (2)the formal, and (3)the universal, need not be dealt with here, as they will come to the fore
in Hegel's discussion of the state. The division of civil society
into these three classes is not particularly troublesome for
Hegel's system. What is of greater interest is the issue of membership in each class, the focus of Hegel's comment on the "folly
of the Understanding" quoted directly above. Hegel states twice
(in paragraphs 202 and 206) that this division of classes is in
accordance with the concept, that it is an essential component of
the structure of civil society. But, he says, "The question of the
particular class to which an individual is to belong is one on
which natural capacity, birth, and other circumstances have their
influence, though the essential and final determining factors are
subjective opinion and the individual's arbitrary will. . . ."[19]

There is a certain tension between Hegel's claim here and
elsewhere that the primary (see the Remark to paragraph 206), the
determining factor in the placement of individuals within classes
is (or should be?) the arbitrary will and his previous statement
that men are created unequal by nature and developed unequally by
(civil) society. (See, for example, the Remark to paragraph 200.)

The inequality, as Hegel stated it, extends even to the realm of moral and intellectual attainment. How can an arbitrary will oppose a necessary inequality, one on which the differentiation of classes rests? Marx's critique of Hegel is in part an attempt to deal with the curious sort of freedom that Hegel grants the arbitrary will in society. The classical anarchists, on the other hand, largely ignored the "necessity" that Hegel attributed to the development of inequality in civil society. Instead, anarchist theory (especially in the work of Stirner and Bakunin) granted the society member a total freedom of arbitrary will, constrained only externally by the state. This issue is one that sharply divides Marx from the anarchists, leading Marx, especially in his critique of Stirner, to characterize the anarchist's neglect of internally developed inequality not as a "folly of the Understanding" but (so to speak) as a folly of ideology. Against Stirner, Marx was to write:

> He seeks to free [the workers] from [the alien "holy"] by defending the individual who has been crippled by the division of labor at the expense of his abilities and relegated to a onesided vocation, against his *own* need to become different, a need which has been *stated to be* his vocation by others. . . . The all-round realization of the individual will only cease to be conceived as an ideal, a vocation, etc., when the impact of the world which stimulates the real development of the abilities of the individual is under the control of the individuals themselves. . . .[20]

Hegel's own account prompts immediate questions, many of which Marx was to struggle with. . . . If an individual is incapable of rising above, say, the immediacy of the substantial class due to a natural or developed defect in mental ability, what sense is there in calling the exercise of his or her arbitrary will a mediating factor in class placement? It is a formal and surely empty sense of "freedom" (see Hegel's Remark to paragraph 206) that is employed here. If the inequality is natural or developed and necessary, so is the position in civil society. Marx was to reject this consequence but was to separate himself from the anarchists (as the above quoted passage indicates) by not rejecting out of hand the role of developed inequality as a mediating factor in society.

Hegel criticizes Plato's *Republic* and the Indian caste system because they either fail to recognize the role of the subjective will in class placement or else restrict this role to the subjective will of the ruling class. The role of the subjective remains an issue in Hegel's system, however, as evidenced by the dispute between Marx and Stirner. It is true, as Charles Taylor and Avineri both point out,[21] that the Hegelian meritocracy is an advance on the old system of hereditary placement. Still, one of the features of life in civil society is the fact that one is born into a certain class and developed according to the feature--and limitations--of that class. Exactly how this fact might limit or affect the exercise of the will is left unclear by Hegel, an unclarity that became a key part of his legacy to Marx.

Moving from the abstract right of needs and need satisfaction to universal right is the movement from the particular needs of persons to persons as members of an ordered society. In this ordered society, according to Hegel, all are equally considered: "A man counts as a man in virtue of his manhood alone. . . ."[22] The structure of this universal right, setting Hegel apart from both the classical anarchists and Marx, is law; and the administration of justice serves as the affirmation of law in civil society. Hegel separates three aspects of the administration of justice: (a) Right as Law, (b) Law as determinately existent, and (c) The Court of Justice.[23]

Law, in Hegel's system, is right become determinate. In its determinacy it becomes universal. This is more than just the legislative action of making rules for a society. As Hegel says: "Making a law is not to be represented as merely the expression of a rule of behavior valid for everyone, through that is one moment in legislation; the more important moment, the inner essence of the matter, is knowledge of the content of the law in its determinate universalty."[24]

Morality is not included in the sphere of positive law for Hegel, however, as he asserts that morality and the dictates of morality are matters of the subjective will. In explaining this,

Hegel invokes a distinction between relationships which are internal and those which are external by nature (see the Addition to paragraph 213). Only those which are external are the proper subjects of positive law. Such internal moral commands as "love your spouse" and those concerning other higher relationships are in the domain of the subjective will and are not proper subjects of positive law.

Even though it is essential for law to become known and have force, Hegel admits a certain contingency within law by asserting the need for force, despite the fact that any codification of law is bound to be incomplete. Reason progresses in law, and this is evidenced by the decreasing significance of formalities in law; yet law at any given point, according to Hegel, must have force.

Hegel presents, essentially, a philosophy of actualized freedom, yet the actualization of this freedom involves determinate law and forceful authority as an integral part of freedom, freedom in a well-ordered society. Marx's inheritance on this point lends limited credence to a separation of Marxian "periods," early and late. For in emancipating himself from Hegel, Marx rejected much of Hegel's position on law and force as a sanctification of authoritarian structures. But, in these early years, as in later, Marx was rejecting specific justifications of authority, nor authority per se. This will be discussed in chapter two and throughout this work. Here it is important to see that Marx attempted to adapt Hegel's pursuit of freedom to a system without the ideological endorsement of certain structures and justifications of authority. For the classical anarchists, any structure and justification of authority was therefore authoritarian, in the pejorative sense. On this point, as on others, Marx's Hegelian legacy separated him from the anarchists, in a fundamental fashion.

The role of the court in the structure of the administration of justice is to institute law in particular cases without subjective, private interests being involved. Thus Hegel terms the court a "public authority."[25] It is not just that this court is a convenient vehicle for instituting the law or that such a legal position is an arbitrary matter. Rather, according to Hegel, the court and other legal institutions are inherently rational and as such are necessary institutions, regardless of their origins. And, since the institution of law and the court is rational and necessary, the enforcement of law by the court is itself necessary-- that is, a duty.

The court is the proper place for the administration of the law, according to Hegel. Since this is so, individuals qua individuals or particulars are never justified in administering the law or taking revenge. The making right of the crime is the duty of the court, where it is in fact objectively the restoration of law and authority and subjectively the restoration of law within the criminal. In the subjective sense, the criminal has a right to be punished, to be reconciled with himself as a subject of the law. In the objective sense, it is the duty of the court of punish the criminal, to reconcile the law with itself, restore right, and so make law and right actual.[26]

Since civil society is characterized by the pursuit of self-interest, Hegel finds it necessary for there to be an external organization, attentive to the subjective will of the criminal which will enforce authority. The organization is the police or public authority (*polizei*). As T. M. Knox notes, Hegel often quite clearly means more than is associated with the English term "police," often intending something closer to "Public authority."[27]

The court deals with actual crimes. The justification for the existence of the police is quite simple: "The point is that the actions of individuals may always be wrongful, and this is the ultimate reason for police control and penal justice."[28] Here Hegel's position, very traditional and accepting of existing legal institutions, separates the Hegelian tradition from the anarchists. It was precisely these institutions, according to William Godwin, Stirner, Proudhon, Bakunin, and others, that promulgated injustice, that played a causal role in leading people to wrongful behavior. Again, the societal institutions seen by Hegel as providing avenues to freedom were seen by the anarchists as external obstacles to freedom. Marx, on the other hand, grasped the internal logic of the Hegelian position, while at the same time rejecting any conservatism implied by that position. This becomes espe-

cially evident in the dispute with Bakunin, where Marx and Engels
were led to assert the necessity of authority, distinguishing legitimate (in the sense of futhering the revolution) exercises of
authority within an organization from the conservative authori-
tarianism that, with whatever justification, has become associated
with the Hegelian position.[29] For Hegel, there is no conceptual
limit to the public authority, as the codification of law varies
with the state of civil society and the perceived need for public
control. The general requirement is that the public authority provides in case of physical conditions or other accidents which may
cause ruin. The question again arises, as it did in the discussion
of the System of Needs, exactly how far is the public authority
obligated to deal with and attempt to rectify the poverty which is
inevitably created in civil society?

Though Hegel has no definitive answer to this question, he is
certain of one thing that sets him apart from both laissez-faire
economic schemes and some of the classical anarchists. Hegel does
not think that care for the poor and otherwise disabled should be
left to private charities, a position shared among the classical
anarchists only by Bakunin (and in a different context, Peter
Kropotkin). To leave to inclination such an important part of society is for Hegel contrary to the rational order of civil society: "Public social conditions are on the contrary to be regarded as all the more perfect the less (in comparison with what is
arranged publicly) is left for an individual to do by himself as
his private inclination directs."[30]

Given the importance for Marx and the anarchists of dealing
with the limits of public authority, it is important to ask: what
is the basis of Hegel's view of poverty and its amelioration?
Hegel attempts to explain the development of poverty through the
description of the expanding mechanism of civil society. Civil
society expands internally as the means of production and needs
continue to multiply and refine, thereby leading to a continual
division of labor and the distress of those at the lowest end of
the economic scale.   The process continues until wealth is
isolated in relatively few hands, while a large number of people
sink into utter poverty. At this point it is possible for a group

Hegel calls a "rabble of paupers" to form.[31] It is only possible
at this point, though, because

> Poverty in itself does not make men into a rabble; a rabble
> is created only when there is joined to poverty a disposition
> of mind, an inner indignation against the rich, against
> society, against the government, &c. . . . Against nature man
> can claim no right, but once society is established, poverty
> immediately takes the form of a wrong done to one class by
> another.   The important question of how poverty is to be
> abolished is one of the most disturbing problems which
> agitate modern society.[32]

Hegel does not offer a solution or even a description of how
this problem is overcome or even stabilized. He in fact shows how
standard remedies for the isolation of wealth either violate the
spirit of civil society or simply do not work. All attempts to re-
lieve the poor through increased production or direct subsidies
intensify the poverty. In a telling phrase, Hegel concludes: "It
hence becomes apparent that despite an excess of wealth civil society is not rich enough, i.e., its own resources are insufficient
to check excessive poverty and the creation of a penurious
rabble."[33] When the situation becomes critical, civil society expands externally, through imperialism, colonialism, and outward
expansion to new markets. Hegel's description of this process (see
paragraph 246) is disturbingly prescient. Still, the question of
poverty is left unanswered--as Hegel acknowledges.

The importance of the Hegelian dialectic of poverty for Marx
and the anarchists cannot be overstated. It is commonplace to con-
nect, both historically and philosophically, Hegel's failure to
find a solution to poverty to Marx's preoccupation with the problem. Marx's eventual rejection of the capitalist mode of production is, in part, a rejection of the factors and structures that
make poverty a crushing dilemma for Hegel. The subtle dialectic
involved here was less clear to Stirner and Proudhon, however.
Especially with Proudhon, Marx can be seen to be offering a solution based on distinctly Hegelian premises--that the dialectic
does result in inescapable poverty, within the capitalist mode of
production. Proudhon, on the other hand, attempts to forge a so-

lution to the problem of impoverishment without altering the basic property relations characteristic of capitalism (and civil society) even though he criticizes certain forms of private property and so ignores the Hegelian statement of the problem. This will be explored in some detail in chapter four. The two positions--with Marx's of distinctly Hegelian parentage--result in widely differing views on the role of the state.

The corporation or trade guild serves for Hegel as a sort of "limited universal." It unites its members and their pursuits within civil society into a common goal. For this reason it is especially suited to the formal class, as the others are already focused on a universal purpose, and it is the bourgeoisie who need a "wholly concrete"[34] universal purpose. It is in fact for them a sort of family, providing for them and protecting them through representing and furthering their interests. It is, as William L. McBride has noted, a "curious admixture of the modern and the Medieval."[35] As a member of a recognized group, furthermore, the corporation gives a person family stability through economic security and recognition of ability and skills *qua* member of the corporation, which Hegel cites as "evidence that he is a somebody."[36] It is the significance of this factor of recognition, so important for both Hegel and Marx, that Stirner disputed. In calling for individualism, Stirner, according to Marx, ignored the recognition that makes possible individuality and freedom.

Hegel has thus presented in civil society a mediating point between the family and the state, as the rational differentiation of human organization. The state is the "true ground" of family and civil society, "although it is from them that the state springs."[37] In bringing forth the state Hegel describes the summit of ethical life.

"The state is the actuality of the ethical Idea, . . . self-consciousness in virtue of its sentiment towards the state finds in the state, as its essence and the end and product of its substantive freedom."[38] "The state is the Divine Idea as it exists on Earth."[39]

In his description of the machinations of civil society, Hegel has presented the picture of a social organization dominated

by the pursuit of interests, by the widespread particularity common to the world of labor and economics. But, as was set out at
the beginning of this chapter, for Hegel the history of the world
is essentially an illustration of the progress of reason; and the
organization characteristic of civil society gives an incomplete
picture of the development of reason--it is not a fully evident
instance of rationality.

Moving to the political sphere, Hegel at last finds the
summit of reason, the "actuality of the ethical idea," in the
state. The picture Hegel finds, however, is not that of any
existing state. For Hegel, existing states were rational only in
so far as they incorporated the particular and the universal in
the reign of freedom. The task for Hegel, then, is to discern,
from the imperfect examples of existing states, the rational
ground of the state as the apex of historical development in the
idea or, as he put it, as the "hieroglyph of the reason which
reveals itself in actuality."[40]

Hegel's evolving view of the state shows a remarkable continuity, from the period of the *Jenaer Realphilosophie* to the
Philosophy of Right. The one exception to this view of the state
as essentially rational is an important one for Hegel's connection
to Marx and the anarchists. In an early programmatic document,
written in 1796, Hegel writes: "Just as there is no idea of a machine, so there is no idea of the state; for the state is something mechanical. Only that which is an object of freedom may be
called an idea. We must therefore go beyond the state! For every
state is bound to treat men as cogs in a machine. And this is
precisely what ought not to be; hence the state must cease to
exist."[41]

At first this appears to contradict Hegel's later praise of
the state as the summit of reason. A careful examination, however, reveals a continuity between this early rejection of a
mechanistic state and Hegel's later support of the state as the
ground of freedom. The state that must be eliminated in this
early passage exhibits many of the same characteristics as the
need based organization of civil society; the regimentation of
labor, the pursuit of particular interests, and the incomplete

development of freedom all characterize what Hegel later called civil society. Thus, this early passage cannot be taken as a rejection of the mature Hegelian conception of the state.

This same passage does provide an instructive contrast to the basic position of classical anarchism, however. In the writings of Stirner, Proudhon, and Bakunin (and, one could add, Kropotkin, Emma Goldman, and others), the state is condemned in an unconditional manner. With classical anarchists, the type of state being condemned is very similar to the type of state that Hegel condemned in the above cited passage. That is, the characteristics of the state and state authority that form, for the most part, the basis of the classical anarchist critique belong to what Hegel termed "civil society," which Hegel condemned--in this early passage. Hegel's later writings displayed an additional, more subtle conception of the state, one which the anarchists, for the most part, failed to address. It is this later Hegelian conception of the state that Marx found both attractive and repulsive and from which he forged his own conception. Here the radically different starting-points--and relative philosophical sophistication--of Marx and the classical anarchists are evident.

During Hegel's Jena period, another set of characteristics became associated with his view of the state, other than the mechanistic, cog creating image exhibited in earlier writings. Hegel came to view the state as having a twofold nature: it served as both a regulatory body and a means of integrating the particular interests of citizens into the universal interest of a single body. The state not only mediates the particular interests of its citizens, it also dialectically incorporates (that is, transcends and preserves) these interests into the higher universal interests of a unified state.

In the *Philosophy of Right*, Hegel's main work on the state, many of the threads of the Jena period are brought together in a complete picture of the rational state. The state is both the end, as traced in philosophical development, and the beginning, as the ground of both family and civil society. As the embodiment of a higher universal interest in human organization, the state both raises particular wills to universality and is the ground of human freedom.   It is this integrative function, the dialectical fusion of the particular and universal, that characterizes the Hegelian state.   "This substantial unity is an absolute unmoved end in itself, in which freedom comes into its supreme right against the individual, whose supreme duty is to be a member of that state."[42]

Thus, the essence of the state is its absolute rationality as the unity of subjective and objective freedom, that is, as the unity of the individual will and universal right. Hegel is critical of both Johann Gottlieb Fichte and Jean-Jacques Rousseau for declaring that the universal proceeds from the aggregation of individuals instead of as a unity of the two, as Hegel himself held.[43]   Whatever the substance or accuracy of these two criticisms, Hegel's point is clear: if the state is truly to serve as the embodiment of human freedom, the compromise of an aggregation of individual wills will not suffice. Instead, Hegel declares, the state must serve as the "inter-penetration of the substantive and the particulars," where "my obligation to what is substantive is at the same time the embodiment of my particular freedom."44   This is accomplished, according to Hegel, by an "identity" of the particular interests with the universal interests of the state.

> [The political] sentiment is, in general, trust (which may
> pass over into a greater or lesser degree of educated in-
> sight), or the consciousness that may interest, both substan-
> tive and particular, is contained and preserved in another's
> (i.e. in the state's) interest and end, i.e. in the other's
> relation to me as an individual. In this way, this very
> other is immediately not an other in my eyes, and in being
> conscious of this fact, I am free.[45]

The most important point to see here, especially as Hegel denies that he is describing any existing state, is the purpose assigned to the state by Hegel. It is the recognition of man (that is, the human being) as a *zoön politikon* and the integration of the particular interests of *homo economicus* into the universal political sphere. Though Hegel asserts the primacy of this politcial sphere, he does not assert, as those characterizing Hegel as an authoritarian have charged, the complete domination of the univer-

sal   interests   of the state. Rather, in true dialectical fashion,
the   state   both incorporates and preserves the legitimate spheres
of both family and civil society. The various mechanisms of civil
society,   as well as the tensions, the poverty, and the inherent
destructive tendencies, remain within the structure of the state,
to a greater or lesser degree, as a particular state fulfills its
mediating function. The state is, so to speak, the keystone of a
human archway, resting on both family and civil society as equally
necessary pillars of support. At the same time, without the keystone of the state, there is no single arch--no single body--and
without this unity, for Hegel, there is no real human freedom.

MARX, HEGEL, AND THE STATE

Marx,   even in his critiques of *The Philosophy of Right*, took
issue not with the *aims* of Hegelian political philosophy, the
ends of integration and community, which to Marx, too, were
vital human needs.   He took issue with Hegel's view that
these aims could be provided for, and men in their social
being satisfied, within the framework of a modern state that
met Hegel's own specifications.[46]

Marx's main extended critique of the Hegelian conception of
the state and of civil society appears in the *Critique of Hegel's
"Philosophy of Right."*[47] In this unfinished manuscript, Marx took
to task, paragraph by paragraph, the sections of Hegel's *Philosophy of Right* dealing with the state. Remaining within the goals
of the Hegelian project, that of the integration of the particular
and the universal, Marx disputed Hegel's claim that a state utilizing the Hegelian model could in fact achieve these goals. Marx
concluded that Hegel had posed the correct questions but had left
the "antinomy" of the external necessity of the state's universal
aim and the "immanent end" of the individual unresolved.[48] A
large part of the problem, according to Marx, is that Hegel mystifies the relationship between the individual ends and universal
ends and among family, civil society, and the state, inverting the
true relationship between civil society and the state.

In claiming that Hegel inverts the true relationship between the particular and universal spheres, Marx pursues the transformative critique of Hegel made famous by Ludwig Feuerbach in *The Essence of Christianity*.[49] Hegel claims that the family and civil society are finite spheres of the state, the realm of particular interests issuing from the concept of the state. To this claim Marx replies: "At this point the logical, pantheistic mysticism becomes very clear."[50] Marx, using the transformative critique, accuses Hegel of making the idea a subject which presupposes (as the state) both family and civil society; according to Marx, the actual relationship is inverted. "Family and civil society constitute *themselves* as the state. They are the driving force."[51] Hegel is mistaken to think, writes Marx, that the idea makes family and civil society into a state, that the idea is the ground and source of necessity. In inverting this real relationship, "(Speculative philosophy expresses this fact as the idea's deed, not as the idea of the multitude, but as the deed of a subjective idea different from the fact itself) 'in such a way that with regard to the individual this assignment . . . is visibly mediated by circumstances, caprice, etc.'"[52]

Marx's critique here is not to be taken as a complete rejection of the Hegelian position, however. Where Hegel holds the idea to be the driving force, the subject, the source of organic unity, Marx holds that the parts of the political constitution are the subject, thus distinguishing the political form of organization from natural organization. To think as Hegel does, according to Marx, is to mystify the true relationship in pursuit of an organic structure that does not exist. The starting-point is actual mind, not actuality in the abstract; the "finite spheres," not the universal. The universal end is the predicate, not the subject--the universal end of the state is developed by actual mind through the utilization of its real powers. With Hegel, "The end of the state and the powers of the state are mystified in that they take the appearance of modes of existence of the substance, drawn out of and divorced from their real existence, the self-knowing and willing mind, the educated mind."[53]

When Marx considers the specific characteristics of Hegel's

modern state, he finds that the general methodological fault of mystification and inversion infects the various aspects of the state. As a key example on the issue of state authority, Marx examines Hegel's view of sovereignty. For Hegel, the clearest indication of the divine element of any state, and the rationality inherent in the idea of the state, is the existence of sovereignty as internal necessity, as a matter of the idea. Though Marx is not as explicit as he could be, the context of his critique clearly implies that Hegel's view ignores the real, existing situation: the fact of the matter is that real sovereignty is more than just a question of the idea, if it is that at all. It is a question, as Marx would see clearly in later writings, of concrete human relations. For the classical anarchists, any conception of a fixed sovereignty, expressed in concrete human relations, entailed patterns of domination, based on either social or economic classes. Marx's critique of Hegel was more subtle than this anarchist position. Though Marx rejected Hegel's view of sovereignty, it is important to see at this point that he did not reject the issue of sovereignty altogether.

The sovereign, or the monarch, in Hegel's state, "embodies" the state in a unique fashion. The monarch is both the universal, unifying element in the state and the subjective element in his position as the sole and final arbiter in decision making. But, according to Marx, Hegel's mystification results not in mere subjectivity being required of the monarch but actual individuality instead.

> Hegel makes all the attributes of the contemporary European constitutional monarch into absolute self-determinations of the will. He does not say the will of the monarch is the final decision, but rather the final decision of the will is the monarch. The first statement is empirical, the second twists the empirical fact into a metaphysical axiom. . . . Thus, because subjectivity is actual only as subject, and the subject actual only as one, the personality of the state is actual only as one person. A beautiful conclusion. Hegel could just as well conclude that because the individual man is one the human species is only a single man.[54]

Hegel embodies sovereignty in the monarch as the necessary subjective element in the state. He is, understandably, completely opposed to the conception of "popular sovereignty." The idea of the sovereignty of the people is contrary to the rational organization of the state, and so Hegel characterizes the democratic impulse as "one of the confused notions based on the wild idea of the 'people.'"[55] Marx's critique of Hegel at this point leads to important claims by Marx concerning what he calls "true democracy."[56] This understanding of democracy is not to be confused with a crude or vague support for "popular sovereignty," where the will of the "people," taken on faith as an indication of the path to some sort of wisdom, directs society in political form--that is, as a traditional political state. What Marx opposed was Hegel's assertion that the modern Hegelian state embodied and integrated the universal and particular interests of the members of society and so provided an adequate account of society. Marx realized that any genuine integration of these interests begins with a reorganization of society as a whole, not just with the political form dominant in modern society nor with the claim that the particular political form of the modern state can integrate particular and universal interests.

Although Marx is not making explicit claims concerning the capacity of the "people" to rule society, he is clearly stating that the human form of social organization, that is, the one which would integrate particular and universal interests, must be based on the concrete relations of the people in a transformed society and not on the character of the state. As Marx commented: "Hegel proceeds from the state and makes man into the subjectified state; democracy starts with man and makes state objectified man."[57] Marx's point is that Hegel reverses the concrete reality of society; that is, Hegel mystifies the actual relationship between the people and the state. This mystification obscures the necessity for transforming the status and condition of human beings in modern society in order to facilitate "true democracy," that society in which human beings regain control over the forces dominating their existence.

While Marx did not dispute the goals of the Hegelian state,

then, he realized that Hegel, in attempting to "write the biography of abstract substance, of the idea,"[58] ignores and inverts the reality of society. The Hegelian state, according to Marx, is not actualized in the person of the monarch but is actually an objectification of its component citizens.

Another example of Marx's critique of specific characteristics of the *Hegelian* state involves the executive or bureaucratic function.   For Hegel, this branch was to work in harmony with the other components of the state, protecting the universal interests of the state. Marx recognized, with acute insight, that in actuality the corporations of civil society in the Hegelian state will be locked in a struggle with the bureaucracy. This struggle results from each side attempting to actualize the latent characteristics of its opposite component contained within itself. And, according to Marx, in real states of that period, the bureaucracy wins:

> The state formalism, which the bureaucracy is, is the state as formalism, and Hegel has described it precisely as such a formalism. Because this state formalism constitutes itself as a real power and becomes itself its own material content, it is evident that the bureaucracy is a tissue of practical illusion, or the illusion of the state. The bureaucratic mind is through and through a Jesuitical, theological mind. The bureaucrats are the Jesuits and theologians of the state. The bureaucracy is *la république prêtre*.[59]

In actual situations of this historical period and in Hegel's state, Marx recognized the possible degeneration of the bureaucracy into a stratified and materialistic corps of civil servants, seeking their own ends and the furtherance of their careers in a closed organization of hierarchical trust. This is only overcome when and if the universal interests really become their particular interests and not simply as in an abstract claim such as Hegel's. What Hegel does not specify is how the civil servant is to be controlled.   In Hegel's hierarchical system, each bureaucrat is responsible to and controlled by his or her superior. One of Marx's questions is: who, then, is to control the hierarchy?

Marx's idea of "true democracy" is of great importance here.

Both in the discussion of the bureaucracy and of Hegel's legislative branch, Marx consistently endorses Hegel's goals while denying that Hegel has provided the necessary mechanisms and correct
methodological ground. As Marx notes, Hegel views consciousness of
the universal aims of the state with high regard (indeed, in the
case of law, with the highest regard), until this consciousness is
empirically located in the Many. With the Many it becomes, according to Marx's gloss of Hegel, "a mere potpourri of the 'thoughts
and opinions of the Many.'"[60] Public affairs in fact are not concerned with the public at all, and that is the problem. So the
legislature is, for Marx, a purely formal, illusory aspect of
public participation within Hegel's state. The legislature is sus-
pect both in its formulation and in the fact that it is, within
Hegel's system, superfluous.

Hegel pictures the Estates of the legislature as the mediating factor between the political and administrative groups and
individual or particular groups. Yet this is the unity in which
the state supposedly exists. How then, asks Marx, can the Hegelian
Estates serve as a mediating factor? "The Estates," according to
Marx, "are the established contradiction of the state and civil
society within the state. At the same time they are the demand for
the dissolution of this contradiction."[61] Thus Marx shows that, in
placing the legislature in such a position, Hegel brings together
and intensifies the internal contradictions present in all existing, non-democratic political states. What Hegel is left with is a
standing conflict between civil society as represented in the
Estates and the political state--a conflict where unity was supposed to have been.

In the historical development of civil society, writes Marx,
class divisions undergo transformations based on money and education, which lead to arbitrary class division. Hegel's recurring
problem--the question of poverty and class mobility--arises again.
Within civil society there are class and social positions, though
these are not always entirely separate. The civil man only rises
above this when assuming the political role afforded by the political, that is, incomplete democracy. In Hegel's system, however,
the Estates prevent this by keeping man in his private role, hence

converting private difference and inequality into class difference and inequality.

Hegel's attempt to develop a unity between the two subjects through the Estates is, according to Marx, mystification and illusion. This mystery is that of Hegelian philosophy in general, of the philosophy of right in particular, and of the modern political state. Hegel falsely conceives of the legislature as the "middle term" between the monarch and the people. This is an apparent unity in mediation. But, as Marx writes: "In general, Hegel conceives the syllogism to be, via its middle term, a *mixtum compositum*. We can say that in his development of the rational syllogism all of the transcendence and mystical dualism of his system becomes apparent. The middle term is the wooden sword, the concealed opposition between universality and singularity."[62] In order to see why Marx opposed Hegel on these points, it is important to see, as clearly as possible, what Marx meant by "democracy" and "true democracy" and how these achieve what Hegel failed to grasp.

In the course of Marx's critique of Hegel's view of sovereignty, Marx makes an unusual statement, though one in complete agreement with his critique up to this point: "The Modern French have conceived it thus: In true democracy the *political state disappears* [*der politische Staat untergehe*]."[63] It is important to clarify the significance of this remark. O'Malley cites this passage as one instance of "Marx's anarchism,"[64] as it has come to be called. It will be seen in the remaining chapters of this work that it is inaccurate to characterize Marx's position, even at this early point, as a type of anarchism. The context of the discussion in which Marx declares that "the political state disappears" in true democracy shows that this "true democracy" is a far more sophisticated and subtle notion than any proposed by the classical anarchists.

Marx's notion of "popular sovereignty" put forward against Hegel's criticism of the "confused notions" and "wild idea" of popular sovereignty is a different sense of popular sovereignty, different from Hegel's usage and from that of the traditional liberal sense. "One can also speak of a sovereignty of the people in opposition to the sovereignty existing in the monarch. But then it is not a question of one and the same sovereignty which has arisen on two sides, but two entirely contradictory concepts of sovereignty, the one a sovereignty such as can come to exist in a monarch, the other such as can come to exist only in a people."[65] The type of sovereignty that "can come to exist only in a people," according to Marx, is that sovereignty characteristic of democracy. In this democracy, as contrasted to Hegel's monarchy, each of the "elements" of society plays a role in determining the "character of the whole" rather than the monarch, seen as an independent element embodying the whole, attempting to determine the whole.[66] Thus Marx claims that democracy as this sovereignty of the people is the "truth of monarchy,"[67] since only in terms of this democracy can monarchy, as an attempt to incorporate and determine the interests of the whole, be understood. What Marx has done is determine, correctly, that Hegel's idea of a sovereign monarchy inadequately accounts for the democratic functions Hegel assigns to the state. Hegel's conception of civil society as the area of society where the particular interests of individuals predominate needed the concept of a mediating state, represented by the monarch, in order to moderate the strains of the pursuit of particular interests and promote the universal interests of society as a whole. In this fashion, the state for Hegel should act as a "democratic" force, furthering the interests of the people in general. As Marx noted, it does not and cannot do this; Hegel's monarchy "is necessarily democracy inconsistent with itself. . . ."[68] In true democracy, rather than the monarch attempting to determine the interests of the whole instead of the interests of the people being represented only in the political sphere of the monarchical state (including the bureaucracy and the Estates)--or, for that matter, in a representative constitution-the constitution or society itself appears as "the self-determination of the people."[69]

Thus, according to Marx, "[D]emocracy is the solved *riddle* of all constitutions" because the determination of the form of society is returned to its original and genuine basis, the "*actual human being*, the *actual people*, and established as the people's *own* work."[70] What Marx is claiming as the basis of true democracy is the primacy of human beings over specific political institutions, or, to put it in another fashion, the fact that human beings are constitutive of political institutions. Where this relationship is distorted, as is the case with Hegel's state, the distortion is still based in democracy, though democracy is then in conflict with itself. This was the case in any particular political framework that Marx had encountered; as Marx put it, democracy is "the *essence of all state constitutions. . . .*"[71] In democracy, where the aspects of the state and the state taken as a whole reflect the self-determination of the people, universal and particular interests are unified. This sense of democracy is only possible where the "state" is organized as the self-determination of society and not, as Hegel had claimed, as an all-encompassing whole or form that claims to govern and organize (or at least mediate) the private, particular aspects of life. Thus, when Marx discusses the claim that "in true democracy, the political state disappears," this must be understood as a claim that the political state as a putative reconciliation of universal and particular interest disappears. Immediately following Marx's comment on the disappearance of the political state, he clarifies this point: "This is correct in so far as the political state qua political state, as constitution, no longer passes for the whole."[72]

What ceases in true democracy is the state as an abstract reconciling power, a conception of the state which Marx held to be a defect in Hegel's monarchical state and in the political republic. In the political republic, the state is still conceived as an abstract entity standing above the particular determinations of the people. Hegel's Estates constitution and the representative constitution share the result of this distortion of democracy, since both are seen as abstractions from actual life, from the real life and determinations of the people. This defect is shared by any state that is merely political since it thereby effects this separation of civil and political life. Thus, when the political state disappears, it is as political state, not necessarily as a state or form of social organization. The disappearance of the political state would mitigate against continued use of the term "state," since it is unclear what sense can be made of a "nonpolitical *state.*" It is, perhaps, best to use "form of social organization" or "organized society" in place of non-political "state." In political states prior to Marx's era, democracy had been distorted in either the false universality of Hegel's monarchy or, as in modern political republics, in the more explicit separation of the political and the civil, the universal and the particular, and the isolation of the pseudo-universal political life in the constitutional state-form.

> [Until] now the *political constitution* has been the *religious sphere*, the *religion* of national life, the heaven of its generality over against the earthly existence of its actuality. The political sphere has been the only state sphere in the state, the only sphere in which the content as well as the form has been species-content, the truly general; but in such a way that at the same time, because this sphere has confronted the others, its content has also become formal and particular. *Political life* in the modern sense is the scholasticism of national life. *Monarchy* is the perfect expression of this estrangement. The *republic* is the negation of this estrangement within its own sphere. It is obvious that the political constitution as such is brought into being only where the private spheres have won an independent existence.[73]

What disappears in true democracy is this merely political state, not the state as such and certainly not every form of social organization. Marx's alleged anarchism is not an anarchism at all. The anarchists advocated abolishing the political state as a means of eliminating the fundamental oppressive force in society. What Marx put forward in this early work was not a call for the abolition of the state but rather an observation that, in the genuine reconciliation of particular and universal interests and of civil life and political life, the merely political state will in fact disappear--it will in a sense become superfluous. For the anarchists, the abolition of the state was an explicit goal and a prerequisite for the type of social change included in Marx's concept of true democracy. At this point for Marx, on the other hand, the abolition of any particular state was not the essential point; every political state up to his time had distorted

its "truth," true democracy, not because it was a state but because it was a merely political state.

Of key importance in understanding Marx at this point is an
examination of his historical approach to the question of the
state.   Even at this early point in his intellectual career, for
Marx it is not simply a question of the abstract concept of the
state but of the development of states throughout history. In
fact, according to Marx, the "state" as such, as an abstraction,
is a modern concept, only possible where private life emerges as a
separate sphere of activity.[74]

In the Greek world, the private individual was absorbed by
the *res publica* and, to put it in Marx's terms, the *res publica*
thus became the "real private affair of the citizens."[75]   In this
state and in "oriental despotisms," where the state is the captive
of an individual will, the merely political state, the state
standing alongside the sphere of private life, did not exist. In
the emergence from the feudalism of the Middle Ages, when civil
life gradually lost its "political character," the private particular interests gained their independence as a non-political
sphere, while the political state organized as the exclusive
sphere of universality. This was an advance over the society of
the Middle Ages which, as a society in which the political perme-
ated the spheres of private activity without reflecting the self-
determination of the people, Marx characterized as the "*democracy
of unfreedom*,"[76] but this advance should not obscure the fact that
this transformation occurred at the cost of the separation of what
then developed as "civil society" and the "political state."

In the emergence from feudalism, the forces of civil society
came to assert their newly realized "independence" against feudal
politics in a way that allowed the distinction between the private
individual and the citizen to act as a destructive force. Where
the political state claims to exclusively embody and promote the
universal and general interests of society while in actuality
being subjected to the powers of civil society, the human interests of those outside of the dominant groups of civil society
suffer.   It is this artificial and illusory separation that Marx
criticized in Hegel and in modern political republics.

Hegel assumed that the state, as a relatively autonomous entity, could actually serve and promote the general interests, mediating the impact of life in civil society. Marx did not accept this view of the political state, as has been seen, since in his view the state is an institution of real people, not an abstract entity, and these real people have their own interests within civil society, as long as the separation is made between civil society and state. As a result, the state is subject to the machinations of civil society even though it proclaims itself as the exclusive sphere of universality. Even if the actual administrators of the political state apparatus attempt to fulfill their duty as state authorities (that is, if they attempt to fulfill the mission of the state), civil society, liberated from the political constraints of the feudal age, would come to dominate social and political life; indeed, the existence of civil society is the precondition of the merely political state.

The advance of this "political emancipation," especially as it developed in the bourgeois revolutions of the eighteenth century, was that it established certain basic rights, albeit in a distorted form, rights including political liberty and equality. These rights were still in distorted form because they had yet to truly embody general, universal interests.[77] As Marx commented in "On the Jewish Question":

> The completion of the idealism of the state was at the same time the completion of the materialism of civil society. Throwing off the political yoke meant at the same time throwing off the bonds which restrained the egoistic spirit of civil society. Political emancipation was at the same time the emancipation of civil society from politics, from having even the *semblance* of a universal content.
>
> Feudal society was resolved into its basic element--*man*, but the member of civil society, is thus the basis, the precondition of the *political* state. He is recognized as such by this state in the rights of man.[78]

It is only with this historical background in view that Marx's remarks concerning "true democracy" can be understood. Given that man as member of civil society is the precondition of the merely political state and given that civil society has the egoistic man, the atomistic individualist as its basis, so long as civil society remains an "independent" sphere of life, any "person, group, or institution that pretends to represent the 'universal [interest]' will really be doing so only to promote its particular interest, and the state will be primarily an arena of conflict."[79] True democracy requires the reconciliation or integration of the universal and the particular, a transformation that will result in the disappearance of the merely political state and not, as the anarchists held, the abolition of every existing individual state in order to achieve "harmony" or "justice." In true democracy, the universal interests will be promoted in actuality, not just as an illusory political form.

The "disappearance," "transcendence," or "withering" of the political state continued as a central theme of both Marx and Friedrich Engels's work, though the idea was developed in a more concrete form in Marx's later works. The idea of the disappearance of the state in what Marx calls in these early works "true democracy" was modified as a result of Marx's realization in the works following the *Critique* that the questions of the preconditions required for true democracy and by whom these preconditions could be met could only be answered by a scientific investigation of the basis of capitalist society, of the nature of class conflict and revolutionary praxis. Especially in *The German Ideology* and the works written during and after 1848 (for example, in *The Communist Manifesto*), this realization led to less use of the terminology of "true democracy," though the core of the concept remained.

True democracy became, for Marx, a society only possible when the conditions of material existence in capitalist society had been transformed by the proletariat so that the interests of one class, the capitalists, are not promoted by the state as the general, universal interest. The state in capitalist society is the expression of the interests of the dominant class, according to Marx, as well as the instrument for preserving the power of the capitalists. The state as pictured here is not a monolithic tool but an "arena of conflict" in which the political struggles reflect the conflicts within the capitalist class and between that class and others. In the absence of class conflict and class rule, the true democratic forces of self-determination could promote the general interests of society. It is important to recognize that Marx's concept of true democracy developed as his concept of communist society and thus to recognize the significance of the admittedly vague concept of true democracy in Marx's development since the concept is so important in his conflict with the anarchists, a brief preliminary attempt at its explication will occupy the remainder of this chapter.

It has been noted earlier that true democracy involves the transcendence of the merely political state in the integration of particular and universal interest, of civil and political man. Intrinsically, then, true democracy is a form of social organization in which the interests of the people are not subordinated to the interests of few, nor are the interests of society conceived as a "whole" in conflict with the particular interests of individuals. Instead, particular and universal are reintegrated, civil and political life brought together. As Marx took pains to note, this has not been the meaning or practice of democracy throughout history. Democracy has typically been a movement against unequal privileges on the part of another group holding lesser privileges. Democracy has been, for the most part, a movement toward power on the part of one group within society and not a movement toward the abolition of particularistic power groups.[80] The former movement has resulted in political democracy, as Marx pointed out, but not in the true democracy he advocated. Marx held that political democracy or "emancipation" was only a step in the direction of true democracy or human emancipation. This true democracy requires, beyond political democracy, the "democratization of economic power," as Robert S. Cohen has noted.[81] The process of true democratization must make actual the values embodied in the concept of democracy; as Engels remarked in *Anti-Dühring*, it must take the values of political democracy and extend them to the socio-economic sphere.[82] True democracy insists on a new socio-economic order, one capable of integrating universal and particular interests and not isolating the universal in the political sphere. This "genuine democracy" means the possibility of all institutions being brought under the control of those who live and work in them; in order for this to happen a revolutionary transformation of the economic and social order is necessary.[83]

The theoretical source for this democratic theory begins with Marx's comments on "true democracy" in his *Critique of Hegel's "Philosophy of Right"* and continues throughout Marx's intellectual development. It is, essentially, a theory in which the members of society, in reintegrating the particular and the universal, the civil and the political man, come to control their own "fate," to be "self-determining" as Marx put it in the *Critique*. This self-determination requires the reappropriation of control over economic life, a project which led Marx to intensive study of the nature of economic forces in society. In order to be self-determining and thus reach true democracy, in order to integrate particular and general interests, humans must transform the actual circumstances of their existence. In order to determine their own history, they must change the circumstances of the present and the inheritance of the past. In *The Eighteenth Brumaire of Louis Bonaparte*, Marx stated: "Men make their own history but they do not make it just as they please; they do not make it under circumstances chosen by themselves, but under circumstances directly encountered, given and transmitted from the past."[84]

The point exemplified in this last quotation is one never learned by the anarchists, as will become clear in the remainder of this work. Even before Marx wrote *Capital*, his notion of the process of transforming society toward true democracy, his theory of revolutionary praxis, fully incorporated the need to change the economic and social conditions of human existence, thereby changing both society and its members. In transforming the conditions of labor, the movement toward self-determination, toward true democracy is begun. As Marx described the nature of labor in *Capital*, humans interact with and oppose themselves to nature and in doing so transform the world--and themselves: "By thus acting on the external world and changing it, [man] at the same time changes his own nature."[85] If the change in society and its members is to be toward true democracy and community, toward Marx's communist society, then it must begin with the transformation of existing economic conditions. In stark contrast, the anarchists conceived of the social transformation as necessarily beginning with the abolition of the state.

Hegel set the tone for Marx's discussion of the state in Marx's early works. In attempting to ground human freedom in the integration of the particular and the universal, Hegel stated the problem that would occupy both Marx and the anarchists: given that Hegel's attempt at this integration in the modern (Hegelian) state had failed, how is true democracy or genuine community possible? Marx gradually emancipated himself from the details of Hegel's solution, though he remained within the framework of Hegelian goals. In the following chapters it will be shown why this was not always the case with the anarchists. Though the anarchists would strive for a "communal individuality" resembling Marx's "true democracy," it will be seen that there are fundamental incompatibilities between the Marxian and anarchist positions, incompatibilities stemming from fundamentally different points of departure. Before this is shown, however, Marx's attempt to formulate his own, more concrete picture of the problem, especially in "On the Jewish Question" and in the *1844 Manuscripts*, will be traced and critically examined in the next chapter.

NOTES

1. Albert Camus, *The Myth of Sisyphus*, trans. Justin O'Brien (New York: Vintage, 1955), p. 49.

2. G.W.F. Hegel, *Berliner Schriften*, 1818-1831, ed. J. Hoffmeister, Band XI (Hamburg: Verlag von Felix Meiner, 1956), p. 8. Throughout this work, all emphases within quotations will be those of the work cited unless otherwise noted.

3. G.W.F. Hegel, *The Philosophy of Right*, trans. and notes by T.M. Knox (London: Oxford University Press, 1967), p. 10. In references to this work, numbers within parentheses refer to the paragraphs in Hegel's text, the remarks appended to these paragraphs, the additions of the Gans editions, or the translator's

notes, as indicated. For more information, see the translator's foreword to *PR*.

4. Ibid., p. 11.

5. Ibid.

6. Witness the polemic against Fries and others in the preface to *PR*, pp. 2, 5.

7. *PR*, p. 123 (184). This is an instance of Hegel's *List der Vernunft*, the "cunning of reason."

8. Ibid., p. 126 (188).

9. Ibid., pp. 126-132.

10. Ibid., p. 127. (Remark to 190.)

11. Ibid., p. 127 (192).

12. Ibid., p. 129 (196).

13. Ibid., p. 129 (198).

14. Shlomo Avineri, *Hegel's Theory of the Modern State* (Cambridge: Cambridge University Press, 1972), p. 146.

15. Ibid., p. 148.

16. *PR*, p. 130 (199).

17. Ibid.

18. Ibid., p. 130 (Remark to 200; my emphasis.)

19. Ibid., p. 132 (206).

20. Karl Marx, *The German Ideology*, in Karl Marx and Frederick Engels, *Marx-Engels Collected Works* (New York: International Publishers, 1975-), vol. V, p. 282.

21. Avineri, pp. 155f; Charles Taylor *Hegel*, (Cambridge: Cambridge University Press, 1975), p. 435 and note 1.

22. *PR*, p. 134. (Remark to 209.)

23. Ibid., pp. 134-146 (211-229).

24. Ibid., p. 135. (Remark to 211.)

25. Ibid., p. 140 (219).

26. Ibid., p. 141 (220).

27. Ibid., p. 360 (note 83).

28. Ibid., p. 146 (233).

29. See, for example, the documents surrounding the dispute between Marx and Bakunin concerning authority and the International, especially "The Alliance of Socialist Democracy and The International Working Men's Association," Karl Marx and Friedrich

Engels, *Selected Works on Anarchism and Anarcho-Syndicalism* (New York: International Publishers, 1972), pp. 105-124.

30. *PR*, p. 149. (Remark to 242.)

31. Ibid., p. 150 (244).

32. Ibid., pp. 277. (Addition to 244.)

33. Ibid., p. 150 (245).

34. Ibid., p. 152 (251).

35. William L. McBride, private communication.

36. *PR*, p. 153 (253).

37. Ibid., p. 155. (Remark to 256.)

38. Ibid., p. 155 (257).

39. G.W.F. Hegel, *The Philosophy of History*, trans. J. Sibree (New York: Dover Publications, 1956), p. 39.

40. *PR*, p. 288. (Addition to 279.)

41. G.W.F. Hegel, "Das alteste Systemprogramm des deutschen Idealismus," quoted in Shlomo Avineri, *Hegel's Theory of the Modern State* (Cambridge: Cambridge University Press, 1972), p. 11. My analysis is indebted to Avineri's own on p. 11.

42. *PR*, p. 156 (258).

43. Ibid., p. 156. (Remark to 258.)

44. Ibid., p. 161 (261).

45. Ibid., p. 164 (268).

46. Paul Thomas, *Karl Marx and the Anarchists* (London: Routledge & Kegan Paul, 1980), p. 50.

47. Marx's *Critique of Hegel's "Philosophy of Right"* appears in slightly differing translations; trans. Annette Jolin, ed. Joseph O'Malley (Cambridge: Cambridge University Press, 1970), and in *MECW* III, as "Contribution to the Critique of Hegel's Philosophy of Law." Both translations will be used here, cited as JOM and *MECW* III, respectively.

48. *MECW* III, p. 5.

49. Ludwig Feuerbach, *The Essence of Christianity*, trans. George Eliot (New York: Harper and Row, 1957).

50. *MECW* III, p. 7.

51. Ibid., p. 8.

52. Ibid., p. 9.

53. JOM, p. 17.

54. Ibid., p. 25, 26.

55. *PR*, p. 182. (Remark to 279.)

56. JOM, p. 31. See passage cited in note 58.

57. Ibid., p. 30.

58. *MECW* III, p. 39.

59. JOM, p. 46.

60. Ibid., p. 61; Marx cites *PR*, p. 195 (301).

61. Ibid., p. 67.

62. Ibid., p. 85.

63. Ibid., p. 31.

64. Ibid., lxii.

65. Marx, *MECW* III, p. 28.

66. Ibid., p. 29.

67. Ibid.

68. Ibid.

69. Ibid.

70. Ibid.

71. Ibid.

72. Ibid., p. 30.

73. Ibid., p. 31.

74. Ibid., p. 32.

75. Ibid.

76. Ibid.

77. See D.F.B. Tucker, *Marxism and Individualism* (New York: St. Martin's Press, 1980), p. 68.

78. Karl Marx, "On the Jewish Question," in *MECW* III, p. 166.

79. T. Kermit Scott, private communication.

80. See Robert S. Cohen, "Marxism and Democracy," in *Marxism and Democracy*, ed. Herbert Aptheker (New York: Humanities Press, for American Institute of Marxist Studies, 1965), p.3.

81. Ibid., p. 7.

82. See Friedrich Engels, *Herr Eugen Dühring's Revolution in Science (Anti-Dühring)*, trans. Emile Burns, ed. C.P. Dutt (New York: International Publishers, 1966), p. 117.

83. Kenneth A. Megill, *The New Democratic Theory* (London: The Free Press, 1970), p. 39.

84. Karl Marx, *The Eighteenth Brumaire of Louis Bonaparte*, in

MECW XI, p. 103.

85. Karl Marx, *Capital*, vol. I., trans. Samuel Moore and Edward Aveling (New York: International Publishers, 1967), p. 177.

2
THE STATE, ALIENATION,
AND HUMAN EMANCIPATION

> Don't you see that in your country they have confused the
> thing whch has neither consciousness nor thought, nor desire,
> nor will; which one picks up, puts down, keeps or exchanges,
> without injury to it, or without its complaining, have con-
> fused this with the thing which cannot be exchanged or ac-
> quired, which has liberty, will, desire, which can give or
> refuse itself for a moment or forever, which laments and suf-
> fers, and which cannot become an article of commerce, without
> its character being forgotten and violence done to its
> nature; contrary to the general laws of existence?
>
> Denis Diderot[1]

MARX'S MOVE BEYOND THE HEGELIAN STATE

To argue at any point that Marx's conception of the state was
static or ahistorical would be misleading. Rather, what the previous chapter has attempted to show is that Marx began from a distinctly historical standpoint, the Hegelian standpoint. It was
precisely this keen awareness of the dynamism of history that allowed Marx to criticize Hegel's conception of the state. The separation of civil society and political life is a historical phenomenon, and thus the emergence of the state in its modern form is
also a historical phenomenon. Hegel's answer to this separation

--the state as mediator of the separated aspects of modern life--
was rejected by Marx, as has been seen, because Marx saw that this
supposed mediation was a false reconciliation and that the supposed reconciliation in fact reinforced the separation. Soon after
his *Critique of Hegel's "Philosophy of Right,"* Marx grounded this
insight in a series of manuscripts, *The Economic and Philosophic
Manuscripts of 1844,*[2] the essay "On the Jewish Question,"[3] and an
"Introduction" to his Critique of Hegel.[4] The purpose of this
chapter is to show the intimate philosophical connection between
Marx's critique of Hegel's conception of the state, discussed in
the previous chapter, and the positive critical results of the
critique found (largely) in the works just mentioned. This will
show Marx's continued development toward a concrete understanding
of the state and thus set the course for an examination of Marx's
disputes with the classical anarchists.

Even before the *Critique of Hegel's "Philosophy of Right,"*
Marx had disputed the ability of the Hegelian state to achieve the
mediation of particularity and universality, while still seeing
this mediation as the goal of societal organization. In some of
his earliest writings that speak of the state, Marx expressed the
conviction: "The true 'public' education carried out by the state
lies in the rational and public existence of the state; the state
itself educates its members by making them its members, by converting the aims of the individual into general aims . . . by the
individual finding his good in the life of the whole, and the
whole in the frame of mind of the individual."[5] Marx was criticizing those[6] who denied that the rational state, the state in
which the particularity of the individual is dialectically integrated with the universal interests of the whole, is "an
association of free human beings who educate one another. . . ."[7]
For the young Marx, as both a student and critic of the Hegelian
political ideal, neither particularity nor universality could be
ignored. A consequence of Marx's position, as of Hegel's, is that
the freedom of the individual cannot simply be absorbed into the
whole of the state.   The preservation of freedom in the
particularity of the individual in the Hegelian framework
involved, as Marx saw, "the state as the great organism, in which

legal, moral, and political freedom must be realized, and in which the individual citizen in obeying the laws of the state only obeys the natural laws of his own reason, of human reason."[8]

As was seen in the previous chapter, Marx rejected the Hegelian model of the state as inadequate for the realization of freedom, of particularity in universality. In Marx's social and political writings of the early 1840s, only the concrete form of the state in which freedom is realized, in which the mediation of the particular and the universal is achieved, constituted the actualization of rationality inherent in the concept of the state. Though the modern political state was not to survive Marx's analysis, the defense of this individual freedom continued throughout his earliest political writings, finding its most explicit form in his *Critique* of Hegel and especially in the essays following the *Critique* with which this chapter is centrally concerned.[9]

In the *Critique of the "Philosophy of Right,"* Marx called this state in which freedom is realized "true democracy." Democracy, according to Marx, is that state in which both elements-- particularity, the individual, and universality, the general--are preserved and at the same time incorporated in the constitution. This is radically different from the Hegelian conception of monarchy, as in democracy "the constitution is constantly brought back to its actual basis, the *actual human being*, the *actual people*, and established as the people's *own* work."[10] In fact, according to Marx, "only democracy . . . is the true unity of the general and the particular."[11] It is only on this basis that Marx could criticize the Hegelian schema, as the false unity of the Hegelian state was inherent in its structure.

In the Hegelian conception, the structure of the rational modern state is based on a concrete distinction between civil society and the state. In this separation, according to Marx, civil society becomes the domain of private property. In so doing wrote Marx, Hegel had inverted the actual relationship of human beings and private property. Rather than grounding private property as object in its relationship to the property owner, Hegel had made property the subject and the owner the objectification of the

"will" of property. Since Hegel had presupposed that the relatively independent economic realm of civil society, with its central institution, private property, would enable humans to act
freely in the political sphere, Marx's criticism is vital. For, as
Marx saw, where the economic activity of civil society and the political activity of civil society are separated and where human
beings become the objects rather than the subjects of private
property, true freedom--the dignity of creative individual devel-
opment--cannot be realized. As Paul Thomas wrote recently:

> When property is given the freedom to act, men are reduced to
> the status of mere objects. Men become the attributes of
> property--even though property is by definition the socially
> crystallized outcome of their own purposive creative activ-
> ity. . . . Far from being the realization or objectification
> of human personality--which had been Hegel's original justi-
> fication--private property actually negated human person-
> ality.[12]

When Marx's attacks on Hegel's notions of private property
are considered in conjunction with his critique of Hegel's political structure, a pattern begins to emerge. If human beings are to
achieve their highest purpose--which was, according to Marx at
this time, the realization of freedom in community (*Gemeinwesen*)
in a democratic state[13]--private property relations in which freedom is negated would need to be transformed. Simply freeing property in the sphere of civil society would negate freedom. Transforming property relations necessitated transformation of the political state that separated economic life from social life and
thus prevented the formation of a true community. Where the form
of the political state prevents the realization of freedom Marx
called "true democracy" and the economic machinations of civil
society obsure and mystify actual economic relations, no real
community can develop. In Marx's early writings, the most cogent
discussion of these problems as they relate directly to the state
is found in Marx's essay, "On the Jewish Question."

ALIENATION AND HUMAN EMANCIPATION

Only when the real, individual man reabsorbs in himself the abstract citizen, and as an individual human being has become a *species-being* in his everyday life, in his particular work, and in his particular situation, only when man has recognized and organized his *'forces propres'* as *social* forces, and consequently no longer separates social power from himself in the shape of *political* power, only then will human emancipation have been accomplished.

"On the Jewish Question"[14]

Ostensibly an essay in response to Bruno Bauer's position on the emancipation of the Jews, "On the Jewish Question" very quickly becomes a key statement of Marx's position on the political state.   Having initiated the critique of the Hegelian dichotomy between civil society and the state, Marx restates the problem in terms of the need for a concrete, human emancipation. This human emancipation is contrasted with a mere political emancipation, where the "abstract citizen" is separated from the concrete conditions of his existence in a partial and illusory political freedom. In these conditions human beings are less than total social beings--political existence being separated from concrete existence.

Contrary to many of his predecessors (including Rousseau), Marx saw this separation of abstract political existence and concrete existence as a distinctly historical phenomenon. Only with the development of the unique characteristics of the modern state in capitalist society could the polarization of the political and socio-economic spheres become so sharply defined. Only with the development of the modern state, where property relations subjugate human beings and the political apparatus falsely claims to represent the universal interests of the community, could this separation predominate. To see the development of Marx's critique of this historical phenomenon, it is important to trace his critique of Bauer.

Marx saw that Bauer had formulated the question of emancipation incorrectly; it was not simply a question of emancipating the

state from religion, as Bauer had proposed, in order to secularize
man.   Bauer had advocated the emancipation from religion as a precondition for the emancipation of the Jews.[15] This position was
based on a more general conception, that of the emancipation of
the state itself from religion. Thus, according to Bauer, the desire of the Jews for emancipation could only be fulfilled when the
Jews renounced Judaism, just as the emancipation of all could only
be achieved when all forms of religion were renounced--especially
in the state. But, asked Marx, *"What kind of emancipation* is in
question? What conditions follow from the very nature of the emancipation that is demanded? Only the criticism *of political emancipation* itself would have been the conclusive criticism of the
Jewish question and its real merging in the 'general question of
the time.'"[16]

In fact, Marx points out, the real question in regard to the
emancipation of the Jews extends beyond the emancipation of the
state from religion and of Jews from Judaism. The civic emancipation of Jews through the renunciation of religion and the political elimination of religion does not eliminate the religious
spirit of both humans and states.

> When Bauer says of the opponents of Jewish emancipation:
> "Their error was only that they assumed the Christian state
> to be the only true one and did not subject it to the same
> criticism that they applied to Judaism. . . ," we find that
> his error lies in the fact that he subjects to criticism *only*
> the "Christian state," not the "state as such," that he does
> not investigate *the relation of political emancipation to hu-
> man emancipation* and therefore puts forward conditions which
> can be explained only by uncritical confusion of political
> emancipation with general human emancipation.[17]

Thus, according to Marx, the emancipation of the state from religion does not therefore secularize (and emancipate) human beings.
What Bauer should have done was to go beyond the level of political emancipation of the state from religion to the question of human emancipation.   For, as Marx argues, man as subject of the
political state is still a "religious" subject. Rather than religion being the cause of "religious" subjugation and alienation, it

is in fact an effect of the "religious" spirit of the political
state that subjugates and alienates humans. Human beings as
"religious" subjects of the state are still examples of religious
alienation--of the separation of humans from themselves in the
separation of abstract citizen and concrete (particular) individual. What Marx termed "religious narrowness" does not cause
the socio-political alienation, secular narrowness, but is itself
caused by the more basic secular narrowness. Religion as an alienating force is "the *manifestation* of secular narrowness."[18]
Bauer's critique of religious alienation is inadequate, then, because the modern political state, even one free from established
religion, continues to incorporate the separation of abstract
citizen and concrete individual. Political emancipation is a
partial, incomplete emancipation.

Marx's comparison of the mediation of religion and that of
the state is especially acute. In effect, the state acts as an
intermediary in the process of political emancipation (as the
mechanism for establishing abstract political freedom) in much the
same way as religion acts as an intermediary between the human and
the divine.[19] As such, the state maintains the alienation of abstract political existence from the particular existence of humans
through the postulation of a false universality.

An allied point that Marx deals with briefly in "On the
Jewish Question" is the nature of private property in the modern,
politically emancipated state. The same type of "contradiction"
exists in property relations as exists in the development of political freedom: though the modern state eliminates property qua-
lifications by extending the franchise to non-property owners, the
subjugation of humans by private property continues. For, writes
Marx, the political state presupposes the continued existence of
the relations of private property. Following Hegel's separation
of the civil and political realms, Marx points out that the state
presupposed the play of particularity--specifically, the relations
of private property--in civil society. Only in the political realm
does the state claim to assert universality.

This separation of the civil and political spheres with its
concomitant isolation of the relations of private property in

civil society and political freedom in the political state is a historical phenomenon. In the movement from the medieval to modern political forms, the operations of civil society became separated from the realm of the common good. As Marx points out, this move toward political emancipation reached its political zenith in the declarations of rights produced in the American and French Revolutions. Rather than, as in medieval political forms, seeking universality in an all-encompassing synthesis of state and religion, the subject of the modern political state seeks universality only in the political sphere. This isolation of universality in the political sphere leaves the private sphere of civil society, and thus private property, free from any universal constraints. The state, according to Hegel, was supposed to overcome this separation in a mediation of particular and universal interests. As Marx's discussions both in his *Critique* and "On the Jewish Question" show, however, Hegel's solution is illusory. The universality Hegel had seen as a necessary component of the rational state is, according to Marx, not attained in Hegel's solution. This universality, the community where human beings are "communal beings,"[20] could not develop because the unrestricted influence of property relations in civil society continued to subjugate and alienate humans beings.

Marx was not condemning political emancipation. Rather, he was attempting to show how Bauer had neglected to see the incomplete nature of political emancipation. "*Political* emancipation is, of course, a big step forward. True, it is not the final form of human emancipation in general, but it is the final form of human emancipation *within* the hitherto existing world order."[21]

Where Bauer had failed (and where many classical anarchists would later fail) was in mistaking this partial and incomplete form of human emancipation for the final and complete form. The political revolutions of the eighteenth century, as well as the developing laissez-faire economic theory had lent strong support to this view. But, as Marx had shown in both the *Critique* and "On the Jewish Question,"

> the so-called *rights of man*, the *droits de l'homme* as distinct from the *droits du citoyen*, are nothing but the rights

of a *member of civil society*, i.e., the rights of egoistic man, of man separated from other men and from the community. . . . In the rights of man, he is far from being conceived as a species-being; on the contrary, species-life itself, society appears as a framework external to the individuals, as a restriction of their original independence.[22]

The result of this situation, according to Marx's analysis, was the reduction of the political, "communal" sphere to a subordinate position.   Political emancipation results in the domination of egoistic man, with the result that "the sphere in which he acts as a communal being is downgraded to a level below the sphere in which he acts as a partial being, and that, finally, it is not man as *citoyen*, but man as *bourgeois* who is considered to be the *essential* and *true* man."[23]

Against this partial and incomplete form of emancipation Marx placed the concept of human emancipation. The subjects of the modern state exist in an alienated condition, one in which civil society predominates. Human emancipation would end this domination and alienation in a reconciliation of the civil and the political. Even so, it is important to point out that Marx was not claiming that the champions of mere political emancipation were correct when they considered man as bourgeois, as atomistic egoist to be the "true" and "essential" human being simply because, under conditions of alienation and partial emancipation, this might appear to be the case. In *The Holy Family*, Marx carefully distinguished between this view and the actual situation, that the supposed "atoms" were in fact alienated communal (human) beings. What Marx wrote is that the actual relationship is one of civil life holding the state together and that, despite the alienated condition that indicated otherwise, it is the real human ties of mutual dependence and interest that bind together civil society.[24]

Given the background of the preceding pages, the statement quoted at the beginning of this section (see note 14) brings Marx's position into sharp relief. Marx has traced the development of the modern political state, where civil society is separated from the political state, and in political emancipation the particular, egoistic interests of civil society are given virtual

free rein. The communal being of human beings is represented in an
alienated and illusory form in the false universal of the political state. Marx's statement concerning human emancipation, examined against this background, helps to illuminate the rather elu-
sive concept of human emancipation and the related concept of communal being. Human emancipation is that situation where the separation of abstract citizen, the political being, from the concrete, particular existence of civil society ends through the mediation of both spheres in the creation of a truly human society.
This dialectical development results in what Marx termed the realization of man as species-being (Gattungswesen), the "unity of man
with man, which is based on the real difference between men, the
concept of the human species brought down from the heaven of abstraction to the real earth, . . . the concept of society."[25]
Though Marx was to elaborate on this concept in his later writings, its use here is fairly clear. Marx, like Hegel, was attempting to state the conditions under which a society of human beings
could live as a genuine community while developing as different
individuals.   Only when the individual has recognized his nature
as a species-being--as an essentially social being--and so transforms abstract citizenship into an internal social force in human
society would human emancipation be complete.

Human emancipation, then, involves the reintegration of the
universal interests of political citizenship with the particular
interests of civil society. What Marx had done is to describe, in
another one of its aspects, what he earlier called "true democracy." Marx's claim that "in true democracy the political state
disappears"[26] assumes importance in this context. What Marx meant
is that the political state as a separate and falsely universal
aspect of human life is transformed and reintegrated into life
through the recognition of man's species-being, his essentially
social nature, and the organization of social forces in accordance
with this nature. It is important to see what Marx thought could
achieve this integration in order to explicate the concept of true
democracy.

Unlike Hegel (and later Ferdinand Lassalle), Marx saw that
the political state was not a separate entity that could achieve

the integration for which all three had hoped. On the contrary, according to Marx's discussion in "On the Jewish Question," the state itself is subordinate to the politically emancipated, depoliticized civil society in the modern era. Unlike the anarchists, Marx did not see the development of the modern state as the development of an omnipotent, autonomous power but rather as the alienated and dominated political expression of civil society. The state in its modern form claims to be the integrative power, but this claim is largely a reflection of its alienated existence. As has been seen, the property relations unfettered in the political emancipation of civil society reach into and come to dominate the political state.

> The political revolution thereby *abolished* the *political character of civil society*. . . . It gathered the dispersed parts of the political spirit, freed it from its intermixture with civil life, and established it as the sphere of community . . . ideally independent of those *particular* elements of civil life.
>
> But the completion of the idealism of the state was at the same time the completion of the materialism of civil society. . . . Political emancipation was at the same time the emancipation of civil society from politics, from having even the *semblance* of a universal content.[27]

The significance of Marx's views on the "emancipation" of the political state in regard to the claims of the anarchists cannot be overstated. Both Bauer and most of the classical anarchists shared a view of the state as a power independent of the relations of civil society. What Marx showed in "On the Jewish Question" is that the modern political state is based on the alienated existence of the state's subjects and the political state--as an effect of the emancipation of civil society--cannot overcome the alienation inherent in the division between civil and political man. This is, as Marx had seen, because the modern political state had progressed as far as it could toward human emancipation in the development of political emancipation.

Before examining the continuity in Marx's other works of the 1840s of the conception of the state just discussed, it should be noted that, in the *Economic and Philosophic Manuscripts of 1844* (hereafter *1844 Manuscripts*), Marx had grounded his description of alienation in the modern state in a profound analysis of the bases of alienation. In "On the Jewish Question," Marx showed how the development of political emancipation in the modern state led to, in Thomas's phrase, "the political and bureaucratic homogenization of individuals. . . ."[28] In the manuscripts of 1844, Marx provides the material conditions for the explication alienation and so grounds the critique of the political state in the forces of alienation found in everyday life.

In an important work on Marx and alienation, István Mészáros characterized the alienation dealt with by Marx in the *1844 Manuscripts* in the following manner:

> Alienation is therefore characterized by the universal exten-
> sion of "saleability" (i.e. the transformation of everything
> into commodity), by the conversion of human beings into
> "things" so that they could appear as commodities on the
> market (in other words: the "reification" of human rela-
> tions); and by the fragmentation of the social body into
> "isolated individuals" (*vereinzelte Einzelnen*) who pursued
> their own limited, particularistic aims "in servitude to
> egoistic need," making a virtue out of their selfishness in
> their cult of privacy.[29]

Composed from April to August in 1844, Marx's *1844 Manuscripts* are at least in part a continuation of his earlier work on Hegel. In these manuscripts Marx's critique of politics becomes concrete or firmly grounded in material conditions and is extended to the economic sphere.

The most important section of the manuscripts for the purposes of this chapter are those dealing with estranged labor and private property and communism.[30] Here Marx's critique of alienation in society comes to the fore, especially as connected to the conditions created by the modern state. In order to place these sections in their proper context, however, relevant material from the other sections will be examined for its connections to the topic at hand.

Marx initially traces the course of the wages of labor in the

economic realm of civil society, which in the modern state is the
realm of capitalist economy. Commenting on Adam Smith's notion of
the normal wage for workers in a capitalist economy as being the
lowest possible wage, Marx writes that the regulation of wages is
the means of maintaining a productive work force: "*The demand for
men necessarily governs the production of men, as of every other
commodity. . . .* The worker has become a commodity. . . ."[31] The
position of the worker in relation to the capitalist as well as
the development of the division of labor reduces the worker to a
market item. Even when the society is prosperous, as Marx points
out, the position of the worker is increasingly degraded. The accumulation of capital by the capitalist with its consequent increase in the division of labor results in an increasingly desper-
ate existence for the worker, as accumulated labor (capital) is
isolated in the hands of the capitalist and the worker's products
become more and more distant and "alien" to the worker. Even in
this prosperous society, ". . . the inevitable result for the
worker is overwork and premature death, decline to a mere machine,
a bond servant of capital, which piles up dangerously over and
against him, decline to more competition, and to starvation or
beggary for a section of the workers."[32]

   In a society where the economic forces of civil society are
not expanding, the condition of the workers is even worse. Con-
sidering the cycles of expansion and contraction in modern industrial society, the worker is in a highly precarious position.
Thus, as Marx states, even though traditional political economy
maintains that "the interest of the worker . . . never stands opposed to the interest of society, society always and necessarily
stands opposed to the interest of the worker."[33] Given the condition of the worker (Marx uses "proletarian"[34]) who has nothing but
his labor to support himself and who is maintained at subsistence
level, Marx formulates two questions that will guide the rest of
the manuscripts and which are of central importance to Marx's conflicts with the anarchists: "(1)What in the evolution of mankind
is the meaning of this reduction of the greater part of mankind to
abstract labor? (2)What are the mistakes committed by the piece-
meal reformers, who either want to *raise* wages and in this way im-

prove the situation of the working class, or regard *equality* of wages (as Proudhon does) [as] the goal of social revolution?"[35] One of the main points of Marx's comment on Proudhon, and in fact the source of the second question, is that labor is not simply an exchange of value, as political economy and some of the anarchists maintained. Rather, under the conditions of capitalism, labor is an appropriation of value by the capitalist. Labor as a "commodity" is life itself; thus, selling labor is selling oneself--that is, slavery.[36]

In capitalist society, according to the political economists cited by Marx, the only motive for the utilization of capital is profit, and this utilization is always where the largest profit is to be found. Though Smith's theoretical device, the "iron hand," provides an explanation of some of the objections to capitalism, it is evident from the passages that Marx extracts from Smith and Jean Baptiste Say and especially his critique of civil society in Hegel that the capitalists are in fact fundamentally opposed to the human interests of society, despite their attempts at explanation. Marx recognizes that the workers constitute the greater (and growing) part of capitalist society and that the control and exploitation of labor and markets, the goal of the capitalists, is in itself contrary to the interest of all others (capitalists and workers alike) in society.

The predatory practices of the industrial capitalists result in the decrease of the importance of older forms of land ownership. Ground rent falls, limiting those able to survive on it. This isolates more land in the hands of the industrials and larger capitalists; eventually, according to Marx, the distinction between capitalists and landowners is abolished, leaving only workers and capitalists in their inevitable conflicts. It is to these conflicts and their basis in the estrangement of labor that we now turn.

The concepts of estrangment (*Entfremdung*) and alienation (*Entäusserung*) are of key importance in Marx's conception of society and the state. Roughly and briefly, Marx's use of "alienation" usually encompasses both the sense of a separation and externalization of something from oneself and the legal sense of the

transfer of something from one person to another, while estrangement usually lacks the legal sense.[37] Both of these concepts are
involved in the phenomenon of alienation, and Marx uses both to
illustrate the relation between capital and labor. For this
reason, Marx turns to the phenomenon of estranged labor as a more
basic fact of political economics than previous political economists had dealt with. "Now, therefore, we have to grasp the essential connection between private property, greed, and the separation of labor, capital, and landed property; between exchange
and competition, value and the devaluation [*Entwertung*] of men,
monopoly and competition, etc.--the connection between this whole
estrangement and the *money* system."[38] This can be seen as the
project of the entire set of manuscripts, but the first and key
step taken is the discussion of "this whole estrangement." Estrangement and alienation have several aspects or modes for Marx:
alienation and objects, alienating activity, alienation and self-
estrangement, and alienation and estrangement from others.

Marx had previously discussed the paradoxical yet highly
"logical" process where the more the worker produces, the poorer
the worker becomes. This takes place because, as more and more
commodities are produced in industrial society, labor, which is
itself a commodity within the modern industrial framework, becomes
less and less expensive for the capitalist. Though it would seem
that greater production would enrich the worker, it in fact gradually impoverishes him by reducing the percentage of profit for
the capitalist on each produced good. Thus, hard work will lead
to overproduction in an effort to generate more profit and, eventually, to lack of work. This process results in the devaluation
of human beings and their world.

This devaluation, according to Marx, occurs when the worker,
in his production of an object, embodies his labor in the object,
thereby giving it new value and power. In this way his labor is
objectified in the labor product. As a result, the object "stands
over against" the worker as an alien thing, an alien power over
the worker in the hands of the capitalist. What is given to the
object, though, is lost to the worker. This Marx calls the "loss
of reality [*Entwirklichung*] for the worker,"[39] a devaluation, as

the worker at once loses value to the object and at the same time through objectification becomes subject to the power of the object. This "appropriation"[40] of the worker, of his value and power, is one aspect of estrangement, the alienation of labor.

Marx is to a certain extent appropriating the Hegelian concept of alienation, though Marx's use of it is novel and radical. Marx quickly goes beyond Hegelian alienation, especially as Hegel expressed it in the *Philosophy of Right*. The difference between the two becomes apparent when Marx extends his use of the term beyond mere separation of worker and labor, beyond a supposed exchange of value. For Marx alienation, the estrangement of humans in all its aspects, becomes a more fundamental feature of modern capitalist industrial society, in that man's essence or species-being is alienated, though this need not be the case in every society in which large scale industry predominates. It is a feature of the capitalist mode of production.

At the core of the interchange for the modern worker is this alienation, this objectification. This is a basic relationship in the worker's existence. As Marx concluded: "All these consequences result from the fact that the worker is related to the *product of his labor* as to an *alien* object."[41]

Alienation, however, is not just evident in the product in relation to the worker. Production itself is an alienating activity whereby the worker alienates himself in the activity of labor. Labor in the capitalist industrial age is an alienating activity, for Marx, in two important senses. Firstly, labor is external, undesirable, "forced" in the sense that it is performed only as a means to the end of survival. Secondly, the worker's labor is "not his own," and so the worker is not completely his "own." This second point is one of the more important aspects of alienation for Marx, the "loss of self."[42]

The most basic form of alienation, the estrangement from self, is perhaps more accurately termed "species-alienation." Again Marx refers to his adaptation of the Feuerbachian concept of species-being in order to explicate this fundamental alienation: "Man is a species being, not only because in practice and in theory he adopts the species as his object (his own as well as

those of other things), but--and this is only another way of ex-
pressing it--also because he treats himself as the actual, living
species; because he treats himself as a *universal* and therefore a
free being."[43] Thus, in addition to the first two aspects of estranged labor, the situation of the worker in modern society is
such that his labor also "estranges the species from the man. It
changes for him the *life of the species* into a means of individual
life.   First it estranges the life of the species and individual
life, and secondly, it makes individual life in its abstract form
the purpose of the life of the species, likewise in its abstract
and estranged form."[44]

Here for Marx species-being sets humans apart from other
beings--it is their essential characteristic. As was seen earlier
in this chapter, species-being is the "unity of man with man," the
realization of which comes about in a truly human society. In the
1844 Manuscripts Marx writes that "free conscious activity is
man's species character."[45] It is in free production that free
conscious activity is exemplified, and so it is in free production
that man's species-being comes to the fore.

It is the constriction of this free production by which estranged labor also alienates the worker's species-being: "Estranged labor reverses this relationship, so that it is just because man is a conscious being that he makes his life activity,
his *essential* being [*Wesen*], a mere means to his *existence*."[46]

The conclusion, then, is that by estranging the worker's
labor and labor products, the worker's species-being (that essential characteristic of a truly human life) is being estranged.
Estranged labor is a process of dehumanization, the reduction of
human worker to an object.

In the alienation of the worker's human essence, the worker
is also estranged from others. This is because the estrangement
of species-being is "realized and expressed in the relationship in
which a man stands to other men."[47] It is not possible to isolate
this crucial alienation--it is in the nature of estranged labor
that the estrangement of a worker's species-being is the basis
from which each worker views others.

As Marx found, it is the capitalist, the master of labor and production, to whom the alien power belongs. The capitalist, given free rein in civil society, accumulates capital through the basic provision of civil society: private property. In concluding the section on estranged labor, Marx gives a seemingly paradoxical but actually dialectical analysis of the role of private property. This analysis is the first step toward appreciating the complexity of alienated labor and the difficulty of its elimination and is an important link to Marx's concept of the state. It is a step that most of the classical anarchists did not take. "The relationship of the worker to labor creates the relation to it of the capitalist. *Private property* is thus the product, the result, the necessary consequence of *alienated labor*, of the external relation of the worker to nature and to himself."[48] Private property, however, is both *cause* and effect, if Marx is correct. The analysis of alienated labor began with the assumption that the worker worked upon private property. This apparent paradox is explained by Marx as the reciprocal relation of alienated labor and private property. The original relation was private property as the effect of alienated labor, this private property later serving as the basis for alienated labor. As reciprocally related, private property is both a product of alienated labor and the cause of alienated labor.

This has very important implications for attempts to eliminate the inequalities of industrial society, including those of Proudhon and Bakunin. Marx claims that Proudhon has not solved the problem by demanding the abolition of private property and equality of wages. Since private property is an effect of alienated labor, alienated labor must also be eliminated (or else, Marx claims, private property will in essence continue). And since equalizing wages would not in itself eliminate alienated labor --wages, according to Marx are a result of alienated labor--this equalization would only make alienation more widespread. The essential alienation of the workers would continue.

The conclusion to be drawn at this point is that both alienated labor and private property must be eliminated. Marx states this objective as "universal human emancipation"[49] represented by the emancipation of the workers.

The "crude" communism of the type advocated by Charles Fourier (and, claims Marx, Proudhon) does not abolish private property but actually makes private property universal. Thus in the section of the *Manuscripts* on private property and communism, it becomes clear that the problem of alienation is not abolished by these theorists--alienation becomes more widespread. This attempt at universality results in "the *community* as the universal capitalist."[50] As Marx and Engels noted in later works, the basis of continued alienation is found in the class society of capitalism not in an abstract relationship between private property and alienated labor. As long as the means of production remain within a class, that is, capitalist system, they continue to bear what Engels termed the "character of capital."[51] Only when this class basis is removed, according to Marx, will fundamental changes in society be possible.

In a similar fashion, theorists such as Bakunin who advocate the abolition of the state as the means of establishing community also fail to eliminate alienation. What communism that merely abolishes the state fails to do is deal with the centrality of the relationship between private property and alienation, and thus such an emancipation is incomplete. Marx's statement of communism brings together the various aspects of Marx's theory of human society discussed in this and the previous chapter--communism as the integration of the particular and the universal ("true democracy"), as the development of universal human emancipation, and as the resolution of estrangement and alienation.

> *Communism* as the *positive* transcendence of *private property*, as *human self-estrangement*, and therefore as the real *appropriation of the human* essence by and for man; communism therefore as the complete return of man to himself as a *social* (i.e., human) being--a return become conscious, and accomplished within the entire wealth of previous development. . . . It is the *genuine* resolution of the conflict between man and nature and man and man--the true resolution of the strife between existence and essence, between objectification and self-confirmation, between freedom and necessity, between the individual and the species.[52]

Marx had formulated a response to his initial, Hegelian problematic.   Communism as Marx described it is essentially social;
and as Marx had consistently maintained, human existence is in its
real, emancipated, non-alienated form social existence. In being
essentially social, communism transcends the merely particular
economic sphere of politically emancipated civil society and eman-
cipates the entire human being. In the *1844 Manuscripts*, Marx describes this development where "need or enjoyment have consequently lost their *egotistical* nature, and nature has lost its mere
utility by use becoming human use."[53] As human essence is reconciled with man, man reconciles with himself and other men.

At this point, Marx makes one puzzling statement concerning
communism. At the end of the section on private property and communism, Marx states: "Communism is the necessary pattern and dy-
namic principle of the immediate future, but communism as such is
not the goal of human development--which goal is the structure of
human society."[54]   This would seem to contradict Marx's position
up to this point.   One explanation points to the discussion of
"crude" communism several paragraphs before, linking this crude
communism with "communism as such." This is not highly plausible,
however, and has serious textual evidence against it. A plausible
explanation is forthcoming, however. Just before the statement
quoted above, Marx had explained that "*real life* is man's positive
reality, no longer mediated through the annulment of private property, through *communism*."[55] This communism is "the negation of the
negation, and is hence the actual phase necessary for the next
stage of historical development in the process of human emancipation and rehabilitation."[56]   Marx's use of Hegelian terminology is
a clue to the possible explanation: perhaps Marx was alluding to a
temporary and intermediate level of communism where, as the negation of the structure of capitalism (which is itself a negation of
real community), the way would be prepared for a dialectical
transformation of human society, the transcendence of both capitalism and its negation. Dirk J. Struik mentions this as a possibility in his notes on this section,[57] and Stanley Moore has
recently discussed this same possibility at some length.[58] What
the structure of this higher stage would be, beyond Marx's dis-

cussion of it as "real life," is not entirely clear--but Marx's statement that the goal of human development is the "structure of human society," taken in concert with Marx's previous statements that the realization of man as species-being is the recognition of man as essentially social, lends support to the view that, in this higher stage, the life of each is made truly social in a genuine human emancipation.

In the *1844 Manuscripts*, Marx grounded his conception of human emancipation, discussed in "On the Jewish Question," in a philosophical analysis of the alienated existence of humans in modern society. In modern society individuals are reduced to commodities, their social power alienated from them as a false and illusory citizenship. Meanwhile, the economic forces of civil society continue unchecked. The political state in modern society exists as the repository of "political freedom," but this state is at the same time based on and the result of the movements of civil society. Can the state ever serve as a mechanism for overcoming the conditions of alienation or of human servitude and institute true democracy and human emancipation? In an article from 1844, Marx notes:

> The *state* . . . will never see in "*the state* and the *system of society*" the source of social maladies. Where political parties exist, each party sees the root of *every* evil in the fact that instead of itself an opposing party stands at the *helm of the state*. Even radical and revolutionary politicians seek the root of evil not in the *essential nature* of the state, but in a definite *state form*, which they wish to replace by a *different* state form.
>
> From the *political* point of view, the *state* and the *system of society* are not two different things. Insofar as the state admits the existence of *social* defects, it sees their cause either in the *laws of nature*, . . . or in *private life*, which does not depend on the state, or in the inexpedient activity of the administration. . . .[59]

According to Marx, the political state is incapable of seeing its role as the political substitute for true community, the development required for the abolition of social distress. The state sees

only the failure of particular governments and not the underlying
domination of the politically emancipated civil society, over
which it does not recognize or assert any control.

> The *contradiction* between the purpose and goodwill of the ad-
> ministration, on the one hand, and its means and possibili-
> ties, on the other hand, cannot be abolished by the state
> without the latter abolishing itself, for it is *based* on this
> contradiction. The state is based on the contradiction be-
> tween *public* and *private life*, on the contradiction between
> *general interests* and *private interests.*[60]

In Marx's writings of this period, the political state in capitalist society is an obstacle to the socialization of human life, to
human emancipation, to true democracy, in so far as it remains
based on and subject to the contradiction between general and private interests. Abolishing the state, as the anarchists advocated, without dealing with the basis of this contradiction would
not, according to Marx, accomplish human emancipation.

CLASS SOCIETY AND THE GROUND OF ALIENATION

In Marx's later writings he never completely abandoned the
conception of the state found in his earlier writings. It would be
more accurate to say that he added to his earlier conception of
the state, as both philosophical investigations and practical
revolutionary necessity demanded. The goals of human emancipation
and true democracy remain, if not always in name and not always as
explicit goals. Though Marx's later works will be discussed in
more detail in the chapters directly concerned with Marx and the
anarchists, a brief outline of his conception of the state up to
the time of The German Ideology is in order.

In the "Introduction" to his Critique of Hegel's *"Philosophy
of Right,"* Marx took an important turn. Working from the existing
conditions in the German states, Marx formulated the conception of
the initiation of human emancipation, of the revolution leading to
human emancipation by a part of society; by one class--the proletariat. When the merely political revolution occurs, a partial

revolution initiated by a part of civil society, only members of
the revolutionary class who share those class interests and resources are emancipated. The result of such a revolution is the
dominance of this class, the domination of other classes by this
class. What Marx saw as the path to a human, general emancipation
in Germany was the emergence of an industrial proletariat, the
"formation of a class with *radical chains*, a class of civil
society which is not a class of civil society, . . . a sphere
which has universal character by its universal suffering and
claims no *particular right* because no *particular wrong* but *wrong
generally* is perpetrated against it. . . ."[61]

By identifying the proletariat, the class without specific
class interests, as the vehicle for change in Germany, Marx presages the development of his view, expressed in later writings,
that the political power of the state serves the ruling class. The
bourgeois revolutions of the eighteenth century were only partial
revolutions, resulting in the ascendence of the bourgeoisie and
the gradual formation of the proletariat, a process described in
the *1844 Manuscripts*. The state resulting from these revolutions
served the interests of the class that created it. It is not
simply that the state is reduced to a crude tool used to dominate
the proletariat but rather that the modern political state in
capitalist society serves the interests of the bourgeoisie by its
very nature, that is, the state is merely political and thus does
not deal with the underlying economic factors. In *The German Ideology*, this is made clear.[62] Only in *The Manifesto of the Communist Party* in this period do the demands of revolutionary propaganda outweigh Marx's careful analysis.[63] There the state does
become the "tool" of the ruling class, though Marx did consistently maintain that the state served the interests of the dominant
class by its very existence as the sphere of illusory universality
and in its representation of the interests of the dominant class
as universal interests. In capitalist society, where the state is
first fully conceived as abstract universality, the interests
served are those of the bourgeoisie.

Still, Marx's development of the concept of the state through
the writing of *The German Ideology* is more closely tied to the

idea of the state as an illusory sphere of universality created by
the political emancipation of civil society than to an unsophisti-
cated theory of the state as merely the device of class rule. Marx
argued that the state allows for the predominance of the relations
of private property by its very structure, but this is quite different from claiming that the state creates these property relations.   To ignore this distinction is to grant the state a sphere
of activity, a power which it does not have in modern capitalist
society.   As will be seen shortly, this is a distinction largely
ignored by the classical anarchist.

Thus the political state in capitalist society, having gained
an abstract "independence" from the other private aspects of real
life, gains only a semblance of the universality it claims as its
domain. Basic rights of equality and liberty are established as
political rights regardless of private position. In separating the
public and the private and political life in the state from economic life in civil society, the forces of capitalist economics
attain their own independence. The class structure of society and
the conditions of production combine to isolate wealth and power
in the capitalists while impoverishing the majority of the
workers. "Abstract (de jure) political equality is accompanied by
real inequality, and abstract freedom is accompanied by real bondage."[64] The state claiming to be the representative of general
interests thus reveals itself as the de facto instrument of the
capitalist class. Marx considered political emancipation a real
advance, since it provided a semblance of universality in political rights and freedoms. At the same time, he recognized that
human emancipation requires the transformation of the "mode of
production and the relations it engenders, a mode of production
which isolates men, forces them into hostile egoism, makes crea-
tivity and productivity a misfortune, and reduces the vast majority to helplessness in the face of the wealth and power created by
their very own labor. . . ."[65]

Marx's conception of the state continued to develop throughout his career. As each conflict with the classical anarchists is
discussed in the next two chapters, the course of Marx's development will be traced in his writings. Up to this point, Marx has

put forward a radical critique of the state in modern society, accompanied by the conclusion that true democracy, human emancipation, and the real community of individuals--the dialectical transcendence of the particular and the universal--could not occur unless the separation and alienation embodied in the modern political state were to be overcome.

NOTES

1. *Supplement to Bougainville's "Voyage"; or, Dialogue between A. and B. on the Disadvantage of Attaching Moral Ideas to Certain Physical Actions Incompatible Therewith*, in *Diderot, Interpreter of Nature* (Selected Writings), ed. Jonathan Kemp, trans. Jean Stuart and Jonathan Kemp, 2d ed. (New York: International Publishers, 1963), p. 164.

2. Karl Marx, *The Economic and Philosophic Manuscripts of 1844*, ed. with an introduction by Dirk J. Struik, trans. Martin Milligan (New York: International Publishers, 1964). Also, see *MECW* III, pp. 229-346.

3. *MECW* III, pp. 146-174.

4. Ibid., pp. 175-187.

5. Leading Article in No. 179 of *Kölnische Zeitung*, in *MECW* I, p. 193.

6. In this case, Karl Hermes.

7. *MECW* I, p. 193.

8. Ibid., p. 202.

9. See, for example, "On the Commissions of the Estates in Prussia" in *MECW* I, p. 296, and "Justification of the Correspondent from the Mosel," ibid., esp. pp. 343-345.

10. Marx, *Critique of Hegel's "Philosophy of Right,"* in *MECW* III, p. 29.

11. Ibid., p. 30.

12. TKM, p. 60.

13. Marx, Letter from Marx to Ruge, May 1843, in *MECW*, III p. 168.

14. Marx, "On the Jewish Question," in *MECW* III, p. 168.

15. The relative merit of Bauer's position on the Jews
--whether he was progressive or reactionary in regard to treatment
of the Jews--is a difficult matter to judge and not directly within the scope of this work.

16. *MECW* III, p. 149.

17. Ibid., p. 149.

18. Ibid., p. 151.

19. See, for example, ibid., p. 154:
Where the political state has attained its true development,
man--not only in thought, in consciousness, but in *reality*,
in *life*--leads a twofold life, a heavenly and an earlthy
life: life in the *political community*, in which he considers
himself a *communal being*, and life in *civil society*, in which
he acts as a *private individual*, regards other men as means,
degrades himself into a means, and becomes the plaything of
alien powers."
Marx elaborates on the "degradation" inherent in the civil sphere
in EPM.

20. *MECW* III, p. 154.

21. Ibid., p. 155.

22. Ibid., pp. 162, 164.

23. Ibid., p. 164.

24. Marx and Engels, *The Holy Family*, in *MECW* IV, p. 120.

25. Marx, Letter from Marx to Feuerbach, August 11, 1844, in
MECW III, p. 354.

26. In the *Critique of Hegel's "Philosophy of Right,"* in *MECW*
III, p. 31.

27. Marx, "On the Jewish Question," in *MECW* III, p. 166.

28. TKM, p. 74.

29. István Mészáros, *Marx's Theory of Alienation* (London:
Merlin Press, 1970), p. 35.

30. In EPM.

31. EPM, p. 65.

32. Ibid., p. 68. Marx's description of impoverishment here
is highly reminiscent of Hegel's account of the same phenomenon in
the *PR*. (See esp. paragraphs 243-245.)

33. EPM, p. 71.

34. Ibid., p. 72.

35. Ibid.

36. See, for example, Marx's excerpt from Eugene Buret's *De la misere des classes laborieuses en Angleterre et en France* (Paris: 1840): "'The working population, the seller of labor, is necessarily reduced to accepting the most meager part of its product. . . . Is the theory of labor as a commodity anything other than a theory of disguised bondage?' 'Why then has nothing but an exchange value been seen in labor?'" (Buret, pp. 43-44) in ibid., p. 76.

37. I am indebted to Dirk J. Struik's note, EPM, p. 58.

38. EPM, p. 107.

39. Ibid., p. 108, translation altered slightly.

40. Ibid.

41. Ibid.

42. Ibid., p. 111.

43. Ibid., p. 112.

44. Ibid.

45. Ibid., p. 113.

46. Ibid.

47. Ibid., p. 115.

48. Ibid., p. 116.

49. Ibid., p. 118.

50. Ibid., p. 134.

51. Friedrich Engels, *Socialism: Utopian and Scientific*, in Marx, Engels, Lenin, *Anarchism and Anarcho-Syndicalism* (New York: International Publishers, 1972), p. 168.

52. EPM, p. 135.

53. Ibid., p. 139.

54. Ibid., p. 146.

55. Ibid.

56. Ibid.

57. Ibid., p. 254.

58. Stanley Moore, *Marx on the Choice between Socialism and Communism* (Cambridge, Mass.: Harvard University Press, 1980), pp. 16-18. See also, for example, Meszaros, *Marx's Theory of Alienation*, pp. 159-161, for an interesting and, I think, fair evalua-

tion of this dispute. Mészáros comments:

> The crucial Marxian distinction is that between communism as a *political* movement--which is confined to a particular historical stage of human development--and communism as comprehensive *social practice*. This second sense is referred to when Marx writes that "this communism, as fully developed naturalism, equals humanism, as a fully-developed humanism equals naturalism." (P. 161.)

D.F.B. Tucker has an interesting account of this same issue in *Marxism and Individualism* (New York: St. Martin's Press, 1980), esp. pp. 79-84.   There is a plethora of literature on this and other issues in the *1844 Manuscripts*.

59. Marx, "Critical Marginal Notes on the Article by a Prussian," in *MECW* III, p. 197.

60. Ibid., p. 198.

61. Marx, "Contribution to the Critique of Hegel's Philosophy of Law. Introduction," in *MECW* III, p. 186.

62. See *The German Ideology* in *MECW* V, esp. p 89.

63. See *The Manifesto of the Communist Party* in *MECW* VI, esp. pp. 486, 503.

64. T. Kermit Scott, private communication. Much of my discussion in this paragraph is indebted to my communication with Professor Scott.

65. Ibid.

3
STIRNER'S EGOISTIC ANARCHISM AND THE CHALLENGE TO COMMUNITY

I have founded my affairs upon nothing
    Hurrah!
And thus to me belongs the entire world
    Hurrah!

Goethe[1]

According to this conception [of the individual], individuals are pictured abstractly as given, with given interests, wants, purposes, needs, etc.; while society and the state are pictured as sets of actual or possible social arrangements which respond more or less adequately to those individuals' requirements. . . . The crucial point about this conception is that the relevant features of individuals determining the ends which social arrangements are held (actually or ideally) to fulfill, whether these features are called instincts, faculties, needs, desires, rights, etc., are assumed as given, independently of a social context. This givenness of fixed and invariant human psychological features leads to an *abstract* conception of the individual who is seen as merely the bearer of those features, which determine his behavior, and specify his interests, needs, and rights.

Steven Lukes[2]

ANARCHISM AND THE UNIQUE

Most studies of anarchist thought, beliefs, or systems (or lack of system) begin with a section devoted to Max Stirner.[3] The secondary literature that discusses Stirner's philosophical and political views is divided as to whether Stirner is an anarchist at all; some want to claim that Stirner makes no substantive political claims at all (an integral part of Stirner's alleged nihilism),[4] while others claim that Stirner supported or his theory implied some sort of proto-fascistic tyranny.[5] The division in the literature is an indication of the strong and conflicting reactions provoked by Max Stirner, the pseudonym of Johann Kaspar Schmidt, a sometime university student and occasional school teacher. Stirner's reputation rests largely on the merits and demerits of one book, *Der Einzige und sein Eigenthum*, originally published in 1845.[6] A careful examination of this work reveals that Stirner was at the very least a supporter of political anarchism and that he regarded the existence of the political state as a fatal impediment to the self-realization of the individual. It will be shown that Stirner's theory extends, albeit imperfectly, from the political realm into the social, demanding the same ruthless independence from societal norms as it does from political control. The first section of this chapter will trace the development of Stirner's system and begin a critical assessment of it as an anarchistic theory. In the course of this section the idea of "political anarchism" will be given a more concrete form.

The second section of this chapter will examine Marx's position (as found in his earlier writings) in relation to Stirner's claims. Contrary to some interpretations of Marx's methodological development,[7] I will in the third section attempt to show that it was at least in part Stirner's strong challenge that led to a modification of some points of Marx's early work. This will be accomplished through an examination of Marx's *The German Ideology* and other works. Finally, this will result in a comparison of Marx's responses to Stirner's position and an assessment of both the adequacy of these responses and their implications for the later conflict between Marx and other anarchists.

Though the object of this examination of Stirner's views is the specific concept of the state found in Stirner's work, it is impossible to isolate this concept from Stirner's system and critique as a whole. Stirner formulated anthropological and psychological models of development, both of which he at various times posits as the source of the form and attraction of the modern state. In turn, Stirner's critique of the modern state reflects (and perhaps depends on) his critique of the more basic structures of authority uncovered in the tracing of the anthropological and psychological development of human beings. More than this, however, Stirner provides an alternative response to the Hegelian and Feuerbachian anthropologies while utilizing several of Hegel's and Feuerbach's notions. Since one of Stirner's more effective and at least partially accurate criticisms of the position represented by Marx in some of Marx's early writings was that Marx did not progress beyond Feuerbachianism, an examination of Stirner's philosophical and methodological groundwork will aid in a thorough evaluation of his critique of Marx.

For Stirner, the origin of all authoritarian structures (the family and the state, for example) is to be found in the psychological and social development of human beings. Accordingly, *The Ego and His Own* has as its introductory section the story of, as Stirner calls it, "A Human Life."[8] This section serves as an explanatory preface for Stirner's specific criticisms of the social and political developments of his day. It also serves as the groundwork of Stirner's own views.

Stirner traces the development of consciousness from the moment of an initial cognitive confrontation. As children, humans are thrown into a world of basic conflict. This has more significance for Stirner than might be expected, however "because each thing *cares for itself* and at the same time comes into constant collision with other things, the combat of self-assertion is unavoidable. *Victory or defeat*--between the two alternatives the fate of the combat wavers. The victor becomes the *lord*, the vanquished one the *subject*. . . . Either the stick conquers the man or the man conquers the stick."[9] Behind the fear and uncertainty inherent in this conflict, Stirner finds a source of strength, of courage, which allows the victor to prevail. Stirner indentifies this courage with other traits of self-assertion: for example, trickery, shrewdness, and obduracy.[10] The discovery of this courage, this basic means of dealing with the mortal combat of human existence, Stirner calls the discovery of mind (*Geist*).[11] This discovery of mind is of key importance to Stirner's political and philosophical system: it is mind that serves as the basis for the triadic development of the ego and egoistic interest. Although Stirner's description of the discovery and development of mind is dependent on a socio-psychological methodology (for example, the "discovery" of mind is linked to the first stages of a child's rebellion against the father figure[12]), he intends for this discovery to have as important a place in his system as Hegel's quite different conception of *Geist* has in his. The youth, having discovered this limitless self, soon encounters its antithesis--reason.   From this important point onward, Stirner's system--as with Hegel's--is dependent on the formation and resolution of conflict. Stirnerian dialectics, however, take a unique course.

When the youth encounters reason, he (for Stirner, always he) abandons his natural attitude of deference to his parents and others and instead submits to the demands of reason and thought identified with the commands of conscience. Where before the world was an opposition of mind and things, the reasoning youth brings forth the mediation of abstract (pure) thought. It is at this state that Stirner identifies the attitude that he will later accuse the "Free Ones,"[13] including presumably Marx, of preserving: "To bring to light the *pure thought*, or to be of its party, is the delight of youth; and all the shapes of light in the world of thought, like truth, freedom, humanity, Man, illumine, and inspire the youthful soul."[14] The realm of pure thought not only inspires the youthful spirit, it is also the beginning of the degeneration of mind or spirit. The elevation of spirit is the result of the conflict between reason and spirit, except that spirit has now incorporated the essential characteristic of reason, the longing for perfection and purity. With this, according to Stirner, a loss or degeneration occurs, for the subsumption of the human spirit in the ideal of the "Holy Spirit"[15]

removes the original subjectivity of spirit, substituting instead
an incorporeal, indeed wholly abstract projection of the demands
of conscience. The result is that the youth, having rejected the
simple life of boyhood, clutters his life with what Stirner vari-
ously calls the "Holy Spirit," the "ideal of spirit," the "general
spirit,"[16] and which he identifies with the internalization and
symbolization of thoughts of "God, Emperor, Pope, Fatherland,
etc."[17] and elsewhere of the ideal of Man or mankind.

All of these abstract thoughts (these aspects of spirit become "alienated" and then internalized as symbolic ideals) merit
the worst treatment from Stirner. They are all ghosts, potential
captors or possessors of spirit even after the youth has matured.
This is, for Stirner, truly a degeneration of spirit, of the unin-
tellectual spirit of boyhood. Stirner goes so far as to characterize this attitude (for it is also an attitude) as a nothing. The
ultimate unreality of these ghosts is the basis for Stirner's
metaphysical and political theories, for if the ghosts (which will
include the ideal of the state and the general welfare of mankind)
are truly unreal, then the egoistic spirit cannot support any
institution perpetuating these fictions.

The transition from youth to man is for Stirner the reincor-
poration of the original physicality of childhood into the youthful concern for thoughts and ideas. The mature man (and here Stirner shifts--in the first of many such shifts--from what purports
to be a descriptive account to an inherently prescriptive account)
discovers or rediscovers corporeality; the realization that the
world does not conform to the ideal of youth, that behind these
ideals one always finds competing interests. The realization of
corporeality referred to here is the discovery that the personal,
the bodily (Stirner, throughout the course of his works, often
seems to mean this literally) interests of the individual are both
the source of the ideals of youth and the means of destroying
their influence. To know them in their "true nature" is, so to
speak, to recapture the power they held over the individual when
they were projected as higher than the individual.

It is at this point that Stirner begins to speak of "egoistic
interest,"[18] those interests to which mature men limit themselves.

Having gone beyond the naive interest of childhood, beyond the idealistic and "ghostly" interests of youth, the mature egoist realizes that he is a physical, though thinking being, an *embodied spirit.*"[19] This is the ultimate human reality for Stirner; this is the center of meaning, interest, and action. "The man is distinguished from the youth by the fact that he takes the world as it is, instead of everywhere fancying it amiss and wanting to improve it, model it after his ideal; in him the view that one must deal with the world according to his *interest*, not according to his ideals, becomes confirmed."[20]

Stirner's account of socio-pyschological development can be summarized as follows: the child (and the childish attitude) concentrates on things, on a naive perception of empirical reality. The youth (and the youthful attitude) concentrates on thought, on a projected idealistic reality. The mature man (and the egoistic attitude) concentrates on both things and thoughts as they apply to him: "'I alone am corporeal.' And now I take the world as what it is to me, as *mine*, as my property; I refer all to myself."[21]

The influence of the Young Hegelians, especially David Strauss, Bruno Bauer, and Feuerbach, is evident in Stirner's curious dialectic.[22] Against Hegel, Stirner relegates the "ideas" of the youth, particularly those ideas of religion, justice, and politics to the realm of rather arbitrary feelings and experience. Though Stirner will later reject Feuerbach's conclusions in the areas of religion and human reality in general, the use of Feuerbach's transformative critique of Hegelian thought is very much in evidence. Feuerbach, in continuing and elaborating on Strauss's critique of Christianity, has concluded: "We have reduced the other-worldly, supernatural and superhuman essence of God to its particular foundations in the essence of man. . . . Man is the beginning of religion, Man is the center of religion, Man is the end of religion."[23] One of the purposes of Feuerbach's critique of religion is to support the recovery of those aspects of man which had been alienated and projected in the image of a deity. To leave these aspects in their alienated form is to impoverish men just that much further. Stirner supports the Feuerbachian project as far as it goes. The primary fault with Feuerbach, according to

Stirner, is that his project does not go far enough. To understand why Stirner regarded Feuerbach's critique as incomplete requires a brief discussion of Stirner's use of psycho-social stages or attitudes (identified by Stirner as Childhood, Youth, and Maturity) in an attempt to formulate an anthropologized history, as history corresponding to the stages in human development. It is in this application that Stirner revives his curious adaptation of Hegel's dialectic and, at the same time, sets the stage for the ensuing conflict with Marx.

David McLellan has argued that Stirner can be viewed as the "last of the Hegelians, last perhaps because he was the most logical, not attempting to replace Hegel's 'concrete universal' by any 'humanity' or 'classless' society."[24] This is not entirely correct. It is correct, as will be seen, that Stirner does not use "humanity" or the "classless society," or for that matter any universal social concept, because Stirner considered all universals-- social, metaphysical, or other--as apparitions or ghosts. Not only did he deny their ultimate reality, he abhorred the enslaving effects of beliefs and attitudes based on such concepts. But to call Stirner "Hegelian" is to miss the crucial difference between the Stirnerian dialectic and the Hegelian dialectic: Stirner was not the most logical of the Hegelians, in the Hegelian sense, because his dialectic was inherently ahistorical. (McLellan seems to recognize this latter point.) This lack of a real historical sense greatly influenced Marx's response to Stirner.

Paul Thomas has written that Stirner's history is "broadly Hegelian;" and, despite recognizing McLellan's own reservations about Stirnerian history as Hegelian, Thomas claims that "Stirner considered the historical process up to that point [that is, what Stirner called the modern era] in Hegelian terms, as the autogenesis of man propelled by spirit or consciousness. Whatever his understanding of Hegel . . . it remains true that Stirner did appropriate a broadly Hegelian approach to history."[25] As with McLellan's original claim of the Hegelian character of Stirner's work, Thomas's point is easily overstated. In contradistinction to Hegel, Stirner did not accept the "propulsion" of anyone by spirit or consciousness as inhabited by ghosts. The "ghosts" were powerful illusions within the individual only because individual humans believed in them.   The ambiguity of this position--how can the ghosts be both unreal and enslaving?--will be discussed below. In any event, though Stirner applies his dialectic to history, he does so quite crudely, as Marx was quick to point out. Nonetheless, this application deserves attention because it is this "history" that brings Stirner into direct conflict with Feuerbach and Marx.

In a near parody of Hegel's *Philosophy of History*, Stirner characterizes the ancient world as corresponding to the attitude of the child, concentrating on the world of things and, through the ancients' basic reliance on the order of a natural system, on themselves as things in the world. The development of the "moderns," the successors to the ancients both historically and dialectically, begins with the Christian era. The characterization of the spirit of Christianity as the chief example of the youthful attitude and of the Christian era as the youth of man provides the basis for Stirner's attack on both Feuerbach and humanism. For Stirner, Feuerbach represented the last philosophical redoubt of Christianity and the religious spirit. And, since Stirner regarded Marx as a variation on the Feuerbachian theme, by extension Marx represented for Stirner the humanized and secularized theological spirit.

Stirner's choice of Christianity in particular and religion in general as the basis for the modern age and for his attack on Feuerbach and the moderns is unsurprising. As many commentators on the Young Hegelians have noted, the critique of religion was the centerpiece of critical thought in the post-Hegelian period.[26] The critique of Christianity was, for Stirner and his contemporaries, an important aspect of the general critique of accepted thought. This critique of religious thought, beginning with David Strauss's *Das leben Jesu* (1835) and continuing with Bauer's *Posaune des jüngsten Gerichts über Hegel den Atheisten und Antichristen* (1841), among other works, contributed to the critical atmosphere in German thought. Feuerbach's *Das Wesen des Christentums* (1841) was perhaps the most significant of the critiques, though there is no need to discuss at this point the question of

its importance at the time among Feuerbach's contemporaries. It
was important to Stirner, so much so that *The Ego and His Own* is
modelled (in form) after Feuerbach's work, and Stirner's work was,
in his own view, the needed rejoinder to Feuerbach's claim to have
provided a radical critique of religious and social thought.

This is not the place for a thorough review of Feuerbach's
views. Some mention of them has already been made; only a few
points need to be mentioned here. The intent of the transformative
critique of religious thought--the reversal of subject and predicate in the relationship between man and God--was for Feuerbach
the demystification of religious thought: "Theology and speculative philosophy make real being and things into arbitrary signs,
vehicles, symbols, or predicates of a distinct, transcendent, absolute, i.e. abstract being. . . . Man--this is the mystery of
religion--projects his being into objectivity, and then again
makes himself an object to this projected image of himself thus
converted into a subject. . . ."[27] By reversing or transforming
this relationship, man recovers his alienated essential attributes. Man becomes the focus of religious thought and theology is
anthropologized.

What Stirner applauds in Feuerbach's critique is also the
basis for further criticism. Stirner recognized the importance of
demystifying religious thought, but only as the first step in
eliminating religious thought altogether. Since the Reformation,
according to Stirner, the spirit and dogmas of religion had become
increasingly internalized, especially within Protestant thought.
The division between the inadequacies of everyday life and the
ideals represented by the alienated essential attributes (love and
justice, for example), previously seen as the external division
between heaven and earth, now comes to be seen as the internal division between the essential and the inessential, the holy and the
base, within the soul or heart. "The heart, from day to day more
unchristian, loses the contents with which it had busied itself,
till at last nothing but empty *warmheartedness* is left it, the
quite general love of men, the love of Man, the consciousness of
freedom, 'self-consciousness.' Only so is Christianity complete,
because it has become bald, withered, and void of contents."[28]

Basically, according to Stirner, those who deny the strictly theological contents of Christianity (say, in favor of anthropology) are still caught in the trap of general ideas: caught in the snare of such ghosts as "Man," "Freedom," "Liberty," and "Equality." As Stirner will elaborate, the individuals who face the future on the boundary between Feuerbachian style of religious thought and the egoistic new world make themselves the pivotal points of their own existences. Even supposedly secular opponents of egoism, according to Stirner, put "spirit" or "essence" or any of a host of fixed ideas at that point, as the internalized "proper self" in a reworked dualism. Stirner's egoist does not succumb to this division, as the egoist grasps himself as the center of a corporeal, embodied spirit: a unique individual.

Feuerbach's specific fault lies in not extending the critical project to the general ideas (man, essence) of non-Christian, even non-theological religious thought to the ideas of what Stirner regarded as liberal humanism. In response to Feuerbach's transformation of the essence of man from the objective essence of God to the objectification of man as God, Stirner contends that such a transformation leaves the reabsorption of alienated facets of the individual incomplete, for it is one and the same to the egoist whether the essence is seen as external or internal to man. With either alternative, the "ghost," "fixed idea," or "spook" of a common essence (and all that such an essence entails), remains to trap and mystify the unique individual. "I am neither God nor Man, neither the supreme essence nor my essence, and therefore it is all one in the main whether I think of the essence as in me or outside me."[29] Feuerbach has not removed the basis of religious thought: "The 'Spirit of God' is, according to the Christian view, also, 'our spirit,' and 'dwells in us.' It dwells in heaven and dwells in us; we poor things are just its 'dwelling,' and, if Feuerbach goes on to destroy its heavenly dwelling and force it to move to us bag and baggage, then we, its earthly apartments, will be badly overcrowded."[30]

This last comment illustrates an important point in Stirner's critique of Feuerbach. Not only does Feuerbach prevent the unique individual from recovering his alienated characteristics (and thus the unique personality), he also brings an essence into direct conflict with the unique ego. The "overcrowding" resulting from this is a destructive and ego-degrading opposition of the ideals of Man (or "humanity") and the reality of men (or "humans"), of the unique individual. For Stirner, Feuerbach is presenting a philosophically developed Christianity: the gods have changed, but the enslavement to religious ideals remains. The love of a super-human God has been changed to love of "the human God, to *homo* as *Deus*."[31]   Thus, according to Stirner, Feuerbach has substituted the sanctity of Man, the generic concept, the "spook" of "every-thing 'truly human,'"[32] for the sanctity of the heavenly God, of the external divine. Feuerbach's essence of man and the qualities associated with that essence--will, thought, and love--become the "fixed ideas" decried by Stirner. Love, especially love of human-ity in general, becomes the secularized credo of the new religious man.   Stirner goes so far as to say that such love is not secular at all: "Even love, in itself the truest, most inward sentiment, becomes an obscure, illusory one through religiousness. . . . Is this different with moral [i.e., Feuerbachian] love? Does it love the man,13 this man for *this* man's sake, or for morality's sake, and so--for *homo homini Deus*--for God's sake?"[33]

What Stirner is placing in opposition is the unique individ-ual or the individual ego and man qua species-being. Though he is unclear on this point, it seems that any concept of species other than a trivial biological notion becomes another link in the chain of "spooks" holding the egoist in check. Also unclear but implied is that this ego is a primitive datum, a given feature of the de-veloped human being. What is very clear is that Feuerbach's idea of a human essence, the notion of species-being (*Gattungswesen*) is just such a spook for Stirner. Any true development of the indi-vidual is self-development; an individual raises himself to his unique individuality: "The species is nothing. . . . Man with [a capital] M is only an ideal, the species only something thought of. . . . *I* am my species, am without norm, without law, without model, and the like."[34]

So far, Stirner's critique of religion, Feuerbachian thought, and ideology (taken in its most general sense) have depended upon all general concepts, all religious, ethical, political, and social universals being mere "spooks" or "ghosts," to use Stirner-ian terminology. This is the crux of Stirner's implicit critique of Marx as well. Since the state for Stirner is the most pervasive and powerful of all ghosts in the modern age (having succeeded the Church in this role), it is important to see just what Stirner means by "ghosts" and what it means to be "possessed," to have one too many rafters in one's head.

Stirner's use of words such as "spook" and "ghost" suggests that those captivated by these things are possessed. Stirner presses this point, though his uses of *Gefangen* here (translated by Steven T. Byington, John Carrol, and many commentators as "possessed") often implies "imprisoned" more than "possessed." Those suffering such spooks are imprisoned within the bounds of a fixed idea and thus are separated from their uniqueness, their particularity. It is, though, like a possession in that spooks gain their reality and efficacy from continued belief in them; they have no independent existence.[35] What then are these spooks?

Most importantly, the spook is the instantiation of the "fixed idea" of ethical, political, and religious thought in con-science, where "fixed idea" encompasses any standard of evaluation external to and applicable beyond the unique individual. Religion, according to Stirner, lives exclusively in the realm of such spooks. Feuerbach's (and for Stirner, Marx's) humanism has creat-ed, in the course of the critique of religion, a new "corporeal ghost,"[36] and has done so in an attempt to bring to earth that which formerly resided in an external realm of ultimate values. Though Christianity began this process by internalizing the ghost (as the sense of sin, of conscience), Feuerbach completes the process by removing the theological content and substituting instead a human essence. This is one of the ghosts in each man, according to Stirner, "Man" with a capital M. For Stirner's ego-ist, however, "Man" as such is a ghost and as a fixed idea sub-jugates the unique in the individual. It is clear from Stirner's discussion at this point that he is not merely criticizing Feu-erbach or other post-Hegelians; the target of stirner's criticisms of spooks and fixed ideas is the entire tradition of what was then modern liberal democratic thought, especially as influenced by the principles of the Enlightenment and the American and French Revolutions. The abstract *citoyen*, just as much as the abstract Man, limits the individual and elevates a ghostly commonality above the "concrete" uniqueness. To see that Stirner aims his critique at this entire tradition requires a further examination of the fixed idea and its possessive force.

In a section entitled "Bats in the Belfry" (or "Wheels in the Head"),[37] Stirner elaborates on the fixed ideas inhabiting the mind in the form of spooks or an extra rafter or two. The comparison that Stirner wants to draw is between the imprisonment or possession of the mind of the insane by delusions and the possession of the supposedly sane man by the ghosts of religion, ethics, and politics. For Stirner, this preoccupation with, this "prepossessedness" by (again, *Gefangen* and *befangen*) fixed ideas is found not only in insane asylums, where inmates are possessed by the idea that they are God, but also in modern life, where the average sane man is possessed by the idea of being a good Christian, a good person, a good citizen. In the sane person, says Stirner, what is (or was) taken as a sign of foolishness and a weak mind in the insane is instead taken as sacred and beyond criticism. It is this comparison, combined with Stirner's curious "historical" dialectic and critique of religion, that illuminates the scope of his attack. Since the development of abstract concepts criticized by Stirner and their internalization supposedly correspond to the development of Protestantism and modern political liberalism, the attack on fixed ideas is an attack on the entire normative framework of what was then modern society. The one exception to Stirner's attack on fixed ideas is one that drew strong criticism from Marx. This exception is the group of fixed ideas common to the economic sphere, including private property and the relations of production. Stirner's only examination of this area is limited to the effect of economic organization on individual, egoistic interest.

It is the political aspect of Stirner's attack which is particularly at issue here. From the context of all of Stirner's works (including his early essays and replies to critics), it is

clear that he regarded the development of liberal political systems, those systems where commerce is freed from political control
to a greater or lesser degree, as having a negative impact on the
unique individual. Stirner compares this development to the development of piety in religious belief.[38] The key example of the
fixed idea for Stirner is the modern political state. The state is
a ghost, a spook that makes itself "corporeal" in the form of
modern abstract citizenship (Stirner's term is *das Bürgerthum*;
Stirner never really distinguishes between the *citoyen* and the
bourgeois) and the demands of political conscience. The rule of
the modern state is distinguished by both mediocrity and fanati-
cism. As one of his key examples of such a state, Stirner claims
that the egalitarian spirit of the French revolutionary state and
its purported goals of liberalism in fact support the fixed ideas
of equality and abstract citizenship at the price of the unique
individual. At the same time that each person is addressed equally
as "citizen," these fixed ideas of the modern political state become sacred talismans of the state.

> This is the dominion of the idea; in others words, it is
> clericalism. Thus Robespierre and Saint Just were priests
> through and through, inspired by the idea, enthusiasts, con-
> sistent instruments of this idea, idealistic men. So Saint
> Just exclaims in a speech, "There is something terrible in
> the sacred love of country; it is so exclusive that it sacri-
> fices everything to the public interest without mercy, with-
> out fear, without human consideration."[39]

Contrary to liberal political theorists, Stirner does not
consider the institutionalization of liberal ideas in the state as
progress. Even when the extreme (and in many ways inconsistent,
though Stirner does not see this) consequences of supporting the
"public interest," exemplified in the actions of Robespierre,
Georges-Jacques Danton, and Saint Just, are mitigated by a strong
and orderly legal system, the state itself remains for Stirner as
the chief obstacle to the progress of the unique individual.
"Authors fill whole folios on the State without calling in question the fixed idea of the State itself; . . . our newspapers are
crammed with politics because they are conjured into the fancy

that man was created to be *a zoon politicon.* . . ."[40] According to Stirner, all of these fixed ideas and especially those undergirding the state need to be brought to light and seen for what they are: apparitions.

The modern state exists on the basis of a secular "ought," on the duty to be a good citizen. What was formerly a religious (for Stirner, Christian) set of duties and obligations is now institutionalized in a secular state. The presupposition that man is a social animal, that a common social bond (such as a human essence) exists, underlies the existence and justification of the state. Stirner asks: why presume that the state is ever jusitifed in interfering in the affairs of the individual? If, as both Hegel and Feuerbach claimed, the state is a political institution separate from religious values, how is sovereignty to be justified? The answer, for Stirner, is that the state rests on the true faith of secular morality and its fixed ideas, including morality, justice, and especially abstract equality. Saint Just spoke of the "sacred love of country" exclusive of human interest because the political ideals of the French revolutionary state were held to supersede the interests of the individual. This "purity of morals"[41] is the means by which the state maintains its authority. Though the state perpetuates violence against individuals and always has the threat of force at its disposal, it need not maintain its authority by force, since the morality is internalized as the political morality of the society.

A criticism of Proudhon by Stirner helps make this point for Stirner: Proudhon substitutes the moral law for the religious law. Though this is a vast oversimplification of Proudhon's position,[42] Stirner's point is important for his case against the state: those who substitute the spooks and fixed ideas of morality, especially political morality, for religious injunctions are just as possessed as the religious, perhaps even more so. For, as Stirner points out in repeated references to Feuerbach and other social critics, they think that they have escaped the dogmatism and limitations of fixed ideas when they eliminate or transform the fixed ideas of religion. Whether the fixed idea is divine or human, it is still for Stirner a general essence, a spook: "It is a question of a supreme essence with both. . . . In the end the relation to the human essence, or to 'Man,' as soon as ever it has shed the snake-skin of the old religion, will yet wear a religious snake-skin again."[43]   The state in its modern form is the most dangerous manifestation of the fixed ideas, as the modern state presupposes and perpetuates the fixed ideas of modern politics, inlcuding "equality" and the worst of the spooks, "Man" or "Humanity." Furthermore, according to Stirner, the modern state reduces the human being to that abstract bearer of rights, the citizen, and so devalues the uniqueness of the individual.

What Stirner is opposing here is more than the political state.   Stirner rarely distinguishes between the political state (as a specific institution) and all of the other societal institutions and practices which are based on social, rather than individual, values (for example, police and educational practices). Paul Thomas has noted that Stirner often considers all political and social practices as using or embodying fixed ideas.[44] Yet this notation by Thomas is intended as a criticism of Stirner: Stirner's critique is said to lack "specificity" and to be "frankly contradictory."[45] As other commentators have noted and as Stirner himself held, such lack of specificity is not only a strength of his position, it is required by his position, by the terms of his arguments.   Thomas is correct when he states that while Stirner's analysis of the state "presents the state . . . as an agent or agency of sacredness and morality, he presents society and religion (not to mention revolution) in almost identical terms."[46]   Stirner's failure to distinguish the various demons haunting the human world will leave him open to Marx's charge that he fails to come to terms with the distinct, identifiable features and natures of state and society. But for Stirner, the reason for his extensive critique of Feuerbach and others--for the discussion linking religious, moral, and political values (and fixed ideas)-- is to show that they suffer from essentially similar defects. Stirner's argument is an attempt at a thoroughgoing critique of ideology, not just of political ideology. As Daniel Guérin has noted: "[The anarchist]--rejects society as a whole along with its guardians. Max Stirner declared that the anarchist frees himself

of all that is sacred, and carries out a vast operation of decon-
secration."[47]

The state itself has a wider scope in Stirner's thought than
in ordinary conceptions of a strictly political institution.
Carroll exaggerates only slightly when he states that for Stirner
"the State . . . represents all organized authority above the influence of the individual. . . . It is defined above all else by
its power."[48] Though it is possible to make some theoretical distinctions between state and society even in Stirner's works, all
institutions and practices in state or society share and are
linked by their common basis in an authority limiting and devalu-
ing the individual's uniqueness.

In discussing everyday morality, the morality of society,
Stirner is clear that the state uses morality as an ideological
tool and that the very existence of the state rests on the moral
principles it perpetuates. In his discussion of Nero, Stirner
touches on the connection between moral principles, the state, and
revolution. The Romans who opposed Nero lacked the courage to
depose him because, according to Stirner, they were too "good."
The fact that the state itself (represented by Nero) rested on a
moral basis prevented any good "citizens" from challenging Nero,
because to do that would have been to challenge the state itself.
Only when one person broke the spell of morality possessing the
good Romans (again, a spook) could a rebellion or revolution take
place. For Stirner, neither Nero nor the "good Romans" had escaped
the limitations of the fixed idea. Condemnation of Nero was from
the standpoint of morality, just as Nero was possessed by the
fixed idea of absolute authority or sovereignty. The paradox that
Stirner wants to demonstrate here is that both Nero and his de-
tractors--and this is the case with all states and their moralistic opponents, according to Stirner--were on an equal footing,
from the egoistic standpoint. Both were caught in the web of
interests inherent in their "fixed ideas."

> Where then in the "good" was the courage for the revolution,
> that courage which they [the Romans opposed to Nero] now
> praised, after another had mustered it up? The good could
> not have this courage, for a revolution, and an insurrection

into the bargain, is always something "immoral," which one can resolve upon only when one ceases to be "good" and becomes either "bad" or--neither of the two."[49]

In the critique of the state, then, Stirner is deliberately challenging the very basis, as he saw it, of law, morality, and society--and he admits it. The spirit of clericalism pervades state and society and their opponents; it is characterized, as the spirit of the youth was characterized before, as living for an idea. The fixed ideas are imparted to children through the state-supported system of education and soon tyrannize the person. Conscience, developed in children by their encounters with society, acts as the repository of the most basic fixed ideas. The worst of these ideas is manifested as the most pernicious spook--"man." In the modern state and society all other ideas soon follow, including the ideas of morality (one ought to promote the truly human in oneself and others) and obligation to the political state (one ought to be a loyal citizen). In making this sort of statement, Stirner challenges the anthropologized religion of Feuerbach and the political theory of Marx. Stirner chose to illustrate how basic he thought his challenge was by once again turning to Proudhon and Proudhon's famous dictum, "Property is theft."

In *What Is Property?* or, *An Inquiry into the Principle of Right and Government*, Proudhon states that just as slavery, in taking from the slave all thought, personality, and power, is murder so property, in enabling non-producers to appropriate the products of others, is robbery or theft.[50] Stirner acknowledges that property may well be theft (though it is difficult to see what sense can be made of the concept of theft within Stirner's framework), but that in itself does not condemn property. It only implies what political and social morality presuppose; that is, that theft is always wrong. Stirner's egoist only affirms the "wrongness" of theft when his interest is directly endangered or when it might be indirectly endangered by the spread of theft as a practice. Any other appeals that Proudhon or others might make in support of the Proudhonian dictum can be no more than the reappearance of the spook and fixed idea of "Man," the fixed idea of a love of humanity in general (in the form of the ideal, "Men ought not steal from one another"), a love that therefore loves no humans in particular. It is the nature of Stirner's conception of fixed ideas that provides for such a widespread critique: any ethics, any religion, and especially any political system appeal to ideas (Stirner would say ghosts) applicable to humans in general or to classes of people. It is in the critique of the modern state, that state founded on the rights and equality of "Man," that Stirner's general critical position becomes clear. Of the basis of this state, he wrote: "He who is infatuated with *Man* leaves persons out of account so far as that infatuation extends, and floats in an ideal, sacred interest. *Man*, you see, is not a person, but an ideal, a spook."[51]

The modern state itself is dealt with by Stirner in three different forms. These three forms (political liberalism, social liberalism, and humane liberalism) are distinguished by the theories underlying each form.[52] The criticisms and descriptions of these state-form's follow from Stirner's general critique of the state just discussed. For the purpose of understanding Stirner's general social critique, it is necessary to deal with only the first two state-forms criticized by Stirner.

Political liberalism, the product of the end of absolute monarchy, affirms the equality of persons qua citizens (again, Stirner's term is *das Bürgerthum*). Only within the state, pursuing the general interest, does each person realize the highest human goals and possibilities. Stirner identifies the introduction of this state-form with the establishment of the National Assembly in France (1789). As the state pursues the general interest, it absorbs individual interests, according to Stirner. When the state established "equality of political rights . . . the State has no regard for my person, . . . to it I, like every other, am only a man, without having another significance that commands its deference."[53] The consequence of such a state, according to Stirner, is that the state absorbs all rights and dispenses them on the basis of qualification as a citizen. Rather than freeing people, political liberalism frees the state. In removing all political intermediaries, the transformed third estate becomes the state; in being identified as a citizen within the state, says Stirner, the individual becomes a "political Protestant."[54] The fixed idea of the monarchical state has been transformed into the idea of the sovereignty of the people, the political facet of liberalism. This corresponds to the result of Feuerbach's critique of religion, as McLellan has pointed out,[55] in that the internalization of sovereignty--sovereignty flowing from the citizens--is just as destructive to the unique individual, according to Stirner, as the internalization of secularized human ideals or essences. "Political liberty means that the *polis*, the State, is free . . . not, therefore, that I am free from the State. . . . It does not mean *my* liberty, but the liberty of a power that rules and subjugates me. . . ."56

The problem with political liberalism, for Stirner, is the same problem afflicting Feuerbach's critique of religion: it does not go far enough. The revolutionary impulse, at least in this situation, is only a desire to replace one domination with another. As Stirner put it, political liberalism challenges "*the establishment in question*" rather than "*the established*."[57] The newly established bourgeoisie engenders the state with those ideals essential to its class, the ideals of abstract equality, the virtue of business and the inviolability of property rights. For Stirner, as for Marx, the establishment of capitalism as the ruling ideology can only end in the domination of labor by the "upright" citizens (identified by Stirner with the bourgeoisie). For Stirner, both are possessed. Labor is possessed by the state's assurance that they are free, despite their status. The capitalists are possessed by the belief that their state is the embodiment of freedom and equality.

Stirner's critique of "social liberalism" brings him into indirect conflict with Marx. The specific target of this attack was the communism of Wilhelm Weitling. (Stirner's categories of political liberalism and social liberalism both include criticisms to which Marx responded.) The critique of social liberalism, as of political liberalism, focuses on what Stirner regarded as the inability of social critics to complete the critique of society. The "communists" want to eliminate the holding of property because the inequalities inherent in property relations deny the freedom

and dignity of the laborer. Stirner, in accordance with his critique of the illusory freedom of political liberalism, concludes
that where political liberalism made the unique individual valuable only as either "Man" or "citizen," social liberalism makes
the individual valuable only as "laboring man." In order to both
liberate and protect laboring man, Stirner saw communism as incor-
porating the worst aspects of political liberalism in a new tyranny: in substituting communist society for the bourgeois state,
the communists use the spook of "Man" (in "laboring man"), thus
entailing the devaluation of the individual found in political
liberalism, and they impoverish the individual by eliminating
property.

Stirner did not deny that the state resulting from political
liberalism supported material inequality. In the last part of his
analysis of this state Stirner declares:

The class of laborers, because unprotected in what they essentially are (for they do not enjoy the protection of the
state as laborers . . .), remains a power hostile to this
State, this State of possessors, this "citizen kingship." Its
principle, labor, is not recognized as to its *value*; it is
exploited, [*ausgebeutet*] a spoil [*Kriegsbeute*] of the possessors. . . . The State rests on *the--slavery of labor*. If *labor* becomes *free*, the State is lost.[58]

Stirner's criticism of the position of the laborer under the
modern liberal, that is, bourgeois state is unrelenting; his criticism of communist society is that the communists have not provided for a true liberation of the individual by basing the concept
of society on labor. For, according to Stirner, the communists are
still possessed by the fixed idea of laboring man. They claim that
only within the context of this idea of laboring man is a truly
human society possible. But, says Stirner, the elimination of
property, the means proposed by the commuacnists, results in the
transformation of the political liberal's fixed idea of man as
citizen to man as "ragamuffin." What Stirner intended in the use
of "ragamuffin" includes both literary name-calling and a substantive claim that the communists seek to impoverish all in order to
transform society. For Stirner, this implied that communists

valued humans only as paupers, only as lacking property. "When the proletarian shall really have founded his . . . 'society' in which the interval between rich and poor is to be removed, then he *will be* a ragamuffin, for then he will feel that it amounts to something to be a ragamuffin, and might lift 'Ragamuffin' to be an honorable form of address, just as the Revolution did with the word 'Citizen.'"[59]

The point of establishing the character of Stirner's critique of social liberalism is twofold. First, the charge that Stirner is just an apologist for bourgeois principles of atomistic, economic egoism be seen as superficial,[60] even if icet turns out, as Marx will argue, that this is the practical result of Stirner's egoism. Secondly, an understanding of why Stirner opposed the modern aspects of the political state and communist society is necessary in order to understand why Marx responded to Stirner as he did. As for the first point, it should be clear that, far from supporting the domination of labor by the capitalist, Stirner in fact argues that such economic domination is the destructive basis of an equally degrading sdfocial order. Still, for Stirner, the society envisioned by the communists he criticized--and for that matter by any truly social theorist--could only dominate, enslave, and absorb Stirner's supreme value--the unique individual. Any state or any society functioning as a state is destructive: only an informal association or union (*Verein*) of egoists, pursuing their own interests in a purely voluntary, non-binding setting could allow for the free self-development of the unique individual. All essences, spooks, fixed ideas, or other principles of organization fall away in Stirner's vision of a thoroughgoing social nominalism:

> The fight of the world today is . . . directed against the "established." Yet people are wont to misunderstand this as if it were only that what is now established was to be exchanged for another, a better, established system. But war might rather be declared against establishment itself, the *State*, not a particular State, not any such thing as the mere condition of the State at the time; it is not another State (such as a "people's State") that men aim at, but their

union,   uniting,   this ever-fluid uniting of everything standing.[61]
Stirner's powerful (though vague) invocation had important implications for Marx's project.

AN OVERABUNDANCE OF RAFTERS

Attempting to assess the historical significance for Marx of
Stirner's work is an extremely difficult task.[62] What is clear is
that Marx devoted most of *The German Ideology* to an energetic and
at times vitriolic page-by-page refutation of Stirner's claims,
dismissal of Stirner's abilities as a historian and philosopher,
and at times defamation of Stirner's character. Something about
Stirner led to this very strong reaction, a "something" that this
section and the next will explore. It is beyond the scope of this
chapter to ashjsess all of Marx's arguments and comments, so the
most important themes will be discussed in some detail.

Marx's technique in his refutation of Stirner's main claims
is ironically fitting: he attempts to show that Stirner's arguments are just as ideological as those criticized by Stirner.
Furthermore, Marx strips Stirner's arguments of their vagueness
and metaphor to reveal an incompletely formed set of ideas--of
individuality, community, and freedom. It is not just in *The
German Ideology* that this takes place, however. Marx's development
prior to the publication of *The Ego and His Own* bears witness to a
continuing and fundamental difference between the two thinkers;
Marx retained many basic aspects of Hegelian thought while Stirner
utilized only a convenient scaffolding of Hegelian method. One
useful way of seeing this is through an examination of Stirner's
basic charge against Marx and other social theorists of his day:
namely, that they were still Feuerbachians.[63]

Carroll has noted that the conflict between Stirner and Marx
(and Engels) provides one of the best examples of the conflict between "man the individual and man the social species-being
(*Gattungswesen* in Marx), man in an elemental state of conflict
with a constraining society and man uniting with man to create an

integrated and harmonious community."[64] This is never clearer than in an examination of Marx's relationship to Feuerbach. Marx, like Feuerbach, never abandoned the basic Hegelian premise that the highest goal of social criticism is the furthering of integration (to use Carroll's terminology) of humans in community. As was seen in the previous chapter of this work, for Marx, in at least the early stages of his thought, this integration was predicated upon a complete human emancipation. Even prior to the *1844 Manuscripts* and "On the Jewish Question," Marx's project was aimed at the betterment of human life. The development of the individual could only be achieved in a general human, social development. In one of Marx's earliest writings (August 1835), he comments: "Man's nature is so constituted that he can attain his perfection only by working for the perfection, for the good, of his fellow men."[65] Elsewhere and later he affirms that the goal of human association is the development and education of one another, especially when that association takes the form of a state.[66]

Marx shared this general concern for human betterment with Feuerbach. In Feuerbach's reappropriation of the human essence through the transformative critique of religion, humans and human concerns once again became the focus of attention, at least among those of their group. What Marx appropriated from or at least shared with Feuerbach in this area was the rejection of Hegel's idealist approach and solution to the problem of the development of individuality in the community of man, that is, in a distinctly human context. What Marx approprianpted from Hegel, however, was the abstract kernel of the idea that this development of individuality is both self-development and self-development through human activity. For Hegel, though, this is still an abstract, mental activity. In the *1844 Manuscripts* Marx noted that Hegel

> grasps the essence of *labor* and comprehends objective man--true, because real man--as the outcome of man's *own labor*. . . . [Hegel] grasps *labor* as the *essence* of man--as man's essence which stands the test: he sees only the positive, not the negative side of labor. Labor is *man's coming-to-be for himself* within *alienation*, or as *alienated* man. The only labor which Hegel knows and recognizes is *abstractly*

mental labor.[67]

This reveals an important point in Marx's dispute with Stirner: Feuerbach did not utilize the Hegelian realization of the importance of labor in individual development, thus distinguishing himself from Marx. For Marx and Hegel labor is an act of autogenesis, though for Hegel this is so only abstractly. As Marx saw, for Hegel the autogenesis is as an alienated subject, though even within this alienated context, it is also the first sign of consciousness of the individual as a human individual. Hegel's formal characterization of labor could not satisfy Marx, of course, but the very notion of labor as autogenesis is foreign to Feuerbach and, more importantly, to Stirner. As was seen earlier in this chapter, Stirner criticized the communist (that is, Weitling's) idea of man as "laboring man" because it posited a spook, a fixed idea, against which the unique individual could only suffer in comparison. Marx, from an importantly Hegelian perspective, however, makes a crucially indifferent point: men come to be human individuals only within the context of labor. This will be one of Marx's main criticisms of Stirner in *The German Ideology*. It is worthwhile to note that Marx held the basis of the criticism before the period of *The German Ideology* and even before the publication of Stirner's work.[68]

As Kit Christensen notes, it is in the combination of Feuerbach's concept of species-being, of the human essence as uniquely human and as the key to the possibilities for human betterment, with the Hegelian recognition of the importance of labor as autogenesis that Marx's early perspective on Feuerbach and the idea of a human essence is found.[69] For Marx, humans are indeed social beings, despite Stirner's misgivings. With Feuerbach, Marx realized that human being necessitated a consciousness of being a member of the human species. Species-being is in this sense the development of the possibilities particular to humans as social beings. But, going beyond Feuerbach, Marx realized that mere consciousness of human sociality could not give a full account of species-being, that the introduction of that distinctively human activity, labor, is vital. Marx notes in the *1844 Manuscripts*:

The positive transcendence of *private property*, as the appropriation of *human* life, is therefore the positive transcendence of all estrangement--that is to say, the return of man from religion, family, state, etc., to his *human*, i.e., *social* existence. Religious estrangement as such occurs only in the realm of *consciousness*, of man's inner life, but economic estrangement is that of *real life*; its transcendence therefore embraces both aspects."[70]

The "real life," the human life estranged by economic activity based on private property, thus requires more than the consciousness of man's sociality for the transcendence of the estrangement. It requires an activity that transcends economic estrangement and incorporates the vital communal aspects of human existence. Species-being, viewed in light of Marx's remarks here, exists less as an essence realized in man's self-consciousness of his membership in the human species than as the communality of human beings, requiring the practical transcendence of alienating economic relations and activity. Human species-being is the activity of human beings free of the alienating conditions cited by Marx: "The whole character of a species--its species-character --is contained in the character of its life activity; and free, conscious activity is man's species-character."[71] Still, Marx did not completely divorce himself from Feuerbach in this area; man's species-being is both free and conscious activity, that is, it is activity characterized by human will and consciousness. It is this characteristic that makes the activity human (as opposed to animal activity).

When Marx's version of species-being is viewed as having both the Feuerbachian element just mentioned and the element of productive transformation essential to practical activity or human labor, it becomes clear that, for Marx, Stirner's support of the conscious self-emancipation of the individual from the spooks of the state and society must be naive and incomplete. While it is true that Stirner recognized the deleterious effects of labor "enslaved" by the laws and practices of capitalist economics, he never saw these effects as intrinsic impediments to the development of a truly human individual. For Stirner, the state, as with any other spook or fixed idea, loses its possessive force and distorting efficacy when it is no longer believed to exist as a sovereign, supra-individual entity. All we have to do to bring down the existing order and usher in the new age of the union of egoists is to reveal the unreality of the fixed ideas supporting the existing order and then make a conscious decision to discard those ideas. For Marx, even at the early stages of his work, any real transformation of existing conditions from the alienated existence of humans under capitalist economics to a human life in which true communal relz|ations exist and individuals cease to be alienated requires more than a mere change of mind. To become a fully human, individual species-being requires the transcendence of the "spooks" (to use Stirner's term) of the alienated consciousness concomitant with (or rather--especially for Marx in *The German Ideology*--as a result of) the transformation of the alienated conditions of real life. This is, in germinal form, the distinctively Marxian notion of praxis, of the conscious transformation of the world--including the transformation of the political conditions--through and in order to develop free, conscious activity.

It might seem that Stirner is in fundamental disagreement with Marx's account of species-being as just discussed. And, in fact, Stirner attacked the Feuerbachian notion of species-being and regarded Marx's use of it (in "On the Jewish Question") as following Feuerbach's usage. There is, however, a fundamental philosophical incompatibility rather than direct disagreement between the Stirnerian and Marxian accounts that can be seen by comparing Marx and Feuerbach on the role of activity or labor and individuality. In one way Stirner is actually much closer than Marx to Feuerbach and other so-called Young Hegelians in that, for Feuerbach as for Stirner, individuality and individual self-consciousness is merely a matter of conscious activity. One becomes conscious of one's species-being and thus individuality for Feuerbach by grasping one's essential humanness; for Stirner one becomes a unique individual by dismissing the fixed ideas from one's mind. Marx's position, to be elaborated against both Feuerbach and Stirner in *The German Ideology*, already represented a distinct starting-point. The development of the individual is both a conscious and a practical activity: human beings constitute themselves as species-beings, as individual and human beings, through their "free, conscious activity." In individual development, an unalienated practical activity enables humans to see themselves as humans, to make objective through their activity the species-beings that they are. The activity is done, according to Marx, in either an alienated context, such as that existing in capitalist economic systems, or in an unalienated, free conscious activity. In this respect, humans forge an objective identity for themselves through their productive activity with the world and other people, an identity both individual and human: "The object of labor is . . . the *objectification of man's species-life*: for he duplicates himself not only, as in consciousness, intellectually, but also actively, in reality and therefore he sees himself in a world that he has created."[72] Through this objectification of human species-life, the producer himself is objectified as an individual.

For Stirner (and this is where Stirner is also distinct from Feuerbach), individuality is not created at all. Whereas for Marx humans create their individual and human identities through their praxis, for Stirner individual identity is present to begin with and is recovered through the elimination of the fixed ideas, the spooks inhabiting an already existent individual. It is worth re-calling one of Stirner's terms for these spooks: *der Sparren*. What the individual has is one too many rafters crowding his head and "his" ego. The point that Stirner wants to make is that the struc-ture of individuality already exists, prior to any activity. The structure has just been overcrowded by the addition of "Man" or "species-being" in the individual identity. For Marx the structure of individuality (although "structure" sounds a bit odd here) is not a preexistent state of every biological human unit. The in-dividual only becomes a human individual through the process of self-objectification. If this self-objectification is carried out in a system where the productive activity engaged in by the work-ers is of the sort described in the *1844 Manuscripts*, then the self-objectification results in an alienated self. It is possible, according to Marx's analysis, to overcome that alienation through the transformation of the social and economic conditions leading to an alienated existence. Even in Marx's early writings, then,

the very notion of what it means to develop and be a human individual is far more complex than the account given by Stirner.

Rather than direct disagreement, this incompatibility leads
to some curious results. The most important of these results for
a critique of the state is that Marx and Stirner are equally critical of the bourgeois political state developed under capitalist
economics but for very different reasons. For Stirner, the bourgeois political state devalues the individual because it values
only the abstract citizen. For Marx, this same state is in itself
less of a threat to the individual than the socio-economic system
that allows and requires such a state. This system organizes productive activity such that the laborer is set against others in an
economic realm where every person is viewed as a means and the
alienated laborer views himself as a means, as a tool of economic
life, while the social character of humans is restricted to the
false and abstract universality of citizenship.

Stirner's condemnation of this citizenship parallels Marx's
but never meets it, since for Stirner the political state itself
is the locus of thwarted individuality, in a sense holding the
unique individual prisoner within the confines of citizenship. On
Marx's account individuality is alienated in the socio-economic
system, the concrete conditions of life underlying the political
state. To regain the power of the unique individual, Stirner
claimed that one need only do away with the political state and
its cultural institutions. Marx, on the other hand, saw the necessity of changing the concrete conditions of real life, the
socio-economic system, in order to make true (that is, human) individuality possible.[73] With this background of Marx's early works
in mind, it is now possible to assess Marx's decisive move against
Stirner: *The German Ideology*.

SAINT MAX

The German Ideology is, as the title suggests, a critique of
Marx's contemporaries, including Feuerbach, Stirner, and Bruno
Bauer. One of the main points of the previous section of this

chapter was to show that elements of this critique were evident
prior to the writing of *The German Ideology* and are in fact com-
patible with much of Marx's development in *The German Ideology*.
Marx was already critical of the ideological position Feuerbach
represented, the key defects of which Marx held to be applicable
to Stirner as well. A Feuerbachian style religious "emancipation"
was incomplete because, as Marx put it in a work written at the
end of 1843 and the beginning of 1844: "Man, who looked for a
superhuman being in the fantastic reality of heaven and found
nothing but the *reflection* of himself, will no longer be disposed
to find but the *semblance* of himself, only an inhuman being, where
he seeks and must seek his true reality."[74] The consequence of
this is that, once begun, the critique of religion becomes a critique of the conditions upon which religion (among other estranged
conditions of life) rests:

> The basis of irreligious criticism is this: *Man makes reli-*
> *gion*, religion does not make man. Religion is the self-con-
> sciousness and self-esteem of man who has either not yet
> found himself or has already lost himself again. But *man* is
> no abstract being encamped outside the world. Man is *the*
> *world of man*, the state, society. This state, this society,
> produce religion, an *inverted world-consciousness*, because
> they are an *inverted world*. [Religion] . . . is the *fantastic*
> *realization* of the human essence because the *human essence*
> has no true realiappeared, is to establish *the truth of this*
> *world*.[75]

It was the failure of the German ideologists, including Stirner,
to realize the implications of the actual conditions of life that
led Marx to *The German Ideology*.

One of Stirner's main ideological faults, as Marx pointed
out, is that he identifies the political state supported by the
fixed idea of "Man" or "human essence" as the source of the oppression of the modern state. Marx, meanwhile, will create an even
wider gap[76] between himself and Feuerbachian humanism and its conception of the human essence, at least in part because of Stirner's own relentless criticism of the idea of essences.

Already in the *Theses on Feuerbach*, written in the spring of

1845, Marx can be seen to be distancing himself from the general approach of Stirner and other "ideologists." An incomplete materialism, humanism, and other Young Hegelian positions are seen in the *Theses* as inadequate and incorrectly formulated. Marx's growing emphasis on the essentially practical nature of human life is itself incompatible with the Feuerbachian species-being. Feuerbach is criticized for isolating the "truly human" facets of species-being in an abstract and non-social context devoid of what Marx calls "revolutionary" and "practical-critical . . . activity."[77]

Though each of the *Theses on Feuerbach* is important in understanding Marx's progression beyond Feuerbach, the most significant in regard to Stirner is thesis number four. After criticizing Feuerbach's lack of a practical basis for his materialism, Marx details in thesis four the implications of this defect. Once Feuerbach has exposed the inverted basis of religion, according to Marx, he duplicates the estrangement of the religious world in his formulation of the new secular basis of the world. The secular basis, the essence of man, becomes "an independent realm in the clouds"[78] because Feuerbach has not established species-being in actual, practical social relations. As Marx then relates in thesis six, "The essence of man is no abstraction inherent in each single individual. In its reality it is the ensemble of the social relations."[79] This is, in many respects, the same criticism levelled at Feuerbach and Marx by Stirner, with the difference that for Stirner there is no essence of man. According to Stirner, Feuerbach's conception of a human essence is a refinement of the religious concept of essence, an abstraction independent of any existing individual humans, though supposedly "inhabiting" each individual. The fixed idea of a human essence, for Stirner, can only be this sort of abstraction. Marx's point in the *Theses*, especially when these are seen as a prelude to *The German Ideology*, can be seen as a partial agreement with Stirner: Feuerbach does succumb to a secular abstraction. The agreement is only partial, however, since Marx's conclusions in the *Theses*, as in *The German Ideology*, point beyond this abstraction. Contrary to Stirner's claims, dismissing the secular abstraction does not leave only "unique" individuals but reveals the actual, practical prerequisites and bases of species-being in the real praxis of humans in society.

The practical consequences of this difference is that Marx and Stirner remain with very differenct requirements for the development of individuality. For Marx, the focus is on the unalienated praxis of humans in community; for Stirner, it is simply a matter of revealing the nature of the abstract "Man" and the state and then dismissing them.

Marx takes up these points in *The German Ideology*. Feuerbach's basic affinity for the Young Hegelian practice of criticizing ideas or concepts, the endless critique of theory, is seen as inadequate. Feuerbach "remains in the realm of theory and conceives of men not in their given social connection, not under their existing conditions of life. . . . He never arrives at the actually existing, active men, but stops at the abstraction 'man'. . . ."[80] Young Hegelianism restricts critique to the abstractions of theory and thus restricts the task of liberation to liberating consciousness from its theoretical demons. Marx was quite correct when he classified Young Hegelians according to method and included Stirner as another one of the abstract theoreticians, if one of the more consistent among them.The Young Hegelians took Hegel's categories and secularized them "by giving them more profane names such as 'species,' 'the unique,' 'man,' etc."[81] (The reference here is to Feuerbach and, of course, Stirner.) By identifying various ideas as the causes of estrangement and the domination of men, these thinkers, according to Marx, made the basis of every dominant relationship "a question of dogmas and belief in dogmas. The world was sanctified to an every-increasing extent [until] at last the venerable Saint Max [Stirner] was able to canonize it *en bloc* and thus dispose of it once and for all."[82] By ignoring the reality of man's practical, productive activity in the real world, these thinkers--and especially Stirner--make it a matter of a change of consciousness, of ideas, concepts and phrases, in order to eliminate the domination of the institutions "represented" by such ideas. This was for Marx both a hopeless project and a negative obscuring and distorting of the real problems. In the words of the famous eleventh thesis on Feuerbach, "The philosophers have only *interpreted* the

world in various ways; the point is to change it."[83] Marx did not
have in mind the elimination of thought and interpretation altogether, as that would have reduced the human beings to the level
of mere animality, according to the terms of his own arguments and
especially his conception of human praxis. What the eleventh
thesis and The German Ideology oppose is the mistaken belief, central to Stirner's argument, that in merely interpreting the world,
philosophers have thereby changed the world.

The best indication of the specific role played by Stirner in
Marx's account is found in the long and often tedious section of
The German Ideology entitled "Saint Max." In the first section of
The German Ideology, Marx had characterized the Young Hegelians,
including Stirner, as the "staunchest conservatives,"[84] and an
understanding of what Marx meant is one way to understand several
of the main arguments in "Saint Max."

According to Stirner, any real, concrete action taken in the
present world to change the social and economic order in order to
achieve a revolutionary goal is doomed to substitute a revolutionary morality for the deposed order. The revolutionary, by submit-
ting himself to a revolutionary organization and then acting in
the name of a revolutionary ideal, allows his uniqueness, his particularity, to be absorbed by the revolution. In other words, the
revolutionary is possessed by a new ideal, a new spook (the revolution and its goals), just as possessed as the supporter of the
existing order. Stirner opposed the idea of revolution with the
act of rebellion (Empörung), a spontaneous reappropriation of the
individual's uniqueness and his self-evaluation above any institutions or ideals. (Stirner speaks of rebellion as characterized by
demands that the rebel sich auf-oder empörzurichten.[85]) The rebels
do not make their rebellion a social or political act, rather they
act for their own (individual, unique) egoistic interests. "The
Revolution aimed at New arrangements; insurrection leads us no
longer to let ourselves be arranged, but to arrange ourselves, and
sets no glittering hopes on 'institutions.' It is not a fight
against the established, since, if it prospers, the established
[including the state] collapses of itself; it is only a working
forth of me out of the established."[86] As was discussed earlier,

the result of such a reappropriation or rebellion is the union or
association of egoists, the only type of association that Stirner
could envision. The association would be wholly subject to each of
its members, each member meanwhile pursuing his own interests and
using the union in order to do so more effectively.

Marx's characterization of Stirner as "conservative" is
directly linked to Stirner's rejection of revolutionary practice
and support of the union of egoists. According to Marx, the theoretical result of such a union is the affirmation, in theory and
practice, of the existing capitalist economic conditions, that is,
the (estranged) relations of production and private property.
Marx's argument for this point has two stages.

The first stage of the argument used by Marx brands Stirner's
conception of private property, egoistic property pursued in association with other egoists, as "nothing but ordinary or bourgeois
property transfigured by his sanctifying fantasy."[87] That is,
Stirner has simply affirmed the existence of exclusive private
property rights as found in capitalism with the added touch of
each person's property as being a "unique" and intimate part of
the egoistic individual's particularity. This insight on the part
of Marx, accompanied by the realization that Stirner does envision
the continued existence of the other aspects of capitalist economy
(the division of labor, for example) in the union of egoists leads
to the next, more important stage of Marx's argument.

Because Stirner does not foresee the necessity of changing
the social and economic conditions and relationships underlying
capitalism but simply advocates an uprising of outraged individuals acting together (not in harmony) to free themselves of the
illusions of the state, he has remained within the Young Hegelian
critique of concepts, ideas, and phrases. Stirner, according to
Marx, changes nothing but his mind. Even worse, the pursuit of
egoism as a supposedly liberating philosophy reinforces (for Marx,
"sanctifies") the real, existing conditions preventing an actual
liberation. "The essence of the matter is this. Bourgeois and,
particularly, petty-bourgeois . . . property is, as we have seen,
retained in the union. Merely the *interpretation*, the '*point of
view*,' is different, for which reason Sancho [that is, Stirner]

always lays stress on the way of 'regarding.'"[88]

Marx's argument here is quite strong. Stirner explicitly re-jects any organized action (political, economic, or other) based on anything other than egoistic interest. And he sees every organ-ized action intent on changing the real social and economic con-ditions as inherently detrimental to egoistic interest; such action is "revolutionary." Even so, Stirner's latter claim, that organized revolutionary activity against the state degrades indi-vidual freedom, is the cornerstone of individualist anarchist thought. Marx's response, that individual freedom in the complete sense of human emancipation is only possible through revolutionary activity that changes the real conditions from which the state emerges, marks the very different starting-points and basic incom-patibility between Marxian thought and (at least Stirnerian) an-archism.

The arguments just cited are one way of viewing the basic conflict between Marx and Stirner, especially in regard to polit-ical action and the state. Within *The German Ideology*, Marx ad-vances the argument. At many points in "Saint Max," Marx repeats his arguments that Stirner's individualism is illusory and that the egoist as individual is a false construction, a pastiche of Young Hegelian and iconoclastic phrasemaking devoid of any basis in the real conditions of life. The division of labor in capital-ism for Marx had consequences for the individual that negated much of Stirner's claimed ability to destroy the power of the state (essentially through thought) and thereby promote individuality. Labor, for Stirner, was inherently egoistic and could be seen to be so by individual laborers once the illusion of the state was seen in its "true form." Marx, on the other hand, saw that the condition of the laborer in capitalism (especially in the division of labor, a key point in *The German Ideology*) is such that labor's estranged nature precluded the development of a fully human indi-viduality and actually threatened the very existence of the labor-ers. In these actual conditions, according to Marx, "the appropri-ation of a totality of instruments of production is, for this very reason, the development of a totality of capacities in the indi-viduals themselves."[89] As Thomas has discerned, Stirner's failure

to appreciate the importance of the division of labor for the individual is a consequence of overlooking the specific nature of
the divison of labor within capitalism. Stirner has instead conceived of the egoistic laborer abstractly, apart from the dehuman-
izing context of the specific form of labor in capitalism. As
Thomas puts it, "What such a view overlooks is that the concept of
'labor' abstracted from any particular kind of labor presupposed
that the placement of individual workers in the productive process
that employs them is no longer considered to be connected with or
expressive of any personal qualities the individual worker himself
might possess."[90] The individual egoist as laborer does not have
an independent existence, if Marx is correct, contrary to what
Stirner thought and what Stirner required in order to make his
egoism coherent.

If the individual egoist as laborer does not have an independent existence, then what sort of existence can it, the ego, have?
Marx's claim, another of his central points in "Saint Max," is
that the unique ego has no real existence at all--it is an
abstraction. As many commentators have noticed, in attempting to
demonstrate the hollowness of Stirner's "unique," the ego, Marx
has turned Stirner's argument against its master. For if the ego
is an abstraction, then Stirner's own position requires him to
reveal its illusory basis. The problem, of course, is that,
given Stirner's dismissal of the real basis of what Marx calls
practical-critical activity, there is nothing left to reveal the
illusion of the abstract ego. As Marx says, "Egoism based on the
egoistic mode of action of these persons must be just as imaginary
as the people themselves."[91] If Marx is correct, then Stirner's
egoism is an empty exercise in ideas.

In defense of Stirner, this reduction of his egoism is only
possible because Marx, in his developing historical materialism,
denies that the individual--Stirner's unique ego--is independent
of material history. For Stirner, the opposite of Marx's claim is
and must be axiomatic. The ego must be an ahistorical, primitive
datum which can be added to by the conditions of real life but
which is not constituted by these conditions. Marx claims that
Stirner's "ego" is just as illusory as Feuerbach's "Man" or "human

essence." But for Stirner the ego is just there; it arises in humans but does not need the self-creation of the human individual
through the practical activity of labor. In this sense, some of
Marx's arguments in *The German Ideology* (and Stirner's possible
responses) reflect and extend what Marx wrote in his earlier works
about what it means to be and become a human individual. Humans
are social beings and only in society can they become human individuals, a point that Marx had maintained for some time. Thus
McLellan is correct when he notes that the arguments have a distinct continuity from the earlier works to *The German Ideology*,
though this later work puts a distinct and in many ways new emphasis on the practical aspects of economic development and ac-
tivity--especially as affected by the division of labor in capitalism.[92] What Stirner neglected in not dealing with the material
conditions of capitalist society is the fact that, as Marx saw it,
egoistic individualism pervades capitalist economic life, but
humans are still far from becoming real individual, communal
beings. Instead, the individual is "entirely subordinated to the
division of labor and hence . . . brought into the most complete
dependence on one another."[93] Rather than fostering individuality,
the system of capitalist organization has organized the real
conditions of life so that individuality is frustrated.

It is very difficult to make a complete evaluation of Stirner
and Marx, largely because they are starting from very different
points. Marx's position is far more complex than Stirner's, resting as it does on a conception of the self-development of individual men in human society, a conception influenced by both Hegel
and Feuerbach. However, there are bases for comparison when the
question is one of political organization and the state.

For Stirner, communism was simply the introduction of another
obstacle to the individual in the form of a new political order.
The communist political order was based on the fixed idea that man
is only "true man" as "laboring man." In being so based it con-
ceals, for Stirner, an antagonism for the unique individual, which
is the basic creative force standing in perpetual opposition to
any general classification. Stirner thought that the communists
wanted to use their drive against private property in order to

gain a better position within society, a position from which they could dictate the course of the laborers. In addition, the elimination of private property impoverishes the egoistic individual, since ownership is the essential characteristic and drive of individuality.

Marx's response rests largely on the claim that Stirner's "ego" is only an ill-formed idea, as it is an abstraction from any of the real existing conditions of society. Only within these conditions can we speak of the development of individuals. Marx's response is the key aspect of his denial that communism is destructive to the individual and that communists want to substitute another "established order." (The practical impact of this denial seems an excellent reason for Marx devoting so much time to Stirner in *The German Ideology*.) As Marx put it, "Saint Max believes that the communists want to 'make sacrifices' for 'society,' when they want at most to sacrifice existing society; in this case he should describe their consciousness that their struggle is the common cause of all people who have outgrown the bourgeois system as a sacrifice that they make to themselves."[94]

In reply to Stirner, then, Marx claimed that communism, rather than subjugating individuals, ends capitalist style individualism and makes human individuality possible. It does so by freeing people from the socio-economic conditions (the "existing society") which preclude the development of a human, universal communality. The political emancipation of the modern era is only a partial and estranged development of this universality. It cannot be "completed," according to Marx, until communism supersedes capitalism and completed only metaphorically, since Marx declared that communism is not a state of affairs or ideal, as Stirner thought, but a "*real* movement which abolishes the present state of things."[95] The opposition between the individual and communist society envisioned by Stirner can only come about if the individual is conceived of as the static, ahistorical entity of Stirner's book.[96] Marx's point is that individuality is not like that at all.

In comparing the two positions, Marx's is clearly superior. It is more complete, more consistent, more coherent, and especial-

ly more in accord with the actual conditions of human life. If opposition to the state is to be more than an empty rebellion, it
must also change the conditions out of which the state arises in
any particular era. Only by recognizing the importance of such
change can any theory claim to be revolutionary. Stirner did not
claim to be a revolutionary and in that he was entirely correct.
He did claim that he provided a unique view of human freedom, of a
way to individual liberation free of any spooks, ghosts, or fixed
ideas. Marx's response to this type of abstract theorizing demon-
strates the incompleteness of Stirner's use of "human freedom" and
"the individual":

> The transformation, through the division of labor, of person-
> al powers (relations) into material powers, cannot be dis-
> pelled by dismissing the general idea of it from one's mind,
> but can only be abolished by the individuals again subjecting
> these material powers to themselves and abolishing the divi-
> sion of labor. This is not possible without the community.
> Only within the community has each individual the means of
> cultivating his gifts in all directions; hence personal free-
> dom becomes possible only within the community. . . . The il-
> lusory community in which individuals have up till now com-
> bined always took on an independent existence in relation to
> them, and since it was the combination of one class over
> against another, it was at the same time for the oppressed
> class not only a completely illusory community, but a new
> fetter as well. In the real community the individuals obtain
> their freedom in and through their association.[97]

Anarchism cannot sustain itself in the abstract, individual-
istic form espoused by Stirner. Those who have followed Stirner
(for example, the members of the "radical right" cited by Gerald
Runkle[98]) have almost without exception defended the existing economic system, capitalism, in the name of abstract principles of
individualism. They have usually not had the relative consistency
of Stirner's denial of all social principles.

Marx's encounter with Stirner can be seen as two steps forward: Marx refined his position on state and society and, at least
in part prodded by Stirner, made clear the differences between the

communist position and Young Hegelianism, including Feuerbachianism. In turn, anarchism passed through its individualist phase. In the period after Stirner, anarchist opposition to the state seldom had the luxury of dismissing the real conditions of human existence and individual development in its search for a complete human freedom.

NOTES

1. From Johann Wolfgang v. Goethe, *Vanitas! vanitatum vanitas!*, Goethes Werke, Band I. Weimar Ausgabe (Weimar: Hermann Bohlau, 1887), pp. 132-133. Stirner uses sections of this poem at the beginning and end of his book.

2. Steven Lukes, *Individualism* (Key Concepts in the Social Sciences) (New York: Harper and Row, 1973), p. 73.

3. See, for example, John Carroll, *Break-out from the Crystal Palace: The Anarcho-Psychological Critique: Stirner, Nietzsche, Dostoevsky* (London, Boston: Routledge and Kegan Paul, 1974), esp. pp. 15-18; TKM, esp. pp. 125-134. There are many others, far too numerous to mention.

4. R.W.K. Paterson, in *The Nihilist Egoist: Max Stirner* (London: Oxford University Press, 1971), supports this view, as does Donald McIntosh, "The Dimensions of Anarchy," in J. Rolnd Pennock and John W. Chapman, eds., *Anarchism: Nomos XIX*, (New York: New York University Press, 1978), esp. pp. 248-253. Though McIntosh refers to John Carroll's Introduction to the abridged version of Max Stirner, *The Ego and His Own*, ed. John Carroll (New York: Harper Torchbook, 1974), for support on this point, Carroll in fact refers to Stirner as "the prototypal anarchist: and as "the anarcho-egoist" (p. 34).

5. This latter claim, puzzling from a philosophical point of view, is less so from a historical one. In much the same way as Nietzsche was appropriated by the apologists of fascism in the twentieth century, Stirner supposedly inspired Benito Mussolini in Mussolini's earlier years. See, for example, James Joll, *The Anarchists*, 2d ed. (Cambridge, Mass.: Harvard University Press,

1980), pp. 154-55, where he quotes Mussolini. A modern proponent of this view of Stirner claims that Stirner is in the anarchist tradition but:

> No elaborate research is needed to establish that the Anarchist tradition is not self-consistent. Practically every point of view other than support of the existing nation state can be found somewhere within it. We should not be surprised to find anarchists wholly supportive of tyranny, as Stirner is.

(Lisa Newton, "The Profoundest Respect for Law," in Pennock and Chapman, *Anarchism: Nomos XIX*, p. 164.) Two brief comments are called for. First, though the space for anarchist theories may be large, it is not without limits; any "anarchist" who supported tyranny would not be an anarchist. Secondly, Stirner did not support tyranny, as will be shown in this chapter. See note 49 below.

6. The translation of Stirner's work as *The Ego and His Own* by Steven T. Byington, ed. James J. Martin (New York: Libertarian Book Club, 1963), will be used throughout this section in conjunction with the amended translation in C-EGO.

7. The sources of and reasons for the neglect of Stirner's influence are documented in David McLellan, *The Young Hegelians and Karl Marx* (London: Macmillan, 1969), p. 134.

8. S-EGO, pp. 9-14.

9. Ibid.

10. Ibid., p. 10.

11. Ibid. It is important to note that Stirner's view of courage as basic to mind is unusual. It presages Stirner's view of the ego, though the initial connection between courage and mind is neither commonplace nor obvious. This was pointed out to me by William L. McBride, private communication.

12. Ibid.

13. See, for example, ibid., p. 138.

14. Ibid., p. 12.

15. Ibid.

16. Ibid., pp. 12, 13.

17. Ibid., p. 14.

18. Ibid., p. 13.

19. Ibid.

20. Ibid., p. 12.

21. Ibid., p. 14.

22. Stirner severely criticized all three, though that does not diminish their influence. Early in his career Stirner wrote a positive review of Bauer's *Posaune* and an article on art and religion in which his indebtedness to Feuerbach is evident. See McLellan, p. 118. There are many stylistic and superficial debts to Feuerbach, including the division of *Ego*.

23. Ludwig Feuerbach, *Sämtliche Werke*, VI, p. 222, cited by McLellan, p. 89.

24. McLellan, p. 119.

25. TKM, p. 131. Had Thomas explored Stirner's psycho-social dialectic in greater detail (Thomas terms it a "curious" section that "has some interesting ontogenetic and phylogenetic implications," p. 130), he might have modified this assertion. James Joll, a lucid interpreter of anarchism, has recognized the ahistorical, anti-Hegelian nature of Stirner's dialectic. See Joll, p. 154.

26. See, among many, CBO, p. 18; McLellan, p. 121.

27. Ludwig Feuerbach, *The Essence of Christianity*, trans. George Eliot (New York: Harper and Row, 1957) xl and p. 29. This was especially true in the period between the publication of Strauss's *Das Leben Jesu* (1835) and the early period of the reign of Friedrich Wilhelm IV (who ascended the Prussian throne in 1840), as has been noted by Lawrence S. Stepelevich, *The Young Hegelians* (Cambridge: Cambridge University Press, 1983), pp. 2-13.

28. S-EGO, p. 25. Though Stirner does not mention Feuerbach by name in the context of this comment (and in fact refers to the progress of Protestant Christianity in general), the reference to Feuerbach's views is unmistakable.

29. S-EGO, p. 33.

30. Ibid. I have omitted Stirner's footnoted reference to several Biblical passages.

31. Ibid., p. 58.

32. Ibid.

33. Ibid., p. 59.

34. Ibid., p. 182.

35. As will be seen, this point is the focus of one of Marx's more important criticism of Stirner. As with Young Hegelianism in general Marx pointed out that according to Stirner "just as we saw in the case of the egoist not in agreement with himself . . . people have only to change their consciousness to make everything in the world all right." *The German Ideology*, part III, in MECW V, p. 282.

36. S-EGO, p. 41.

37. Ibid., p. 43; C-EGO, p. 58. Stirner's term is der Spar-ren (rafters), referring to the German colloquialism, einen Sparren zuviel haben, to be not quite right in the upper stories, to have one too many rafters. As Stirner has said, in the pos-sessed (referring specifically to Feuerbach's critique of theo-logy), the "earthly apartments" become quite overcrowded. See the passage cited in note 30 above.

38. Ibid., p. 48. The comparison uses Friedrich Christoph Schlosser's Geschichte des achtzenten Jahrhunderts (1823), in which Schlosser traces the influence of rationalism and political thought prior to the French Revolution. Stirner cites:

> Holbach's company constituted a regular plot against the tra-ditional doctrine and the existing system, and its members were as fanatical on behalf of their unbelief as monks and priests, Jesuits and Pietists, Methodists, missionary and Bible societies, commonly are for mechanical worship and orthodoxy. (Schlosser, p. 519, in S-EGO, p. 45.)

See also Carroll's note 4 in C-EGO, p. 61. Schlosser's historical oversimplification is Stirner's philosophical overgeneralization, though that cannot be debated here.

39. Ibid., p. 77.

40. Ibid., p. 44.

41. Ibid., p. 46.

42. See any of the works of Proudhon and the next chapter of this work. Stirner does have his point against Proudhon, one that Marx was to take up. Stirner cites Proudhon's remark, "The moral law is eternal and absolute. Who would dare today to attack morality?" Pierre-Joseph Proudhon, *De la Creation de l'ordre dans*

l'humanitié, ou principes d'organisation politique, (Paris, 1843), p. 36; cited by Stirner, in S-EGO, p. 47. Both Stirner and Marx answer the challenge.

43. S-EGO, p. 47.

44. TKM, p. 133. Curiously, Thomas follows this with an extensive list supposedly distinguishing state from society in Stirner's work. The list can be misleading: many of the characteristics cited are used interchangeably by Stirner.

45. Ibid.

46. Ibid.

47. Daniel Guérin, *Anarchism from Theory to Practice*, trans. Mary Klopper (New York: Monthly Review Press, 1970), p. 13; see the passage cited from *The German Ideology* in note 82 below.

48. CBO, p. 50.

49. S-EGO, p. 54. Stirner's statements that "A Nero is a 'bad' man only in the eyes of the 'good'" and "Nero was no viler than his time, in which one could only be one of the two, good or bad" (p. 54) may in part account for Lisa Newton's claim that Stirner supports tyranny (see note 5 above). The discussion of Stirner's view in the text of this work has shown that Newton's position is untenable. The tyrant is just as "possessed" as the servant, if not more so: the tyrant thinks that he is free of morality. Stirner concludes that "Nero became very inconvenient by his possessedness" (p. 55).

50. Pierre-Joseph Proudhon, *What Is Property? An Inquiry into the Principle of Right and Government*, trans. Benjamin R. Tucker (New York: Dover Publications, 1970), p. 11. Much more will be said about this in the next chapter of this work.

51. S-EGO, p. 79.

52. TKM argues that "Stirner says very little about forms of the state, beyond the propositions that any state is a despotism. . . ." (P. 133.) In light of the fifty-three pages Stirner spends on these three forms alone, this remark is rather puzzling. It is true that Stirner's three state-forms are less descriptions of coherent political theories or existing states than means of attacking aspects of the state in general, but this seems to be the case with most political polemics.

53. S-EGO, p. 102.

54. Ibid., p. 104.

55. McLellan, p. 122.

56. S-EGO, p. 107.

57. Ibid., p. 110.

58. Ibid., p. 115.

59. Ibid., p. 117.

60. See, for example, the Preface to Marx-Engels, *Anarchism and Anarcho-Syndicalism*, (New York: International Publishers, 1972), esp. p. 9.

61. S-EGO, p. 223.

62. There is a good summary of this complicated task in Kit Christensen,"The Concept of 'Species Being' in the Works of Feuerbach and Marx" (Ph.D. dissertation Purdue University, 1982), esp. p. 180.

63. I owe much of my discussion of this point to Christensen, ibid., pp. 109-199.

64. CBO, p. 60.

65. Karl Marx, "Reflections of a Young Man on the Choice of a Profession," in *MECW* I, p. 8.

66. See Karl Marx, "Leading Article in No. 179 of *Kolnische Zeitung*," in *MECW* I, p. 193. This comment is prior to the critique of the state in capitalism found in "On the Jewish Question."

67. Karl Marx, *Economic and Philosophic Manuscripts of 1844*, in *MECW* III, p. 333. I take it that Marx means that Hegel does not recognize that the alienated nature of labor persists and hence it remains negative. On p. 342 Marx comments:

> Because [Hegel's] exposition is *formal* and *abstract*, the supersession of the alienation becomes a confirmation of the alienation; or for Hegel this movement of *self-genesis* and *self-objectification* in the form of *self-alienation* and *self-estrangement* is the *absolute,* and hence final, *expression of human life*--with itself as its aim, at peace with itself, and in unity with its essence.

68. The *1844 Manuscripts* were finished at about the same time as Stirner's *Ego* was published, in late 1844.

69. Christensen, p. 115.

70. *1844 Manuscripts*, in *MECW* III, p. 297. See also "Contribution to Critique of Hegel's Philosophy of Law. Introduction," in
MECW III, where Marx states, "The criticism of religion ends with
the teaching that *man is the highest being for man*, hence with the
categorical imperative to overthrow all relations in which man is
a debased, enslaved, forsaken, despicable being. . . ." (p. 182).

71. Ibid., p. 276.

72. Ibid., p. 277.

73. There are many passages within the *1844 Manuscripts* and
"On the Jewish Question" where Marx emphasizes the need for a complete, not just political emancipation. The sections on "Estranged
Labor" (beginning on p. 270 in *MECW* III) and "Private Property and
Communism" (beginning on p. 293 in *MECW* III) are two important
sources in the *1844 Manuscripts*. In the latter section, Marx comments that in a communism in which the political state is eliminated without eliminating the underlying private property relations, emancipation is still incomplete. Though there is an awareness of the "transcendence of human self-estrangement" still this
communism "has not yet grasped the positive essence of private
property, and just as little the *human* nature of need, [thus] it
remains captive to it and infected by it." (P. 296.)

74. Karl Marx, "Contribution to the Critique of Hegel's
Philosophy of Law," in *MECW* III, p. 175.

75. Ibid.

76. This gap is a progression from one stage of Marx's
thought to another, not, as some have held, a "break" of some
sort. See Louis Althusser, *For Marx*, trans. Ben Brewster (New
York: Vintage, 1970).

77. Karl Marx, *Theses on Feuerbach*, original version, thesis
1, in *MECW* V, p. 3.

78. Ibid., thesis 4, p. 4.

79. Ibid., thesis 6, p. 4.

80. Karl Marx and Frederick Engels, *The German Ideology*, part
I, in *MECW* V, p. 41.

81. Ibid., p. 29.

82. Ibid.

83. Marx, *Theses on Feuerbach*, Thesis 11, *MECW* V, p. 5.

84. Marx and Engels, *MECW* V, part I, p. 30.

85. S-EGO, p. 316.

86.   Ibid.   One of the more interesting brief commentaries on Stirner is included in Albert Camus, *The Rebel*: *An Essay on Man in Revolt* (New York: Vintage, 1956), pp. 62-65. Camus notes, with a mixture of wonder and trepidation, that Stirner attempted the most basic metaphysical rebellion, extending even to the rebellion of revolution.

87. Marx and Engels, *MECW* V, part III, p. 367.

88. Ibid., p. 406.

89. Ibid., part I, p. 87.

90. TKM, p. 152.

91. Marx and Engels, *MECW* V, part III, p. 120.

92.   McLellan, p. 132. He does greatly exaggerate the point when he claims that there "is nothing new on alienated labor in the *Heilige Familie* and in the *Deutsche Ideologie*. . . ." The terminology of 'alienation' does drop out, but, if nothing else, the attacks on Stirner show that Marx had a more developed sense of the origin of estrangement in the capitalist system, especially in the division of labor and the material conditions of life. He also had a more developed sense of the consequences.

93. Marx and Engels, *MECW* V, part I, p. 86.

94. Ibid., part III, p. 213.

95. Ibid., part I, p. 49.

96.   On this, at least, I am in agreement with Carroll (CBO, p. 67). Carroll comments, in apparent support: "Stirner's egoist morality, his theory of individual action, reflects an a-historical conception of man, who need be neither modern nor civilized." This is true and revealing--as Marx held, there is in Stirner's work a lack of modernity and of a sense of community.

97. Marx and Engels, *MECW* V, part I, p. 77.

98.   Gerald Runkle, *Anarchism: Old and New* (New York: Dell Publishing Co., 1972), pp. 228-255.

4
PROUDHON'S MORAL VISION AND THE POVERTY OF PHILOSOPHY

By all means let us [that is, Marx and Proudhon] work together to discover the laws of society, the ways in which these
laws are realized and the process by which we are able to
discover them. But, for God's sake, when we have demolished
all *a priori* dogmas, do not let us think of indoctrinating
the people in our turn. . . . Let us set the world an example
of wise and farsighted tolerance, but simply because we are
leaders of a movement let us not instigate a new intolerance.
Let us not set ourselves up as the apostles of a new religion, even if it be the religion of logic or of reason.

Proudhon[1]

The Parisian gentlemen [attending the first Congress at
Geneva] had their heads full of the emptiest Proudhonist
phrases. They babble about science and know nothing. They
scorn all *revolutionary* activity, . . . all concentrated,
social movements, and therefore also those which can be
carried through by *political means*. . . . Under the *pretext
of freedom*, and of anti-governmentalism or anti-authoritarian
individualism, these gentlemen . . . actually preach ordinary
bourgeois economy, only Proudhonistically idealized!

Marx[2]

I have received a libel by a Doctor Marx. . . . It is a tis-

sue of abuse, calumny, falsification and plagiarism. Marx is
the tapeworm of socialism!

Proudhon[3]

PROUDHON, MARX, AND THE PHILOSOPHICAL TRADITION

If the egoistic individualist branch of anarchism settled into re-
pose after the brief notoriety of Stirner, anarchism itself was
far from dead. Those students of political theory who deny that
Stirner was an anarchist often place the birth of modern anarchism
in the writings of Pierre-Joseph Proudhon, a near contemporary of
Stirner.[4] Though Proudhon claimed the title of "individualist,"
his individualism is quite different from Stirnerian egoism. Where
Stirner held that all values and supra-individualistic goals were
traps for the unique ego, Proudhon based his individualism and his
anarchism on an unwavering belief in the value of justice, the
concept of which he held to encompass a large number of normative
concepts, including equality, liberty, reciprocity, and mutuality.[5]   It is from this essentially moral belief in the value of
the components (or, as Proudhon would have it, aspects) of justice
that Proudhon formulates all of his substantive positions on the
state, society, economics, and ethics itself. Through a careful
examination of Proudhon's substantive positions, his conflict with
Marx on the issues of the state and social change will be brought
to light.

     In a sense, Stirner was correct in calling Proudhon a moral-
ist. For Proudhon, however, his moralism was the result of a
"rigorous" scientific investigation of the bases of human society.
Proudhon's goal was the preservation and improvement of human
society because he saw an improved society as a prerequisite for
the complete and widespread improvement of individuals. Only with
the complete transformation of social and economic relations (and
the elimination of strictly political relations) could the individual fully exercise his autonomy, according to Proudhon. Given
this starting-point, Proudhon eventually advocated the abolition
of the political state, the transformation of the workplace from

the capitalist wage-labor model to a worker possessed and managed workshop and the reform of educational practices, among other points.   Such a moral vision, combined with the inconsistencies and occasional perverse idiosyncrasies of Proudhon's thought was bound to bring Proudhon into conflict with Marx.

Proudhon's earliest major work, *What Is Property? An Inquiry into the Principle of Right and Government* (1840), is in many ways limited by the young Proudhon's agrarian and provincial viewpoint. Despite these limitations, however, this seminal work contains most of Proudhon's major points, albeit in an undeveloped form. These ideas were elaborated and refined though not fundamentally altered throughout Proudhon's career, especially in the *System of Economic Contradictions, or the Philosophy of Poverty* (1846), the *General Idea of Revolution in the 19th Century* (1851), and *Justice in the Revolution and the Church* (1858). The general course of his development was to an increasingly modern viewpoint: Proudhon came to realize that the establishment of justice in society necessarily went beyond the reorganization of (rural) property and village trade relations. With this sophistication came an occasional inconsistency and a gradual moderation of his radical rhetoric and of his optimism concerning the possibilities for change.

The guiding theme of Proudhon's moral vision throughout his career was the vital and positive character of individual work, of labor performed in a self-controlled and unconstrained environment. Proudhon came to view individual labor as a means of effecting the moral transformation of society, through the near redemptive power and effects of direct productive action. It was the perversion of the nature of labor that Proudhon opposed. Here Proudhon's enduring vision of a society built according to the standards of, as James Joll has put it, "sturdy, independent, self-supporting peasants"[6] is in evidence. Proudhon was attracted to the simple (and often naive) common sense of the Franc-Comtois peasant, where labor was a virtue in itself, even though debt or rent expropriated much of the product of the laborer. The only just bases of labor for Proudhon were liberty, the ability to labor as one pleases and to contract freely, and equality, the ability to escape the disadvantageous workings and especially the domination of the regime of capital and property.

What Proudhon concluded from his examination of labor and society was that society must be completely transformed (that is, the social and economic bases of society must be transformed) in order to achieve justice in labor and social relations. He occasionally opposed efforts to ameliorate the effects of the capitalist economic order (especially the organization of labor by non-laborers) not, as Marx and some others would have it, because he was defending bourgeois values but because he saw these reforms as (at most) marginal gains for the dispossessed. Proudhon may have been "defending" bourgeois values in *Marx*'s sense; when Marx accused Proudhon of being a *petit-bourgeois*, he did so in part as an *ad hominem* attack and in part as an accurate description of what Marx saw as the essence and effects of Proudhon's moral vision. What Proudhon supported was broad-based change, beginning at the local level but in a radical fashion, eliminating the power of capital and property gradually but thoroughly. What he opposed was the creation of a new hierarchy in the process. Proudhon also opposed any large-scale cooperation with the existing proprietors and government officials. The contaminating effect of this cooperation and the prolongation of the regime of property and hierarchy outweighed, in Proudhon's eyes, the advantages to be gained.

Proudhon not only opposed any cooperation with what he regarded as the "enemy" and the reformism entailed by such cooperation, he also opposed the retention of any property relations (which included the ownership of capital) that might conflict with the norms and goals of justice. Thus, Proudhon opposed the continuation of property relations regulated by any hierarchical authority, even if a particular hierarchical system, in violating Proudhon's first aspect of justice, the standard of liberty, intended to use the reorganization of property relations to attain equality, his second major aspect of justice. Labor and society could only be just if they were both equal and free, in the specific senses intended by Proudhon. Neither liberty nor equality could be sacrificed in the service of its counterpart.

The result of this undeviating orthodoxy in regard to his conception of the standards of justice was that Proudhon found

himself opposed by nearly every social and revolutionary thinker
of his age.[7] Not only did Proudhon oppose the utopians, especially
Fourier, Saint-Simon, Etienne Cabet, and Louis Blanc, on the
grounds that they simply changed the appearance of the injustices
perpetrated upon the laborer, but he also opposed the "liberal"
democrats and revolutionaries of his time, on the grounds that
neither group addressed justice in its entirety. The former
ignored the demands of real equality, while the latter attempted
to institute equality through a denial of liberty.

What Proudhon proposed instead of the inequalities of capitalism and what he saw as the unfreedom of any revolutionary hierarchy was a society ordered by economic self-organization and
cooperative enterprise, rather than one organized by any external
power, be it the power of capital and property or the power of the
state. Again, the basis of such an ordering had to be the individual laborer and the personal, moral change on his part in his relations with other workers. In the second volume of the *System of
Economic Contradictions*, Proudhon declared "Whoever appeals to
power and to capital for the organization of labor is lying, because organization of labor must be the overthrow of capital and
power."[8]   The overthrow of the regime of capital and property and
power would enable work, the "first attribute, the essential characteristic of man"[9] to come to the fore, eliminating the exploitation of the laborer and the reduction to poverty entailed by that
exploitation.   Just how Proudhon proposed to effect the overthrow
of the exploiters will be examined in detail in the second section
of this chapter; it will suffice at this point to show the basic
reasons for the conflict between Proudhon's moral vision of a just
order and Marx's revolutionary program.

As just noted, Proudhon's concept of the nature of human
beings and their purpose in an ordered society is intrinsically
linked to individual labor. It is through labor that human beings
come to be fully human. Labor serves as the means to survival and
common labor in society is the means to survival in a complex, di-
verse society. At the same time, the effect of individual labor
upon the laborer is at the basis of Proudhon's moral vision.
Throughout Proudhon's writings, his antipathy toward proprietors

and speculative capitalists is very clearly a rejection of two
things. First, he rejects the material inequalities resulting from
the domination of property and capital because these inequalities
degrade the dignity of the autonomous individual laborer, a dignity inherent in labor itself (hence one of Proudhon's famous "contradictions"). Workers recognize their dignity in their labor
while being exploited as laborers. Secondly, since labor is both
individually and socially necessary, the degradation of the
laborer weakens and degrades society. The laborer sees the dis-
parity between the social purposes of work and the practical results of modern wage-labor; the productive capacities generated by
entire societies past and present, generated as the creative and
sustaining forces of society, are now appropriated by a relatively
small class. This cannot but weaken the social fabric, according
to Proudhon. Despite these limiting and distorting forces, individual labor itself is never completely degraded and alienating
for Proudhon. For, at the core of the laboring act, the laborer
remains--and in fact affirms--his autonomy and dignity as a human
being. It is because of this morally redeeming and affirming characteristic of labor that Proudhon saw the social and economic
transformation, the realization of a just order, as proceeding
freely from the moral conversion of the individual laborer. Though
James Joll exhibits a rather facile understanding of Marx's historical dialectic in the following quotation, Joll does put quite
succinctly the basis of Proudhon's theory, and thus the basis of
the conflict between Marx and Proudhon:

> If, for Marx, the proletariat was to be the class destined by
> the immutable laws of history to triumph, for Proudhon the
> proletariat was to be the class whose toil and sufferings
> were to make possible a new moral as well as a new social
> order. The sense of the dignity of labor, and the necessity
> of preserving it from the degradation imposed by machines and
> the exploitation imposed by the capitalist system, runs
> through all Proudhon's work, and this idea of the worker's
> duty to himself and his mission to the world is the basis of
> all subsequent anarchist thought.[10]

Proudhon's moral vision of the personal and social virtues

of individual labor is quite different from Marx's conception of labor. The examination of Marx's view of the self-development of humans through labor, begun in the last chapter, will continue in the second and third sections of this chapter. As in the last chapter, it will be seen that Marx's initial premises were radically different from his anarchist opponent, and thus that the conflict between the two philosophers--and between their plans for social change--was inevitable. Though the conflict was inevitable and fundamental, several basic points concerning Marx and Proudhon have been distorted or confused in the literature. Mention will be made of some of these points here, with the details of each point to be explored in the next two sections of this chapter.

The first misconception surrounding Proudhon concerns his status as a radical, as a moralist, and as a utopian thinker. Marx claimed and many Marxists claim that, in the same manner as Stirner, Proudhon was a defender of bourgeois values masquerading as a radical.[11] Proudhon was a radical, in the sense that he attempted to give an account of a complete--that is, radical-- transformation of the structures, relations, and especially values of existing society. When Marx and others accused Proudhon of being an apologist for the bourgeoisie, however, they usually had something more than his motives and goals in mind. What this chapter will show is that Marx's criticism of Proudhon as a reactionary depends on a prior critique of the moral basis of Proudhon's views. Proudhon was a reactionary in Marx's eyes because, in part, he was a bourgeois moralist. Proudhon was also, in the eyes of many of his critics, a utopian. What the second and third sections of this chapter will show is that Proudhon was a radical, though in a different sense than Marx recognized; that he was a moralist, though hardly bourgeois; and that he was most certainly not a utopian. Henri Mougin has commented that "the petty-bourgeois Proudhon opts for equilibrium, for mutual support of conflicting forces; the bourgeoisie is not to be abolished, but preserved by means of class collaboration."[12] As an anticipation of my analysis, I will only comment that Mougin is only partly correct; Proudhon did opt for equilibrium. Mougin's error comes after the semi-colon: the equilibrium (synonymous for Proudhon

with the balance of liberty and equality) does not involve class
collaboration with the bourgeoisie but rather the destruction of
the bourgeoisie as a separate class concomitant with the elimination of the existing structures of inequality in class society.

Another misconception about Proudhon's work paints him as a
forerunner of modern fascism.[13] When Stirner was accused of advocating a type of fascist tyranny, the accusation was based on a
general misreading of Stirner's text and purpose. With Proudhon,
the accusation stems from a selective reading of his works, concentrating on Proudhon's occasional intemperate remark (especially
in his unpublished writings) concerning races and the need for
order. These interpreters of Proudhon usually cite the journal en-
tries concerning racial relations, his ambiguous position during
the American Civil War, and especially his alleged support of
Louis Napoleon in the formation of the Second Empire. There can be
no adequate explanation for Proudhon's personal prejudices (except, of course, that he was a bigot); but the use of his putative
Bonapartism as a means of drafting Proudhon into the authoritarian
or more specifically fascist camp is inexcusable, as Bonapartism
is not equivalent to fascism and, in any event, Proudhon was
specifically anti-Bonapartist. In the second section of this chapter I will examine the tentative and limited support that Proudhon
considered giving to Louis Napoleon, why he did not give that support, and why it would have been impossible for him to give any
support and remain even relatively consistent.[14] At this point,
it will suffice to refer to the consistent anti-authoritarianism
of Proudhon's works and his stress on the importance of economic,
social, and moral change, not political opportunism.

It has proven advantageous to Marxists, fascists, and many
others to portray Proudhon as a veiled supporter of their respective ideologies. Proudhon's own inconsistencies and ambiguities
lend aid to the various distortions. Proudhon exaggerated, digres-
sed, and delighted in contradicting his own claims made in earlier
works or even in earlier chapters. Still, there is a consistent
train of thought throughout Proudhon's work, one that allows distortions to be seen as such and one that allows for a relatively
unambiguous portrait of Proudhon to emerge. The best place to be-

gin such a portrait is with Proudhon's philosophical precursors.

Anarchism of the sort espoused by Proudhon has been, like existentialism, an aspect of many thinkers' statements in the history of philosophy. There is no need to trace every strain of anarchist thinking, as this is no more productive than such an enterprise is when dealing with existentialism. Still, there are definite precedents for Proudhon's theories. It is important to see the moral basis underlying these precedents in order to see why Proudhon advocated the particular moral principles encompassed by his vision of social justice. For it is truly a moral vision that Proudhon formulated.

It is at least clear that Proudhon inherited the confidence in progress, enlightenment, and a rational social order found in the works of Condorcet, Montesquieu, Jeremy Bentham, or even Rousseau. This must be asserted with some caution, however, since none of these thinkers combined this confidence in human rationality and possible goodness with an anarchist style critique of political authority, hierarchical institutions, and the existing socio-economic structures. Even Rousseau, praised in many places by Proudhon, remained a political theorist; in *The Social Contract*, it is through political order and education that reform takes place. Though claimed by many anarchists as their own, Rousseau remains within the mainstream of political theory.[15]

What Proudhon did adopt from the Enlightenment, in his own unusual way, was the confidence in knowledge, education, and human progress. Remaining an optimist about human progress throughout his life, Proudhon tempered this optimism with an acute critique of the real, material factors blocking this progress, in addition to a critique of the moral weakness preventing the establishment of a just order. For Proudhon these two factors had to be changed before a progressive order could be established. Changing these two factors required educating workers about the nature of a just moral order and providing demonstrative examples to others in the form of mutualist, cooperative enterprise.

One of the predecessors to Proudhon's anarchism is William Godwin. Though there is no strong evidence that Godwin's works had a direct influence on Proudhon, it is clear that many of Proudhon's doctrines are derived from his understanding of Godwin's views, even if the understanding was second or thirdhand.[16] Godwin's rejection of political reform as a means to a just society separates him from the mainstream of political theory. When this antipathy toward politics--in his *Enquiry Concerning Political Justice* it is actually a condemnation of government--is combined with his rejection of legal institutions and property, Godwin can be seen as a forerunner of Proudhonian anarchism. Godwin's utopian solution to the problem of social justice bears the moralistic mark of his Calvinist upbringing. This basing of the social order on an underlying set of moral principles (latent or explicit) links Godwin's anarchism to that particular type proposed by Proudhon. Unlike Stirner or Bakunin, Proudhon's principled anarchism requires an extensive set of moral precepts. For that reason, it is useful to explore the connection between Godwin and Proudhon, as this connection will bear directly on the fundamental differences between Proudhon and Marx.

Godwin rejected politics and government as means of effecting social change. This rejection was both moral (in the common traditional sense, principled) and practical. In an early work Godwin characterized elections as "a trade so despicably degrading, so eternally incompatible with moral and mental dignity that I can scarcely believe a truly great mind capable of the dirty drudgery of such vice."[17] And in his *Enquiry* he concluded, "It is scarcely possible to conceive a political institution, that includes a more direct and explicit patronage of vice [than the ballot]."[18]

As with Proudhon, Godwin's objection to political activity and the resulting practical legitimation of government rested not only on moral sentiment but also on the practical objection that the illusion of political participation inherent in the electoral process perpetuated social and economic injustice. Godwin argues for a system of equality where a just (that is, equal) distribution of "the good things of life"[19] would encourage the eradication of the moral weaknessess of those currently living under the regime of property. As long as inequality of property is perpetuated and in fact justified by the political equality established in universal (or near universal) suffrage, humans will continue to act in immoral and undignified ways inconsistent with real equality, the mean spiritedness of class conflict and the dependence upon property for social position will continue.

> Observe the pauper fawning with abject vileness upon his rich benefactor, speechless with sensations of gratitude, for having received that which he ought to have claimed. . . . Observe the tradesman, how he studies the passions of his customers, not to correct, but to pamper them, the vileness of his flattery. . . . Observe the practices of a popular election, where the great mass are purchased by obsequiousness, by intemperance and bribery, or driven by unmanly threats of poverty and persecution.[20]

Godwin's rejection of political activity extends to a rejection of government, as it is government that perpetuates the illusion of equality and thus enables property (and the commercial sensibility) to dominate social life. Godwin was confident that a just, egalitarian order would eliminate the need for the coercive function of government. Since happiness results from virtue and the just social order is based on and encourages virtue, such an order will result in a satisfied society. In such a society man's nature will be uncorrupted by the greed and hypocrisy of the inegalitarian society. According to Godwin, the original purpose of government was to provide security against the weakness, "vices," and greed of men, but government eventually embodied and perpetuated these same traits.[21] Once government and the regime of property are eliminated, the causes of vice will disappear, and the happy, virtuous society will emerge. Once people are convinced (through education) that the virtuous path is the rational path, human reason will adopt the virtuous path and eliminate the institutions perpetuating the causes of vice.[22]

This criticism of government and politics--that they are both undesirable and unnecessary--is characteristic of most anarchists and was specifically embraced by Proudhon. The result of this sort of critique of politics is the critique of government, since for both Godwin and Proudhon it is the modern state which encourages viciousness through its policies, as well as directly oppressing the rebellious and those without property. Godwin extended this critique to positive law and all legal institutions, claiming that laws were framed and especially enforced so as to aggravate the inequality and viciousness found in politics, government, and commerce.[23] In Godwin's rational universe, law is another obstacle to virtue because it prevents the development of virtue. It does so by sanctioning an unjust social and economic order and then branding violations of that order "crime." Removing law thus removes another obstacle to virtue and happiness. Proudhon's critique of law relies more on the immorality of the unequal application of law than on the inherent limitations of a system of law. Still, the two thinkers shared a hatred of law, especially in its unequal application and the resulting favoring of one class over another. And, for both Godwin and Proudhon, the critique of law leads to and requires a third step: the critique of property.

One of the best ways to see the importance of Godwin's critique of property in a critical look at Proudhon is to compare the Malthusian doctrine which was formulated in response to Godwin and against which Proudhon argued. Though Proudhon was concerned about the effects of unlimited population growth, it was for quite different reasons than Thomas Malthus. Proudhon proposed to deal with the problem in a traditional fashion. Both Godwin and Proudhon abhorred the presuppositon of Malthus's position: namely that an unequal distribution of essential goods in the face of scarcity requires not an egalitarian redistribution, but rather a recognition of the primary rights of property owners. As Malthus put it: "A man who is born into a world already possessed, if he cannot get subsistence from his parents on whom he has a just demand, and if the society do not want his labor, has no claim of *right* to the smallest portion of food, and, in fact, has no business to be where he is. At nature's mighty feast there is no vacant cover for him."[24]

Malthus's statement was intended in part as a reply to Godwin's egalitarianism. For, as Godwin would have it, the claims of property are part of the problem, not the solution. Property rights ensure an unequal distribution of resources, leading the dispossessed into "crime" and envy. Moreover, the desire for exclusive property and the accompanying competitive spirit obscures

the need for an observance of rational values, the most basic of
which is that each is entitled to equal access to and use of resources. Godwin's optimism (shared by Proudhon) protects him from
Malthus's rejoinder: if goods and resources are available on an
egalitarian basis with scarcity being an unassailable fact, more
total misery would result than had the unequal but "efficient"
system been preserved. For Godwin, as for Proudhon, the elimination of exclusive property will produce a change in desires (reducing them in certain areas) such that scarcity will cease to be
a problem. When each person is convinced that the accumulation of
large amounts of unused property is unnecessary and inefficient
(and for Godwin and Proudhon, immoral), then all will be provided
for.

For both Godwin and Proudhon, then, exclusive property is objectionable from both moral and practical perspectives.[25] From
what Proudhon considered the practical, economic perspective, he
condemned Malthus for sanctifying the existing economic system and
its results as the only true economic order:

The error of Malthus, the radical vice of political economy,
consists, in general terms, in affirming as a definitive
state a transitory condition,--namely, the division of
society into patricians and proletaries; and, particularly,
in saying that in an organized, and consequently *solidaire*,
society, there may be some who possess, labor, and consume,
while others have neither possession, nor labor, nor bread.

In short, the theory of Malthus . . . is a *reductio ad
absurdum* of all political economy.[26]

From the moral perspective, Proudhon adds: "Some who are extremist
disciples of Malthus, speak out boldly against Justice. First and
foremost, and at any price they demand wealth, of which they hope
to have their share. They attach little value to the life, liberty and intelligence of the masses."[27] Speaking directly to Malthus
he added, "Man certainly does not come into the world as a usurper
and intruder; a member of the great human family, he seats himself
at the common table; society is in no way a mistress who can
accept or reject him."[28]

If Godwin's eccentricities are put aside and his critique of

politics and government, law and legal institutions, and property
are seen as central to his type of anarchism, then the philosophical connection to Proudhon is clear. For reasons that will be
dealt with below, Proudhon extended his critique of property beyond what Godwin had thought advisable. For although Godwin advocated an almost Stirnerian rejection of supra-individual cooperation or institutions, Godwin had not drawn the ultimate conclusion
of a thoroughgoing individualism. Even so, Godwin rejected any
cooperation that did not prove of immediate benefit to the individual, this rejection sometimes reaching absurd proportions.[29]
For Proudhon, cooperation and a strongly interdependent human
society were the keys to a truly social anarchism that at the same
time conserved and fostered individual freedom. The philosophical
link between Godwin and Proudhon is strong, then, but not without
exception.

The 1789 Revolution and its aftermath was claimed by Proudhon
and others as a watershed for Proudhonian style anarchism. Both
Proudhon (in many of his works) and Peter Kropotkin emphasized the
importance of the initial revolt and the rebellion against authoritarian principles.[30] At first glance, this claim does not seem
unusual, as many social reformers and revolutionaries have allied
themselves with the cause of the French revolutionaries. It is unusual, though, since anarchism and anarchist motivations played an
extremely small role in the Revolution. None of the major partici-
pants followed Godwin in advocating the abolition of government,
property, or law. The influence of the Revolution upon Proudhon
and anarchism generally must remain inspirational; it was proof
that something could be done, as Kropotkin seems to stress.

Unlike other revolutionaries, however, Proudhon's attitude
toward the Revolution and especially the Terror (and the ascendan-
cy of Bonaparte) was always colored by his abhorrence of the violence of the revolutionary period. As Godwin's anarchism gave the
example of a moralistic rejection of authority, so the violence of
the Revolution reveals another important difference between Marx
and Proudhon. Unlike Marx, Proudhon rejected revolutionary violence. If true change is only possible when the moral regeneration
of individual workers occurs, revolutionary violence (and its as-

sociation with the "immorality" of harming others and destroying goods can only be counterproductive. For this reason, and because of the extreme nationalism and limited social and economic change achieved or even attempted by the initial revolutionaries and especially their heir, Bonaparte, Proudhon's enthusiasm for the French revolutionary tradition was always muted.

There are other important precursors of Proudhon's thought, particularly François-Noël Babeuf and Fourier. Since Proudhon offered direct and penetrating criticisms of these two figures in several of the works to be considered in the next section of this chapter, an examination of their significance will await that section.

THE PROUDHONIAN VISION AND THE JUST ORDER

The fundamental, decisive idea of this Revolution, is it not this NO MORE AUTHORITY, neither in the Church, nor in the State, nor in land, nor in money?

No more authority! That means something we have never seen, something we have never understood; the harmony of the interest of one with the interest of all; the identity of collective sovereignty and individual sovereignty. No more Authority! That means debts paid, servitude abolished, mortgages lifted, rents reimbursed . . . the State suppressed; free credit, equal exchange, free association, . . . no more centralization, no more governments, no more priests. Is not that Society emerged from its shell and walking upright? No more Authority! That is to say further: free contract in place of arbitrary law; voluntary transactions in place of the control of the State; equitable and reciprocal justice in place of sovereign and distributive justice; rational instead of revealed morals; equilibrium of forces instead of equilibrium of powers; economic unity in place of political centralization. Once more, I ask, is not this . . . a complete reversal, a turn-over, a Revolution?
                                                        Proudhon[31]

The statement quoted directly above gives as good and concise a summary of his developed views as Proudhon ever gave. The one addition that might be made to Proudhon's list of the ideas and conditions of the Revolution is one that led to the strongest arguments between Marx and Proudhon, Marx and Bakunin, and Marxism and anarchism in general: no more authority in the development of the Revolution itself. Proudhon's arrival at this position followed a long, self-correcting period of conflict and changes in his philosophical direction. There is, however, a core to the Proudhonian conception of justice and social change, one that requires an unqualified rejection of the political state. In this section I will isolate the components of this core in Proudhon's early life, in his critical works on property, and finally in his later works on politics, justice, labor, and revolution. In the course of this critical analysis I will develop what can be seen as the "Proudhonian vision": the just society, developed from individual moral education and regeneration, based on cooperative and mutualist enterprises associated at the local level, free of external coercion and hierarchy and providing the setting for the codevelopment of individual freedom and complete equality. Once this vision is clarified, Marx and Proudhon (and Proudhonism) will be subjected to a critical comparison. This will be the subject of the third section of this chapter.

It would be interesting if not particularly edifying to trace the source of the his vision in his early childhood, in his love of nature and childhood freedom, in his peasant background.[32] (Accounts of Proudhon's childhood and youth are strangely reminiscent of Stirner's account of the stages of human development.) The one fact about Proudhon's background that helps establish the origin of this essentially moral vision is his father's business practices. When forced to open a small tavern (events of the Napoleonic Wars had made such a move a matter of survival), Claude-François Proudhon proved to be a singularly unsuccessful entrepreneur. The main reason for the elder Proudhon's gradual failure was that he refused to charge the market price for his products. Charging that price would mean taking a profit beyond his costs and living expenses. Claude-François charged the "Just Price," a practice which, with the collaboration of his fellow businessmen who charged extraordinarily high prices for supplies and food during the 1817 famine in eastern France, led to the elder Proudhon's bankruptcy by 1818. During this period the younger Proudhon was undoubetedly aware of the unusual nature of his father's business practices, the idea of a just economic order based on a mutually observed set of moral principles, the essence of the Just Price, must have made a strong impression. Proudhon later remarked: "I realized perfectly the loyalty and the regularity in the paternal method, but I also saw to no less a degree the risk it involved. My conscience approved of the one; my feelings for our security pushed me towards the other. It was an enigma."[33]

The first evidence of Proudhon's vision--especially its key component, anarchism--seems to have arisen when he was offered the editorship of the Fourierist paper in Besançon, *L'Impartial*. Proudhon had met Charles Fourier in 1829 while supervising the printing of Fourier's *Le Nouveau monde industrial et sociétaire*. Fourier's utopian "socialism" had made some impression upon the young Proudhon, though to what extent it is difficult to determine. Proudhon apparently discussed Fourier's phalansterian theories with the master and accepted the idea of a "scientific" approach to social theory. Proudhon also adapted Fourier's serial law theory as a "scientific" means of reconciling individual freedom and collective aims. Whatever the initial influence, Proudhon criticized Fourier's theories throughout his writings.

When Proudhon was offered the helm of the Bisontin voice of Fourierism, he declined. The offer of employment had been qualified by a suggestion that Proudhon would be advised to guide the paper in an objective manner, both to avoid the official censor and to avoid offending the Fourierists. In an undated letter to Just Muiron (who had offered the position), Proudhon rejected the offer and the suggestion:

Why should we not profess publicly an absolute pyrrhonism towards all ministers, past, present and future? Why should we not invite the population to make themselves capable of managing their own affairs and of preparing the way for a confederation of peoples? Let them see, through instruction, science,   moral   health and patriotism, how to dispense with all ministerial and constitutional hierarchy. . . .[34]

Proudhon's suspicions concerning the nature of systems of authority and the intent of those who directed them continued to develop after this point. In Proudhon's first published work (*Essai de grammaire generale*, printed as an appendix to Abbe Bergier's *Elements primitifs des langues*, 1837), Proudhon attempted to demonstrate the linguist primacy of "*moi*" and its equivalents, rather than the then-accepted primacy of "*être*" and its equivalents.[35]   Proudhon as linguist and philologist presages Proudhon as anarchist and individualist; Proudhon attempted to derive (in the fashion of an autodidact, as Woodcock has noted) a comprehensive philosophical stance on the position of the individual in the social order from the allegedly universal structures of language. The individual was primary, the institutions of society secondary and limiting. It is a position highly reminiscent of Stirner's egoism and it is significant that Proudhon later rejected the essay as, among other things, "feeble."[36] It is still significant, though, that at this point in his career, Proudhon had established one important facet of the Proudhonian vision: the focus of any liberating philosophy must be the individual and the cultivation of individual freedom.

Proudhon's newly established position as a published author enabled him to convince the directors of the Besançon Academy that he deserved the Suard pension, a limited scholarship. This is important in the development of the Proudhonian vision for two reasons. First, the award gave Proudhon time to study and consider the pressing social problems of his day. For some time before this Proudhon had begun to consider the position of the poor, of the laborer. He had been coming to the conclusion that the poor were severely constrained in the development of their freedom because of their positon within the economic order. Secondly, in his application to the academy, Proudhon enunciated this concern for the poor laborer:

Born and brought up in the working class, still belonging to it, . . . above all by the community of interests and wishes, the greatest joy of the candidate, if he gains your votes, will be to have attracted in his person your just solicitude for that interesting portion of society, to have been judged worthy of being its first representative before you, and to be able to work henceforward . . . for the complete liberation of his brothers and companions.[37]

Surprisingly, given the conservatism of the academy and the tone of Proudhon's application, he won the award. One year later, he restated his determination to seek the liberation of the working class, this time writing of the task as a specifically moral project: Proudhon wanted to work for the "moral and intellectual betterment" of the workers, to "propagate among them the seeds of a doctrine which I regard as the law of the moral world. . . ."[38] This marks the beginning of Proudhon's specifically moral vision of the nature of social change, which he was to pursue first in his critique of the institution of property.

In 1839 Proudhon began his attack on property, an attack which he would come to see as basic to his attack on the state and all other social institutions. The attack began not with the celebrated *What Is Property?* but with an obscure essay submitted to the Besançon Academy for consideration in a prize contest. The topic of the essay contest was "On the utility of the celebration of the Sabbath, with regard to hygiene, morality, and familial and civic relations."[39] Proudhon's essay of the same title was less a discussion of the utility of the Sabbath than an initial discussion of the problem of establishing a truly fraternal society that was based on individual freedom.

Proudhon began his attack with the assertion that the Mosaic legal tradition is not only a source of law but also a source of socio-economic reform. Proudhon argues that Moses as a national leader attempted to mold, through the establishment of common principals and customs (including the celebration of the Sabbath), a society bonded by more than mere political obligation. This society would be bonded by a community of faith, interest, and desire. What Moses sought, according to Proudhon, was social unity-- the cohesion of a fraternal society. One of the preconditions of such a society is the establishment not only of common practices

but of equal conditions as well. Especially in a society characterized by the threat of scarcity and external attack, the development of social cohesion demands that all share equally the re-
wards and the deprivations suffered by any member of the society.
Thus, according to Proudhon, the celebration of the Sabbath (among
other practices) signified both the community of opportunity (all
would labor and rest on the same days) and the community of hope
(all would join together in hope of avoiding danger to any individual)--thus presenting a solid social front.

Proudhon's essay is not an especially strong argument or exposition. What is more interesting is the emphasis that Proudhon
put on the ideal of fraternity, the "going beyond" society as a
mere collection of individuals. Devoid of its questionable historical context, Proudhon's use of *fraternité* is stronger than any
sense given to it in 1789 and afterwards. For Proudhon not only
claimed that liberty, equality, and fraternity were desirable
goals but that in fact *fraternité* required *egalité*. Proudhon had
already proclaimed the importance of liberty and later would attempt to show that a fraternal society must also embrace individual freedom. This would then become the cornerstone of his theory
of justice: the coexistence and mutual development of individual
liberty and socio-economic equality, leading to a truly fraternal
society. The coherence of the Proudhonian moral vision depends
upon Proudhon's success in reconciling in practical terms the conflict between the inegalitarian demands of individualism and the
egalitarian demands of a fraternal society. At this point it is
important to see that Proudhon's vision did embrace both sides of
the conflict. In fact, Proudhon extended his demand for equality
such that true equality became incompatible with the holding of
exclusive property.

In the establishment of the Commandments, Proudhon held, the
Hebrews had in actuality established the basis of the complete
equality of conditions. Proudhon claimed that the injunction
against theft included a prohibition against unequal conditions
("Thou shalt not steal" meaning "Thou shalt not lay anything aside
for thyself"[40]), since unequal conditions, laying more aside for
oneself, was theft in a truly communal, fraternal society. If

scarcity and prosperity are to be shared equally, then the establishment of exclusive property rights which provided for and defended inequality of conditions constituted the establishment of
the right to theft. And, for Proudhon, such rights also degraded
the social cohesion of the society by protecting the inequality of
opportunity and material possessions.

Proudhon's vision here is still a moral one. His demand for
equality of conditions is based on the conviction that fraternity
as social unity is a legitimate goal, against the claims of those
such as the Malthusians and the Utilitarians. Proudhon asserted
that, contrary to Malthus's claims, the right to an equal share of
the goods and obligations of society is the primary right since,
as Proudhon maintained, each person is an integral part of the society and has as much right to the goods of society as any other
person. Each person is equal in humanity and in the right to as
good a life as the society can provide for all. Against Fourier
and Saint-Simon Proudhon defended his arguments against inequality, claiming that no society could hope to eliminate suffering
unless it scrupulously observed the basic human rights he had out-
lined.

The result of this preliminary critique of property, then, is
that Proudhon's defense of egalitarianism could only lead to a
complete condemnation of exclusive property and its abuses. In
this preliminary essay Proudhon claimed that "equality of conditions is . . . the aim of society" and that "[p]roperty is the
last of the false gods."[41] In his own eyes forever the iconoclast,
Proudhon made his most famous attack against this false god and
its chief priest, the state, in *What Is Property?*

It was in *What Is Property?* that Proudhon stated many of his
objections to the economic order based on property and to the political order supported by and legitimating the economic order.
This critique of property differs in emphasis from that of Proudhon's earlier prize essay because *What Is Property?* stresses the
practical economic inconsistencies of the regime of property in
addition to the moral objections advanced in the prize essay. It
was this emphasis on the "scientific" and economic aspects of
property that earned Proudhon the preliminary admiration of

Marx.[42]   It is also in *What Is Property?* that Proudhon is clearest on those issues on which he and Marx might have agreed; at the same time, it is in this same work that the lines of disagreement are most clearly drawn.

One important clarification needs to be made at this point: Proudhon was not opposed to property per se; rather he was opposed to the abusive use of property, the ability of the proprietor to exploit the propertyless, especially through the imposition of rent and the accumulation of profit and interest. It was this un-earned income, acquired only by means of exclusive property that Proudhon characterized as theft. Proudhon supported individual possession and use, so long as the possession and the opportunity for use conformed to that basic principle of Proudhonian justice--equality. In Proudhon's second *mémoire* on property, the *Letter to M. Blanqui on Property*, Proudhon made clear the object of his at-tack. In the Preface to the combined edition of the two *mémoires*, Proudhon responded directly to the economist, Jérome-Adolphe Blanqui. Blanqui had objected to Proudhon's radical attack on property itself. While admitting that property was frequently abused, as Proudhon had claimed, Blanqui did not think such abuse to be inherent in the institution of property.

> I agree with you in one thing only; namely, that all kinds of property get too frequently abused in this world. But I do not reason from the abuse to the abolition. . . .

> I feel as deeply as you, sir, the abuses which you point out; but I have so great an affection for . . . the majestic and imposing order of human societies,--that I sometimes find myself embarrassed in attacking certain abuses. I like to re-build with one hand when I am compelled to destroy with the other.[43]

Proudhon quickly corrected Blanqui's mistaken impression of the intent of *What Is Property?* With the exception of Blanqui's defense of the institution of property as "the most powerful motor of the human mind"[44] and the foundation of any society, Proudhon agreed that the chief obstacle was the sum of the abuses of prop-erty. "M. Blanqui acknowledges that property is abused in many harmful ways; I call *property* the sum of these abuses exclusively.

To each of us property seems a polygon whose angles need knocking
off; but, the operation performed, M. Blanqui maintains that the
figure will still be a polygon . . . while I consider that this
figure will be a circle."[45]

In other words, Proudhon objected to property because of its
abuses, and these abuses he considered inherent in the notion of
exclusive property. The elimination of these abuses thus requires
the transformation of property itself. The nature of this transformation, its principles, methods, and goals, explains much of
the conflict between Marx and Proudhon.

Proudhon's famous dictum that, just as slavery is murder, so
"[p]roperty is robbery!"[46] echoes throughout his social and political theories. Proudhon's use of the slogan is original, even
if the slogan itself originated elsewhere. There are traces of
such sentiments in many thinkers prior to Proudhon, including
Blaise Pascal and Rousseau. Pascal's comment was directed toward
the origin and institution of exclusive property: "*Mine, Thine.--*
'This dog is mine,' said those poor children; 'that is my place in
the sun.' Here is the beginning and image of the usurpation of all
the earth."[47]

With *What Is Property?*, the objection to property, to the sum
of the abuses of property--as acts of theft--is defended as both a
twofold moral objection (in a fashion similar to Proudhon's
earlier prize essay) and as an economic objection. Proudhon
objected to rent, interest, and profit because these denied the
worker the product of his labor and because they perpetuated the
unjust (and immoral) inequality of conditions. As an economic objection, Proudhon argued that property is "impossible," that it is
an institution founded on inconsistent principles.

Proudhon directed these objections toward the non-producer,
the proprietor who accumulated property so as to avoid labor. One
result of this emphasis is a certain provincialism in *What Is
Property?*, where "property" is most frequently seen as the property of the rural landlord or the small town bourgeoisie. Still,
Proudhon's principles, amended as they were in later years, serve
as the instruments of a broader challenge. "Property" would come
to be seen as all exclusive holding of property beyond possession

and control for direct use. Proudhon never objected to such possession and control; he defended the rights of possession and use
as the guarantors of individual liberty and initiative.

In attacking the prevailing theories of property, Proudhon
insisted that he was not building a new system, nor did he desire
disciples. What he wanted was the recognition of the demands of
justice; as he saw it, the meanings of *"[j]ustice, equity,* [and]
liberty"[48] had been obscured by previous attempts at social reform. What he wanted in place of such attempts was knowledge, understanding. Proudhon reveals here a concern that would remain
constant: if people could demonstrate the efficacy and consistency
of the just order, the just order could be established throughout
society. Though Proudhon would advocate more practical proposals
for reform, he never lost his fundamental trust in the power of
enlightenment. Proudhon's own program at this point was both
simple and grandiose: "I ask an end to privilege, the abolition of
slavery, equality of rights, and the reign of law. Justice, nothing else; that is the alpha and omega of my argument: to others I
leave the business of governing the world."[49]

So far, Proudhon's moral vision remains consistent, if vague.
Justice, the coexistence of equality and liberty without the rule
of government, is the goal. Proudhon's apparently inconsistent appeal to the "reign of law" is best understood as an appeal to that
moral law upon which, according to him, justice is founded. Proudhon remains an anarchist; he does not make at any point in his
career an unequivocal appeal to positive law or government.

In trying to specify the nature of justice and so clarify the
character of his moral vision, Proudhon developed the idea of a
sense of immanent justice inhering in the conscience of each person.[50] Religion cannot be the sole source of social ills, as some
reformers of the early nineteenth and late eighteenth century had
held; the source of misery and inequality lies rather in "man himself": "that is, volition and conscience, free-will and law,
eternally antagonistic. Man is at war with himself: why?"[51]

In answering his own question, Proudhon rejects the traditional response, namely, that man's nature suffers from the defect
inherited from an original sin. Human nature is at war with it-

self, it has been perverted, according to Proudhon, but the source of the perversion lies less in the misty past of the species and more in the history of economic relationships.

Human beings, according to Proudhon, have a natural, immanent sense of justice. This sense of justice has been expressed in various ways, all of which Proudhon saw as variations of the Biblical "Golden Rule": "All the most reasonable teachings of human wisdom concerning justice are summed up in that famous adage: *Do unto others. . . ."*[52] This is the guiding principle of human interaction, the central focus and regulator of conduct. Law and government reflect this sense of justice more or less accurately at various stages in history, usually less so. The reason that this sense of justice and its two latent principles, liberty and equality, have been obscured by government and law is that those in power distorted the sense of justice--both the concept and practice of justice--in order to maintain their position. The concept of justice expressed in legal and political relationships and especially the practice of justice expressed in economic relationships has thus set man's immanent sense of justice against itself. Conscience rebels against the officially recognized guiding principles of public life, the pursuit of personal interests and power.

In the modern age, which Proudhon saw as beginning with the 1789 Revolution, the opposition between the sense of justice and the established unjust practices became attentuated. In advocating democratic political principles, the revolutionaries of the modern age simply extended the opposition between justice and societal practice, for they institutionalized the same type of principles (such as sovereignty of the will and the inequality of wealth) previously relegated to private relationships. The extension of political democracy was thus seen by Proudhon as the illusion of justice, the illusion of equality and liberty. Democracy multiplies the number of wills included in the expression of sovereignty and extends the role of will instead of removing will as the governing principle of society, democracy is "the sovereignty of man instead of the sovereignty of the law, the sovereignty of the will instead of the sovereignty of the reason; in one word, the

passions instead of justice."[53]   The legacy of the Revolution,
what Proudhon termed the "three fundamental principles of modern
society,"[54] includes the extension of the "despotism" of political
sovereignty or the rule of will over reason, the expression of
democratic sovereignty in the political and legal spheres only
while the inequality of wealth and economic station was sanctioned
by establishing civil relationships (including paid public offices) that perpetuated inequality, and above all the legitimation
of property. It is in the revolutionary government's confirmation
of the rights of the proprietor--both in 1789 and 1830 these
rights were held above the claims of "justice"--that Proudhon saw
the main danger to the establishment of a just order, the main
reason for the continued distortion of the immanent sense of justice.   The true legacy of the revolutionary period is less the extension of the authority of humans over one another or the continuation of civil inequality (though these were important results of
the revolutionary governments) than the continuation of the regime
of property, embodied in the revolutionary Declaration of Rights
and eventually in the *Code Napoléon*.

Proudhon's critique of property is important for his critique
of the state for several reasons. The state violates justice by
exercising its will (monarchical, democratic, or otherwise) over
the individual, but it can do so, it can maintain its sovereignty
and power, only through its continued defense of property. Proudhon initially criticizes two common theories of property and
later any justificatory theories of property in order to show that
the distortions of justice--and the continued existence of the
state--are intimately connected. The two theories that Proudhon
attacks at first attempt to account for property as either a civil
or natural right. Property as a civil right is based on occupation
plus the sanction of law; as a natural right, on labor plus the
sanction of law.

Though Proudhon frequently confuses even his own distinctions
in the course of his critique, he actually wants to attack three
different justifications of property as the exclusive right to
use, abuse or dispose of a given resource or entity: (1)property
as a natural human right, (2)property as an established civil

right, and (3)property as a right created by labor. (Proudhon occasionally combines the first and third senses; even more occasionally he confuses the first and second senses.) The principle
of property common to all three senses is that a property right
includes the right to use, abuse, and dispose of the property.
Against this right of exclusive property Proudhon opposed the
right of possession and use.

Property as a natural human right is shown by Proudhon, quite
convincingly, to be essentially unlike other putative human
rights. For most people, property as a "right" exists as an ideal
or goal, not a reality. It is a strange human right that can be
exercised by only a small percentage of human beings. For those
who are capable of exercising their right to property, this supposedly inviolable right is repeatedly violated by other proprietors, legal institutions, and even governments.

This critique of property as a natural right leads to the
critique of property as an established civil right. Proudhon does
not dismiss the claim that property as a civil institution was initially intended as a means of ensuring a civilized social order,
free from brute force as the means of distributing basic goods. In
fact, Proudhon claims that property originated in the desire to
ensure equality. The transformation of mere possession into exclusive property gives each proprietor an equal status as a proprietor, if not an equal amount of property. The result of this
transformation, however, according to Proudhon, was the institutionalization of inequality. Proudhon delighted in this "contradiction": property rests on equality (as a justification) and violates equality (as a result). The resolution of the contradiction
is, for Proudhon, the "annihilation" of property.

In a similar fashion, Proudhon disposes of the claim that
labor is the foundation and justification of property. Though
Proudhon does not mention John Locke in his arguments against this
claim, he clearly has a Lockean style defense of property in
mind.[55] Rather than labor being the foundation of property, "in
the order of justice, labor *destroys* property."[56] In response to
the claim that labor mixed with the land creates a property right,
Proudhon claims that the only right thus created is the right to

the products of labor, not a right to the land, trees, and seas.
Labor by itself, claims Proudhon, never changes possession into
property. In the unjust order, in the oppressive society, this
transformation requires the sanction of civil law and the enforcement power of the state.

One of the results of the claim that labor is the foundation
of property is that the wage-laborer and the tenant farmer should
own or be granted title to the land or other property with which
they work. Rejecting the rejoinder that the property is already
owned (Proudhon has little difficulty showing that the laborer increases the value of the property without receiving even that increased value as wages or as a decrease in land rent), Proudhon
finds another "contradiction" in the institution of property:
labor, supposedly the "just" basis of property, is in fact ignored
when it is convenient for the proprietor to do so.[57] Proudhon's
critique of the payment of wages as the justification for the system of proprietorship in many ways parallels Marx's account, Proudhon notes that the capitalist enjoys the values created by the
laborer, paying only individual wages, and then only as much as is
required to ensure the laborer's continued productivity. "The
laborer's wages exceed but little his running expenses, and do not
assure him wages for tomorrow; while the capitalist finds in the
instrument produced by the laborer a pledge of independence and
security for the future."[58]

Given this admittedly brief summary of Proudhon's critique of
the traditional defenses of property, what did Proudhon suggest as
a substitute for property? If property prevents equality of conditions, as Proudhon claims, then it is unjust; it is robbery or
usurpation legitimized by the state. If property is unjust, then
it cannot be a basic human right and it cannot serve as the foundation of (a just) society. Proudhon gives an example of a basic
human right that is in accord with justice: liberty. Unlike property, liberty is inviolable. "Liberty is the original condition of
man; to renounce liberty is to renounce the nature of man: after
that, how could we perform the acts of man?"[59]

In a like manner Proudhon claims that equality of rights and
conditions is inviolable or, more to the point, at least ought to

be inviolable in the just society. He bases his critique of property as a whole on the claim that property violates this aspect of
justice as it creates and perpetuates inequality. And, as has been
seen, justice is the "alpha and omega" of Proudhon's vision and
argument. In place of the unjust regime of property, Proudhon
advocated the societal defense of legitimate possession, where
legitimacy has two conditions. First, for any possession of goods
within a society to be considered legitimate, there must be a
roughly equal distribution of goods and real property within the
society as a whole; secondly, individual possession is legitimate
only where each possesses as much as that person (or family), can
use.   Only by eliminating property and its "contradictions" will
the distortion of our immanent sense of justice end. And, only
through the end of the regime of property will the unjust practices of the property-based state end. In this way man will be
returned to that human nature which Proudhon assumes to be essentially both libertarian and egalitarian; in this way the regime of
property will be replaced by the reign of justice.

Proudhon's view of human nature and his characteristic moral
fervor in demanding the natural justice due humans is well illus-
trated in his charge to proprietors at the conclusion of an example of how property, even when considered in abstract form as an
equalizing force, in practice corrupts and eventually degrades.
"In this century of *bourgeoisie* morality, in which I have had the
honor to be born, the moral sense is so debased that I should not
be at all surprised if I were asked, by many a worthy proprietor,
what I see in this that is unjust and illegitimate? Debased crea-
ture! galvanized corpse! how can I expect to convince you, if you
cannot tell robbery when I show it to you?"[60]

It is fine for Proudhon to expound his moral vision, to condemn property as immoral and therefore unjust, and to advocate the
establishment of justice through the development of liberty and
equality in both social and economic life. What such an account
lacks up to this point is a specific analysis of the underlying
causes of injustice and especially the means by which justice is
to be established. It is in giving this account that Proudhon completes what I have called the "Proudhonian vision," connecting his

critique of property with his critique of politics and the state.

The right created by labor is, according to Proudhon, the right to possess and use. Labor establishes value, but this value is "mortgaged in advance by society,"[61] as labor uses both the accumulated talent and the shared resources of society, past and present. Proudhon saw labor as an individual effort that was the result of the collective contributions of other laborers, past and present, and the collective effort of society in utilizing common natural resources. This collective effort allows and supports specialized individual labor. The capitalist exploits the laborer by taking an unequal share of the created value which is due not to the holders of property titles, but to society as a whole. This conception of labor as social labor precludes any but an egalitarian distribution of goods, since the right to a larger share of goods than others receive can be based only on a unique, singular productive contribution. According to Proudhon, none of us makes such a contribution, we all stand on the "shoulders" of past efforts, balanced in our positions by the efforts of those around us. The breakdown of modern economic society results from the capitalist's believing--and acting on the belief--that he can stand alone, that he has the right to control more than others, thus causing those around him to fall into poverty.

Indeed, the situation is worse than that with the capitalist proprietor. While all other laborers balance each other in their efforts--to continue my metaphor--the proprietor drops his hands, demanding an unequal share for no labor: "The proprietor, producing neither by his own labor nor by his implement, and receiving products in exchange for nothing, is either a parasite or a thief."[62]

What is to be done? According to Proudhon, property is the "mother of tyranny,"[63] the basis of man's domination of other men. As long as property exists, the schemes of the Saint-Simonians and those of the Fourierists are doomed to failure. As long as property exists, the organization of labor for political purposes and action is futile. For as long as property exists, justice is impossible. Political rights and civil equality are subordinated to the demands of property; the "market" becomes the enforcement

mechanism of the proprietor, ensuring destructive economic inequality. The competition of the marketplace is the means by which
the proprietor pursues his most effective and refined robberies:
"Now, what is competition? A duel in a closed field, where arms
are the test of right."[64]

The underlying causes of injustice (according to Proudhon)
have already been dealt with in a limited fashion. At this point
they need clarification. Property, in one sense, causes injustice,
but it can do so only because of the perversion of human nature,
the distortion in both theory and practice of the natural human
tendency toward (or sense of) liberty and equality--justice. Humans are, for Proudhon, both rational and social animals--animals
needing society. The practice of justice is the following of social principles, which Proudhon identifies with the actualization
of right. Justice, then, is the rational adherence to social principles, to the demands of liberty and equality in our dealings
with others. Our rational natures allow and demand of us not only
the conformity to such principles but the recognition of their
validity and binding force. We differ from other animals in that
we have a higher, unique degree of sociability, a social instinct
or nature such that we tend toward and are conscious of the character and force of the principles of liberty and equality. Our
reflective reasoning powers, when combined with our natural pre-
dilection for liberty and equality, form the core of justice in
the "recognition of the equality between another's personality and
our own."[65] This is justice in the true, human sense--justice
which recognizes in the equality of the other the complex interdependence of human society, the need for a constant, reciprocal
interchange of ideas and actions. Justice is only possible when
these principles of liberty and equality--in effect, a type of
social and economic proportionality--are mutually recognized and
established. "*Sociability, justice, équité*,--such, in its tri-
plicity, is the exact definition of the instinctive faculty which
leads us into communication with our fellows, and whose physical
manifestation is expressed by the formula: *Equality in natural
wealth, and* [in] *the products of labor.*"[66]

It is this basic conception of human beings and human society that motivated much of Proudhon's claims against property, the state, religion, and any other institution that distorted the natural sense of justice. Proudhon was to modify his view of human nature in his later years; the conflict between the social and the egoistic in each person, recognized by Proudhon at the outset as largely the result of the history of social and economic "perversions," came to be seen as an unavoidable characteristic of human beings. Proudhon would then advocate the sublimation of egoistic desires through the pursuit of just, cooperative, social goals. (Presumably, the effort involved in such pursuits and the habits formed in just practice would mitigate the effects of egoistic desires.)

Throughout Proudhon's career, the emphasis was on enlightening people, on educating them as to the just course. Proudhon saw the movement from instinct and the egoistic will to intelligence and the recognition of justice as the mark of progress in the individual and in human society. The means of effecting this progress was education. Only in this fashion could the demands of both liberty and equality be met; equality and just economic practices could be encouraged (through demonstrations of their rational superiority) without undue restrictions of liberty.

It is for this reason--that liberty and equality must be reconciled in the realization of justice--that Proudhon rejected the communism of Babeuf and others of the early nineteenth century. Proudhon thought that the advocates of communism were attempting to recreate the initial form of social organization (that is, the primitive form) against which the regime of property had been instituted as a counterbalance. Both communism and property share the proprietary prejudice, however, as both require the submission of one aspect of justice in the service of the social order. Property requires inequality, while primitive communism requires individual submission to the community and hence denies liberty. This denial of liberty reflects what Proudhon saw as the essentially proprietary nature of communism: "The members of a community, it is true, have no private property; but the community is proprietor, and proprietor not only of the goods, but of the persons and wills. . . . Life, talent, and all the human faculties

are the property of the State, which has the right to use them as
it pleases for the common good. Communism is oppression and
slavery."[67]

The attempt at ending the inequalities of property results in
the suppression of liberty in the system of primitive communism,
an acceptance of the equality of conditions instead of the equality of opportunity to develop individual excellence, according to
Proudhon.

If both the capitalist socio-economic order and political
system and the attempts at primitive communism were "impossible,"
that is, unjust and self-destructive, what was left for Proudhon?
In his reply to Blanqui, Proudhon claimed that any reformation of
property would transform property itself; it would make the polygon of property a circle.[68] In his critique of communism, Proudhon
claimed that any reconciliation of the demands of individual reason and will with communism would be communism in name only.[69] The
only course Proudhon saw between the two obstacles to liberty and
equality was anarchism:

> What is to be the form of government in the future? I hear
> some of my younger readers reply: "Why, how can you ask such
> a question? You are a republican." "A republican! Yes: but
> that word specifies nothing. *Res publica*; that is, the public
> thing. Now, whoever is interested in public affairs--no mat-
> ter under what form of government--may call himself a repub-
> lican. . . . "What are you then?" "I am an anarchist."[70]

Proudhon's anarchism was intended as a synthesis of communism
and the demands of property (not property itself), the movement
from the domination of man to the scientific administration of the
world of things. Property would end in equality, the practice of
political sovereignty would end in the sovereignty of reason, all
ending in a scientific socialism in which justice prevailed as the
primary normative social standard. Though Proudhon elaborated his
central thesis in his later works, emphasizing specific economic
solutions rather than abstract formulae, all of the central anarchist themes and tenets are found in his early work, *What Is
Property?*[71]

In the second memoir on property, the explanatory essay for

What Is Property? (*Lettre à M. Blanqui*), Proudhon elaborated both his critique of property and his anarchism, he was anxious to protect what he saw as the legitimate rights of possession for use and free contractual transmission while eliminating the abuses of exclusive property and the state. Proudhon also made a new claim in the *Lettre*--that the development toward justice was the course of history and he was illustrating future probabilities, not advocating change through violent revolution. This was the first of many such disclaimers for Proudhon. He made it a point against all revolutionists, including the utopian socialists and Marx, to deny that Proudhonism was a revolutionary political theory that entailed or even allowed violence as a means of social change.

In the last of Proudhon's major writings on property, the *Warning to Proprietors* (largely a reply to Fourierist criticism of Proudhon's demand for equality, the *Warning* was addressed to Victor Considérant), Proudhon abandoned any hope of an existing government leading the way to a just social order. Though government was roundly condemned in *What Is Property?*, Proudhon had left some theoretical space for a limited course of reform led by government, a space especially evident in the letter to Blanqui. In the completion of his anarchist turn, in the *Warning* Proudhon directed the full force of his moral vision against the non-producing class of society and against government as irremediably tainted. In passages reminiscent of the defiant appeals to working class solidarity found in his application for the Suard pension, Proudhon declared that the only avenue left clear for real social change led directly to the working class and that the course of this change required the elimination of property and of property's political arm, the state.

Proudhon's moral vision shares many features with a number of thinkers who preceded Proudhon, especially with Locke and Rousseau.[72] Proudhon's vision is unique, as I will now show in a critical analysis of the implications of the claims of *What Is Property?*, claims evidenced beyond this early work in Proudhon's continuing preoccupation with morality, politics, and labor. Proudhon's sense of "justice" and "freedom" encompasses far more than previous thinkers claimed or would have thought justifiable.

Proudhon was not a utopian, as was seen in part by comparisons between Proudhon and other utopians. Proudhon's moral vision was also a practical vision, the critique of property and the state in his early years gave way to a practical consideration of the obstacles to change and the best method for removing these obstacles. Proudhon was not a utopian in the sense that he did not engage in purely theoretical speculations. If Proudhon was a utopian, it was in the sense that he was not "scientific" in Marx's sense. Proudhon's account of the process of social change was not firmly grounded in the actual historically developing conditions of society. In that sense, perhaps, Proudhon was utopian. The first major obstacle that Proudhon attempted to deal with was human nature. Paradoxically, Proudhon insisted that humans have a relatively fixed, unchangeable nature. The paradox is found in Proudhon's continuing claims that human nature tends toward equality and liberty. Proudhon came to see that his simplistic attitude could, without correction, be classified as utopian. This part of human nature--the immanent sense of justice--is only part of the story. In his later writings Proudhon developed a view of human nature in which the sense of justice--represented by the demands of conscience--is in constant conflict with its egoistic counterpart. Traces of this view appear in the early works, but it is not until the *System of Economic Contradictions* that Proudhon's assertion that humans are psychological egoists is fully developed. The paradox of a human nature that is both psychologically egoistic and tending toward equality provides both a difficult problem for Proudhon and a glimpse at his own confused and divided thought. By the time of the later works (especially the *System*), Proudhon not only admitted the truth of psychological egoism, he also softened the view expressed in *What Is Property?* that humans are distinguished as creatures by their unique degree of sociability. Though he never dismisssed the role of the sense of justice (as some have claimed), he did come to see that role as under constant threat from the overwhelming influence of egoistic desires.[73]

This developing realization resulted from two problems recognized by Proudhon. First, Proudhon came to realize that social constraints--the laws, customs, and the values supported by the ideological apparatuses of the modern world--had been integrated into the egoistic aspect of the individual personality. Egoistic desires are then adopted as one's own, rather than being presented to conscience as foreign or introduced desires. In *What Is Property?*, Proudhon had held that the false values could be discerned by the individual as foreign to his or her true nature, once the individual had understood the actual just order. In the later works this view was modified, as Proudhon saw that his psychology was simplistically voluntaristic and ahistorical and that the system of political and economic inculcation was both pervasive and thoroughly persuasive. Secondly, Proudhon recognized that the individual need for social integration prompts the acceptance of societal norms, often without the need for extensive persuasion. This need to be accepted within one's own social group would prompt the acceptance of societal norms even if those norms were, as Proudhon held, unjust.

The sense of justice in each human being is thus threatened by egoism and social constraints, but Proudhon saw this threat as less of a question of one aspect of human nature being inherently stronger than the other than as a question of balancing the two, of equilibrium:

> The man who lives in misery . . . shares his master's corruption; like him, he gives everything to pride and luxury, and if he sometimes cries out against the inequality from which he suffers, it is still less from zeal for justice than from rivalry in desire. . . .
>
> The dissidence and harmony of the human faculties . . . [are] two faces of our nature, ever adverse, ever in course of reconciliation, but never entirely reconciled. In a word, as individualism is the primordial fact of humanity, so association is its complementary term. Both are present constantly, and on earth there can be no love without justice.[74]

Proudhon saw these two aspects of human nature as complementary and as jointly necessary (though in imbalance not sufficient) prerequisites for a just order. The path to justice followed a balancing of the two, where the sense of justice (or principle of association, of egalitarian community) prevented the abuses of unrestrained egoism without extinguishing what Proudhon saw as the natural expression of the other aspect of justice--liberty.

This view of human nature was developed by Proudhon, as by Stirner, in a reworking of the history of human relations and of the repression of justice. The most important part of this "history" is the conclusion that Proudhon draws from what he considered to be the overwhelming evidence of a distortion of human nature, a deliberate imbalance of the two aspects of human nature in the service of an oppressive power. Though Proudhon acknowledged that government had replaced religion as the dominant power in society, he stressed that it had done so only through the perpetuation of economic inequality and a consequent self-estrangement from the poor and dispossessed. The oppressed classes, according to Proudhon, have learned all too well the lessons of the bourgeois revolutions, despairing of community values and association, the oppressed adopt the values of the oppressors, becoming practically (though not always formally) indifferent to political institutions, instead pursuing individual gain. Given this fairly pessimistic view of social development, it is unclear how Proudhon could envision any substantial social change. How did Proudhon propose to effect the "equilibrium" of interests necessary for the reign of justice?

The answer--an important answer in Proudhon's philosophical debate with Marx--is that, in actuality, history points toward the reign of justice, not away from it. According to Proudhon, authoritarian institutions served a useful purpose in the past, since they helped instill in humans the kernel of justice--the idea, however distorted, of the rule of right. Despite themselves, these Institutions (especially religion, property, and government) planted the seeds of their own destruction by disciplining and educating the people. According to Proudhon, continuing education will enable the oppressed to remove the last of the obstacles to justice, the authoritarian institutions themselves. "Government was progressive when it defended a society against savages. There are no more savages: there are only workers whom the government continues to treat like savages."[75]

Once people saw the superfluity of government and its allied institutions, Proudhon thought that they would be able to emancipate themselves from the state without reverting to a presocial or even bourgeois egoism. History is on the side of the social revolutions, but the final step cannot be left to history. For--and this is one of Proudhon's main sticking-points with Marx--the final transformation, the end of oppression and the beginning of justice must originate in the personal transformation of the individual worker. History is a series of authoritarian institutions creating the conditions of their own superfluity, only to be replaced by new authoritarian powers. In a fashion curiously reminiscent of Stirner, Proudhon saw the final transformation, the end of authoritarian institutions in toto, as the result of an individual (for Proudhon, moral) transformation. For Proudhon, history provides us with a lesson: all movements away from authority have resulted in only limited gains and distorted goals because the moral basis of authority remained intact in a distorted sense of justice within the majority of the society. Each person must eventually effect a personal moral change in order to end this distortion. As Robert Hoffman put it: "Man must make himself, through the deliberate efforts of each of us. . . . The true enemy is neither hostile ruling classes nor the natural world around us that technology strives against so mightily. Victory over ourselves is the real goal; somehow, Proudhon is sure, we will win."[76] Proudhon's own statement of the same point is uncharacteristically clear: "Then let us work to make ourselves better, to think justly; let us seek frugality and flee sloth. With that we shall shorten the trial and be reborn superior to our fathers."[77]

The keys to this personal transformation involve the use of moral education in order to overcome the obstacles posed by the state and by man's own egoistic desires in addition to the self-organization of labor in just, reciprocal economic units. Both of these keys to the success of his moral vision rest on the ethics of justice adopted by Proudhon. If human nature in its perverted form is an obstacle to justice, it is so only because it is evidence of a distorted morality.

Though Proudhon began in a sort of naive ethical naturalism, there is evidence from the time of *What Is Property?* onward that he had adopted an intuitionist, deontological stance. Each human being is capable of intuiting the just course of action, using the dictates of an enlightened conscience. Just actions and the principles of just actions are both intrinsically just, an action being just (and hence good) if it conforms to the immanent sense or principle of justice found in human nature. This highly personal intuitionism, with each person intuiting the justice of particular actions and obligations, seems hopelessly vague and conflict ridden. It is one step from such an intuitionism to a very weak relativism, one similar in practical content to Stirner's position. Proudhon avoids taking that step, however, by integrating a subtle adaptation of Kantianism and a faith in moral education into his ethical theory.

As Proudhon stated in *What Is Property?*, the result of the best human teaching concerning justice is found in the principle of reciprocity, of treating others as you would be treated.[78] Proudhon established this basic sense of justice as his primary norm, avoiding Stirnerian relativism by grounding all claims about justice, and social progress on this primary norm. James Joll has noted, correctly, that Proudhon uses this primary norm in the same way that Immanuel Kant used the categorical imperative as the basis of his ethical philosophy.[79] Though there are significant differences between the two ethical principles, Proudhon uses the concept of justice as a many hued reciprocity as the ultimate test of any action and of any society. Kant's use of the categorical imperative as a fundamental moral principle for his system is similar, though Kant's principle is a test of maxims, not of actions or societies. Justice, as "mutuality," as "balance," as "equilibrium,"[80] is the single intrinsic good for individuals and societies for Proudhon, the standard against which individual actions and social structures are judged.

Proudhon avoids relativism, it is true, in taking this step. He does so, though, despite the claims of his supporters, at the cost of a retreat into vagueness. Unlike the logical coherence and rational basis of the Kantian system, Proudhon's social ethics suffer from both an infirm foundation and a lack of conceptual consistency. The number of expressions Proudhon used to convey his

core concept of justice expresses less a breadth of application
than a conceptual confusion as to what such a vague standard could
mean in application. Such a diffuse primary norm is at best a
foggy ideal, grounded less in history (as Proudhon thought) than
in the ideological embrace of a determinate notion of the nature
of human beings. Granting these problems, such was the norm Proudhon chose. Even if we accept this primary norm at face value,
however, a question remains: how is this ethical standard to be
implemented?

As has been noted, Proudhon emphasized the individual acceptance of justice, the personal moral transformation of the worker
and capitalist alike. He recognized that this was inadequate, however, and supplemented his moral exhortation with strong support
for moral education. Since we must convince others of the primacy
of justice and thus of the need to respect other persons as social
and economic equals, education as a demonstration of the superiority of justice must be one of the main emphases (if not the main
emphasis) of any program for social reform. Proudhon rejected the
educational apparatuses of authoritarian institutions (including
those of the Church and of any government) because of the history
of such institutions as distorters of the sense of justice and
because of inherent problems in the use of any authoritarian
agency as a means of liberation. Proudhon's moral stance requires
ultimate respect for the autonomous individual and the demands of
the individual conscience. Proudhon's adapted "Kantianism" pro-
hibits the inculcation of moral values through the use of external
authority; the individual must adopt the principles of justice (of
liberty and equality) as his or her own. Both religion and government establish and perpetuate their values through explicit or implicit displays of authority and thus violate the principles of
justice as well as the reciprocal respect for autonomy found at
the core of the concept of justice. Justice must be demonstrated,
rather than inculcated, much as Socrates "demonstrated" the extent
of Euthyphro's ignorance of piety without dogmatically asserting a
positive position on the subject.[81] Though Proudhon's "demonstration" would have a more explicit conclusion than Socrates's in the
Euthyphro, the demonstration would stop short of indoctrination,

or so Proudhon thought.

Proudhon rejected indoctrination in favor of a rational demonstration of the Socratic sort. Proudhon was certain that such a
demonstration could succeed, as he was certain of what he regarded
as the factual and logical superiority of a just order when com-
pared to any unjust system. Proudhon dismissed previous attempts
at demonstrating this superiority; he could not consistently advocate the presuppositions implicit in the supposed demonstrations
of the compatibility of individual interest and social justice in
the fashion of either Shaftesbury or David Hume.[82] The superiority
of justice could not be demonstrated by an appeal to self-interest, according to Proudhon; rather, the demonstration must show
the general utility of a just order apart from the demands of
self-interest. By showing that a logical economics and general
prosperity require a just order (as he had attempted to show in
What Is Property?), Proudhon thought to appeal to the immanent
sense of justice in each of us.

When we are shown the practical advantages for all of a just
order, Proudhon thought that our latent egoism would be overcome
by our inherent sense of justice. Proudhon thought that these demonstrations could be accomplished by a specific use of propaganda;
the internalization of a properly informed collective opinion
would hasten the acceptance of justice as the prevailing norm.
Proudhon recognized the danger of such a stance, since he usually
condemned the use of ideology as antithetical to liberty. He
reconciled this conflict with his basic moral stance by claiming
that he was appealing to an existing aspect of human nature rather
than distoring that nature, as religious and other authoritarian
ideologists did in imposing unjust values by a wholly external
force. Proudhon claimed that such a stance was not inconsistent;
the influence of such moral education "would never be transformed
into an obligatory law for the will without an emotional predispo-
sition which makes social relations that embrace the subject
appear to him as . . . a sort of secret commandment from himself
to himself."[83]

Through moral education, however vague Proudhon left the details of such education, justice as the primary norm was to be

propagated in all its aspects. This entire system of morality and education had one goal: the replacement of the oppressive features of society, hierarchy in government, and inequality in the economic sphere by an egalitarian society devoid of the domination of humans by humans. Any other social order would be unjust. Government and law are inherently unjust, as is religious domination and economic domination. Any authoritarian institution or practice violates the central demands of justice since it inhibits freedom and preserves inequality. For these reasons Proudhon condemned representative government in any form as simply broadening the base of oppression. He also opposed attempts at representative democracy because he claimed that, once elected, representatives are corrupted by the authoritarian system in which they work. People must be both equal and free, and any state, no matter how wide the suffrage and how extensive the recall mechanisms, retains illegitimate sovereignty. Though Proudhon opposed statism and any worker participation in either elected government or the electoral process (for the reasons just stated), he did not oppose order. In his mature writings, Proudhon put forward several proposals for social order, an order which would be less than a political system and more than a laissez-faire anarchy.

In denying the necessary connection between government and order, Proudhon thought that he could provide instead a plan for social organization that would maintain order without compromising either liberty or equality. Such a non-political organization would both contain excessive political conflict and allow maximum freedom for individuals and small groups to establish the just relations precluded by political organizations and political activity, these relations proceeding from and maintaining the elimination of hierarchy and inequality. Proudhon rejected the classical capitalist economic system, as was seen in the analysis of *What Is Property?* Capitalism as the guiding economic and social principle, the minimalist state "governed" by market mechanisms, is an illusory substitute for a more moderate and at the same time more insidious political order; the market breeds inequality through the manipulation of the propertyless weakened by the strong proprietors. In the end, according to Proudhon, the practical contradictions of capitalism prevent the market from being the true guiding force. In the end, political coercion is needed to support the controlled inequality bred by the supposedly "free" market system.

The key to Proudhon's new society, the positive result of his moral vision, is the establishment of a just society through freely chosen and maintained contract. The injustices of capitalism and communism--as Proudhon saw them, the suppression of equality and liberty, respectively--could be mediated in a society where humans were free to contract for their needs. Since previous social forms were deficient in that they preserved injustice through authority and hierarchy and since most proposed new forms preserved the unjust basis of previous societies, the solution as Proudhon saw it was the removal of authority and hierarchy. In such a society contract is between equals, binding equally on both parties and based on an equality of exchange. Proudhon wanted to establish just such a society through the locally based enterprises operating on such a model which he endorsed and in which he participated. Such a society would be mutualist in its economic and social relationship, its members living in equality and liberty and having undergone the personal moral transformation which Proudhon deemed necessary for such a venture. "It must be based on a law of *exchange*, a theory of MUTUALITY. . . . It will make both capital and the State subordinate to labor. Through the genuine nature of exchange it will create true solidarity between peoples. The theory of mutuality, . . . that is to say exchange in kind, . . . is the synthesis of the notions of private property and collective ownership."[84]

A problem arises with the formulation of Proudhon's solution: if mutualist exchange, free contract, is to be the basis of the new society, what is to prevent the exchanges from degenerating into the inequality of exchange inherent in capitalism? (Proudhon had given a vivid account of just such a possibility in *What Is Property?*) Why should any individual respect the interests of another as one's own (and thus act justly, on Proudhon's account) if one can strike a better deal through, say, syndicate combination or monopoly? In short, how can contract be and remain free and equal? Is Proudhon's theory of contract more than an ideologically refined version of laissez-faire capitalism?

Proudhon's reply to such charges has two aspects, both of which were important in his debate with Marx, as these charges were just the sort lodged against Proudhon by Marx. First, Proudhon's theory of contract was intended to be quite different from the Hobbesian theory or even from that of Rousseau. Proudhon agreed that destructive egoism prevails in the capitalist economic system and that sovereign political authority then acts as a regulatory power for the economic system. But, Proudhon argued, it is the system of economic relations themselves, in distorting the immanent sense of justice, that perpetuates the destructive egoism. Once the system is changed, the egoistic tendencies will begin to disappear, accompanied by a personal moral transformation on the part of the workers. Then the need for a regulatory sovereign as the arbiter of disputes between the "public good" and egoism will disappear. Proudhon characterized the principle of this change as "the ancient law of retaliation, *an eye for an eye*, . . . as it were turned upside down and transferred from criminal law . . . to economic law, to the tasks of labor and to the good offices of free fraternity. On it depend all the mutualist institutions. . . . I will even go as far as to say [that the mutualist principle acts] as a kind of religion. . . ."[85] So the first part of Proudhon's answer is that free contract in a mutualist society will be devoid of the unequal and oppressive features of the present society, encouraging the balance of forces in human nature to turn toward justice. The mutualist principle, as the guiding feature of such a society, will help ensure the equality of exchange.

The second part of Proudhon's answer also relies on the mutualist principle and the change that the acceptance of such a principle by a large number of the workers would signal. Where mutualism prevails, power to utilize resources and access to resources are equalized. Proudhon was never clear about how this was to be done, but he seemed to think that mutualism would prevent the degeneration of society into a new unjust order by mandating equality of access and use-rights for all basic resources and goods. Each small group of laborers would hold and use certain

essential goods, the intent being to prevent monopoly, especially
in basic food stuffs and other essentials. In addition, each group
would have equal access to natural resources within the society as
a whole, the amount used determined by an egalitarian distribution
among all members of the society. (Proudhon seems to have thought
of this distribution as proceeding along rather crude mathematical
lines, after determining the available amount of a given resource,
the groups would then divide the amount by the number of citizens
in the society.) The point of this system, the central thesis pro-
pounded by Proudhon here, was to decentralize power and resources,
decreasing the possibility of economic dependency between groups
while increasing small group interdependence--the need for mutual
aid between and among groups, for cooperation. This system would
then reflect, on a societal scale, the essence of Proudhon's moral
vision, that each person should respect the interests of others as
one's own, since in such a society the interests of other groups
would be inextricably linked with those of every other group.
Proudhon thought that the important first step in this process
required workers to adopt the principles of justice as their own,
thus ensuring the success of the groups and of the society. Then,
according to Proudhon, this process required workers to realize
the vastly increased power of their labor when they combined, when
they joined together in collective enterprise. Workers could then
begin to transform their economic situation by bargaining as a
unit with employers, eventually reaching a stage of equality where
the employer-employee distinction would be transcended by association in mutualist enterprises. (These enterprises would include
the former employers as new workers. It is interesting to note
that this was the process followed in Spain in the 1930s, where
factory owners were given the opportunity to particiapte as fellow
workers in the newly mutualized enterprises.)

The equality advocated by Proudhon differed, in his eyes,
from the sterile isolation of atomistic egoism as well as from the
equally sterile collective institutions of communism, though again
Proudhon used this latter term in reference to the primitive com-
munisms of the early nineteenth century for most of his career.
Proudhon sought to avoid both extremes by advocating social diver-

sity and interdependence, where the mutualist society promoted diversification in occupation and production. In this way Proudhon attempted to account for the possibility of mutualism becoming a stale and static force in the economic life of a given society. Without this diversity Proudhon thought, such staleness was inevitable and along with this staleness would come the reintroduction of government regulation as a short-term solution.

In order to combat the contingencies of contractual life, Proudhon added another aspect to his ideal of justice. In addition to measures already discussed, actually as the basis of those measures, Proudhon advocated the rule of commutative justice in all contractual exchange. This is the core of Proudhon's reply to criticisms of his theory of contract: only with equivalent exchange can contract remain both free and equal. "The social contract is an agreement of man with man; an agreement from which must result what we call society. In this, the notion of *commutative justice*, first brought forward by the primitive fact of exchange, and defined by the Roman law, is substituted for that of *distributive justice*. . . . The future hope of humanity lies in this substitution."[86]

In formulating a policy reminiscent of his father's use of the Just Price, Proudhon adapted the standard of commutative justice, the means of measuring value for exchange as the cost of production. Proudhon thought that this standard would produce relatively small differences among workers, because he held that differences in productive capacities were relatively small among people, though these differences were exaggerated and aggravated by the system in which people worked. In any event, Proudhon thought that these differences were less than differences in talent, prestige, and cunning, which were the typical standards guiding production and exchange. What inequality remained could be ameliorated in the non-mutualist, completely giving context of familial love. Though this last point is unconvincing and has certain sexist overtones, Proudhon did think that the family would serve as the ultimate means of fostering justice, both in developing the sense of justice within the family unit and in softening the minor inequalities of commutative justice. Both aspects of the family are important in developing the mutualist sense: "The more I love, the more I will be afraid to displease, and as a result, the more I will respect myself; now, the more vivid this self-respect becomes, the more strongly will I feel it sympathetically in others; and consequently, the more just I will be."[87]

Such was the basic development of Proudhon's moral vision, capped by his support of the family hearth and the power of love. A limited critique of the implications of Proudhon's vision for his anti-statism has been given throughout this section. This limited critique will be continued in an examination of the conflict between Proudhon's moral vision and Marx's growing realization of the need for a concrete social theory based on a realist assessment of the possibilities and requirements for change.

MARX, PROUDHON, AND THE POVERTY OF PHILOSOPHY

A revolution which is inspired by state socialism and adopts this form, even "provisionally" and "temporarily," is lost: it takes a wrong road down an ever steeper slope. . . . All political power inevitably creates a privileged position for those who exercise it. Having taken over the Revolution, mastered it, and harnessed it, those in power are obliged to create the bureaucratic and repressive apparatus which is indispensable for any authority that wants to maintain itself, to command, to give orders, in a word: to govern.

Voline[88]

Proudhon's moral vision, in summary form, consists of the call for justice in all social and economic relationships. Justice, as the coexistence of equality and liberty, is grounded in an immanent sense of justice evident in human nature but which is realized fully only in the absence of the distortions of unjust authoritarian institutions (especially the state, religion, and the capitalist economic system). Only with the elimination of these false orders and hierarchies can liberty emerge. In addition, true justice requires the presence of just--that is, reciprocal, mutualist, and egalitarian--economic and social relationships.

The transformation of society was to be accomplished by a moral transformation in the workers (and, eventually, in the non-producers as well), instigated and supported by social criticism. This criticism, using moral education as a demonstrative tool, enlightens workers and illuminates justice without directing the transformation. This moral transformation, supported by criticism and education and the loving context of the family and the workshop, would be accompanied by a parallel transformation of economic life in accordance with just, mutualist principles. The authority and hierarchy of both government and the capitalist economic order would thus be bypassed, rather than fought directly. Political organization, tainted by the need for authority and compromise of principles, was to be avoided in favor of the mutualist self-organization of labor. Beginning in small, local groups, workers would organize themselves, not for political action but for economic change.[89]

Eventually, Proudhon came to see his moral vision resulting in an international federation of such groups, based on the interests of labor rather than national or corporate interests. Labor was to be the main vehicle for social transformation; to produce is to work toward justice, in however small a fashion. Work promotes respect for self and others. From this basic idea of the value of labor, Proudhon saw the self-organization of workers along non-exploitative lines as following quite naturally. Any organization would be from below, by the workers, preserving liberty by preserving decentralization and a lack of hierarchy while promoting equality and mutual respect.

Given this moral vision, Proudhon could not but oppose any revolutionary movement which placed political organization and violent change above the Proudhonian version of the organization of labor by labor and above Proudhon's change by demonstration, work, and economic self-reorganization. Thus Proudhon consistently opposed Jacobinism, Blanquism, and--unavoidabley--Marxism. The point Proudhon continually raised against all such movements was that political power is illegitimate, inherently illegitimate, that it rests in and perpetuates inequality and force. Even a "transitional" state could only sustain itself by either allying itself with the "proprietor" (loosely speaking) or else by adopting unacceptable dictatorial methods and powers. The state, in whatever form, could only perpetuate injustice. Liberty and equality suffer as a consequence. Paul Thomas put it well when he commented that, for Proudhon, the state "is no mere instrument; it can dictate to society so long as society refrains from sweeping it out of existence. 'Liberty' and 'government' were to Proudhon quite simply zero-sum alternatives. . . ."[90]

Proudhon's program for the elimination of the state can only be seen as a gradualist program, for two reasons. First, the building of the just, mutualist society (and thus socio-economic order) is possible only through the transformation of the personal and economic relations of the workers, especially in small, locally based units. This process takes time. It is, after all, a moral transformation, not a cataclysmic revolutionary change. Secondly, the building of a just, mutualist society can only come about through non-political means; that is, by non-institutional, non-hierarchical means. Workers must not use the state or its political mechanisms, since the key to the transformation is education by example and demonstration. What the workers do and say in their efforts should be an example of the type of society being built. It is unsurprising, then, to find that Proudhon opposed all political participation, even though he participated in the French state at one point (to his eventual and perpetual regret). Given the nature of Proudhon's moral vision, it is also unsurprising that Proudhon and Marx clashed so violently.

Marx met Proudhon in Paris in 1844. From all appearances the meeting and subsequent discussions were friendly enough, though the later writings of both men tend to obscure their initial cordiality. They had certainly heard of each other before 1844, though Marx was more likely to have been familiar with Proudhon's writings than Proudhon with Marx's work. (Proudhon did not read German.) Much effort has been expended on attempting to establish which writer was a greater influence on the other; as with Proudhon's originality in using the slogan "Property is theft," such scholarly effort is interesting but neither strictly relevant nor

terribly important.[91] Though the specific conflicts in their works
are important, I am in complete agreement with Robert Hoffman concerning the problem of "influence": "The differences between the
two men were too great for them to influence each other signifi-
cantly. A common interest in socialism and the philosophy of Hegel
brought them together briefly, but that was in reality a rather
vague basis for close intellectual bonds. They had little else."[92]
Marx dealt briefly with Proudhon in *The Holy Family* and in the
1844 Manuscripts, as well as in occasional references to Proudhon
as one among several socialist theorists.[93] Marx's references to
Proudhon in the works prior to *The Poverty of Philosophy* (1847)
are generally positive in character; Proudhon is seen as one of
the "sharper" social critics in Europe. Still, the comments must
be seen within the context of Marx's work as a whole--his project
--and within this context they appear as qualified and guarded. In
most of Marx's works after 1847, Proudhon is at least mentioned
and criticized in passing and often in detail, evidence that Proudhon and Proudhonism continued to bother Marx and Engels long
after Proudhon's death. Proudhonism strongly influenced the French
labor movement long after his death, an influence that forced Marx
and Engels to deal with the French Proudhonists in the First International. After the dissolution of the First International,
Proudhonism continued to influence the French and (to a lesser
degree) the Belgian labor movement through the development of late
nineteenth--and early twentieth--century syndicalism.[94] In this
section I will show why Proudhon's influence proved so enduring
and how Marx and Proudhon's respective political theories reflected fundamental differences in their philosophical beliefs.

Marx's early comments on Proudhon and Proudhon's influence
recognize the value of Proudhon's emphasis on property as the
underlying basis of oppression. Proudhon is praised as an antidote
to the dogmatic communism of Cabet, Theodore Dézamy, and
Weitling.[95] With Fourierism, Proudhon's socialism was seen by Marx
as a necessary reaction to dogmatic communism. Marx seemed to
regard the early writings of Proudhon and Weitling as incomplete
statements of a truly emancipatory theory, each lacking a complete
understanding of the sources of oppression and their possible

remedy. In the *1844 Manuscripts*, Marx clarified his view of Proudhon: in several brief but important references to Proudhon, Marx
pointed out that he was to be praised for advocating the primacy
of labor over private property. Still, Proudhon had only grasped
the nature of labor and its estrangement from a limited perspective. According to Marx, Proudhon failed to grasp the more fundamental source of estrangement in modern society. Though "Proudhon
has decided in favor of labor against private property," Marx un-
derstands that the contradictory role of labor in political economy ("labor [is] . . . the real soul of production; yet to labor
it gives nothing, and to private property everything") "is the
contradiction of *estranged labor* with itself, and that political
economy has merely formulated the laws of estranged labor."[96] For
Proudhon to advocate any increase in or equality of wages is to
ignore that wages themselves reflect and are products of estranged
labor. Indeed, according to Marx, such an enforced increase of
wages "would therefore be nothing but better payment for the
slave, and would not win either for the worker or for labor their
human status and dignity."[97] The enforced equality of wages "only
transforms the relationship of the present-day worker to his labor
into the relationship of all men to labor. Society is then
conceived as an abstract capitalist."[98] Though Marx, in these
early works, criticizes many other views held by Proudhon, all of
his criticisms mirror this last quotation: Proudhon was not radical, that is, Proudhon had not seen social problems through to
their source. Marx's praise of *What Is Property?* must be seen in
light of this fundamental criticism of Proudhon.

     At first glance, Marx's praise of *What Is Property?* seems to
result more from a misunderstanding of Proudhon's intent than from
a genuine appreciation of Proudhon's achievement. In a letter to
Feuerbach (dated August 11, 1844), Marx criticized Bruno Bauer's
"one-sidedness" in Bauer's claiming that criticism must be the
purely theoretical pursuit of "an ironical ice-cold *sophos*."[99]
Proudhon, the subject of such criticism, is contrasted positively
with Bauer's stance, since Proudhon's point of departure is that
of a "practical need."[100] Marx's praise of this starting-point is
unusual, since the practical need or needs used by Proudhon in

What Is Property? scarcely reflect either Marx's methodology or
his critical position. This unusual praise, continued in *The Holy
Family*, reflects in part Marx's ambivalent attitude toward
Proudhon. Though Marx considered Proudhon's achievements and prag-
matic stance to be an advance over the accomplishments of Bauer
and others, he could not endorse the uncritical presuppositions of
Proudhon's stance--among these presuppositions is Proudhon's emphasis on the efficacy of the use of the sense of justice (as
equality and liberty) in order to effect social change. Though
What Is Property? is an important work within political economy as
Marx saw it, its arguments are limited by their inability to deal
with the presuppositions of political economy as a whole. Still,
Proudhon "takes the *human semblance* of the economic relations
seriously and sharply opposes it to their *inhuman reality*. He
forces them to be in reality what they imagine themselves to be,
or rather to give up their own idea of themseleves and confess
their real inhumanity."[101] In so doing, Proudhon exposes the internal contradictions of private property and its concomitant
economic relationships. Though Marx is ready to praise such an
accomplishment (as he did in *The Holy Family*), it is only because
Marx saw Proudhon's work as a necessary first step in the eventual
critique of political economy in general. It was only a first step
because Proudhon had not extended his critique of property to the
more subtle forms of property, including the creations of property
("wages, trade, value, price, money, etc.").[102] More importantly,
Proudhon had failed to extend his critique of property to the
basic economic relationships involved in the use of "possession":

> Proudhon's wish to abolish not having and the old way of hav-
> ing is quite identical with his wish to abolish the practi-
> cally estranged relation of man to his *objective essence* and
> the *economic* expression of human self-estrangement. But since
> his criticism of political economy is still captive to the
> premises of political economy, the re-appropriation of the
> objective world itself is still conceived in the economic
> form of *possession*.

> Proudhon . . . opposes *possession* to the old way of hav-
> ing, to *private property*. He proclaims possession to be a

"*social function*". What is "interesting" in a function, however, is not to "exclude" the other person, but to affirm and
to realize the forces of my own being.

Proudhon did not succeed in giving this thought appropriate development. The idea of '*equal* possession' is the
economic and therefore itself still estranged expression for
the fact that the *object* as *being for man*, as the *objective
being of man*, is at the same time the *existence of man for
other men*, his *human relation to other men*, the *social behavior of man to man*. Proudhon abolishes economic estrangement *within* economic estrangement.[103]

Proudhon had gone as far as he could within the bounds of political economy and had made considerable progress in going that far.
Specifically, Proudhon had forced the apologists of capitalist
economy to face the implications of their system. At the same
time, Proudhon would not or could not go beyond the economic
categories of possession and, especially, contract. In *The Holy
Family*, Marx commented that Proudhon had attempted to defend a
truly free contract, where political economy had held this freedom
to be "only nominal and illusory. . . ."[104] Although Proudhon
attempts to make political economy consistent, truly to institute
the idea of a free exchange, he does so, according to Marx, without recognizing the estrangement inherent in the contractual relationship.[105]

It was this inability to generate a truly radical theory,
providing for fundamental change, that Marx found objectionable in
Proudhon's work. In contract, in consideration of wages and interest, in the relationship between capital and labor, Marx saw
Proudhon as reaching only partial and incomplete solutions to
fundamental problems. This view of Proudhon was reflected in
Marx's later works, though in a much less generous and more bitter
fashion. In the first volume of *Capital*, Proudhon's socialism,
especially his theory of exchange, of free contract, is ridiculed
as the "working out" of a "Philistine Utopia," based on an illusory theory of directly exchangeable commodities.[106] Here, as well
as in the *Grundrisse* and *Theories of Surplus Value*, Proudhon is
seen as an essentially reactionary force: Proudhon could not (or

would not) move beyond the bounds of political economy. From this
it can be seen that Marx and Proudhon were unable to avoid a
direct conflict. Though the outlines of the philosophical conflict
have already been traced in the earlier works of the two thinkers,
the personal and acute philosophical conflict came after the writing of *The Holy Family* and was far more dramatic.

On May 5, 1846, Marx wrote to Proudhon from Brussels.[107]
Marx's purpose in writing was to establish a correspondence committee in Paris, to be led by Proudhon. Marx's letter had more to
say:

> It will be the chief aim of our correspondence, however, to
> put the German Socialists in contact with the French and
> English Socialists. . . . An exchange of ideas will ensue and
> impartial criticism be secured. It is a step which the social
> movement should take in its *literary* expression in order to
> free itself of its *national* limitations. And at the time for
> action it is certainly of great benefit to everyone to be
> enlightened on the state of affairs abroad as well as at
> home.[108]

Though several aspects of the letter were quite provocative
(Proudhon was an ardent Frenchman), the most important point for
this work--and for Proudhon as well in his reply--was Marx's
veiled reference to the "time for action." Proudhon's reply
focused largely on this phrase.

> Do not let us fall into your compatriot Martin Luther's in-
> consistency. As soon as he had overthrown Catholic theology
> he immediately...set about founding a Protestant theology.
> Let us not make further work for humanity by creating another
> shambles. [See also note 1 of this chapter.]
>
> I must also make some observations about the phrase in
> your letter, "at the time for action." Perhaps you still hold
> the opinion that no reform is possible without a helping *coup
> de main*, without what used to be called a revolution but
> which is quite simply a jolt. I confess that my most recent
> studies have led me to abandon this view. . . . I do not
> think that this is what we need in order to succeed, and
> consequently we must not suggest *revolutionary* action as the

means of social reform because this supposed means would simply be an appeal to force and arbitrariness. In brief, it would be a contradiction. I put the problem this way: *How can we put back into society, through some system of economics, the wealth which has been taken out of society by another system of economics?* In other words, through Political Economy we must turn the theory of Property against Property in such a way as to create what you German Socialists call *community* and which for the moment I will only go so far as calling *liberty* or *equality*. Now I think I know the way in which this problem may be very quickly solved. Therefore I would rather burn Property little by little than give it renewed strength by making a Saint Bartholomew's Day of property owners. . . .

This, my dear philosopher, is my present position. I may be mistaken, and if that happens and you give me the cane, I would cheerfully endure it while waiting for my revenge. I must add in passing that this also seems to be the feeling of the French working class. Our proletarians are so thirsty for knowledge that they would receive us very badly if all we give them to drink were blood. To be brief, it would in my opinion be very bad policy to use the language of extermination. Rigorous measures will come right enough; in this the people are in no need of exhortation.[109]

In this letter Proudhon expressed his basic optimism, his view of the goal of justice as liberty and equality, and especially his abhorrence of the possibility of wasting revolutionary activity in an effort doomed to increase either the strength of the proprietors or the power of a new hierarchy. (Not incidentally, Proudhon also demonstrated his inability to predict the actions of the French working class. Two years after this letter was written, his Parisian proletarians thirsting for knowledge staged a considerable "jolt.") Marx's cane came down quickly and without mercy as a response to Proudhon's *System of Economic Contradictions, or the Philosophy of Poverty,* entitled *The Poverty of Philosophy: Response to "The Philosophy of Poverty" of M. Proudhon.*

Marx's response, *The Poverty of Philosophy,* is revealing both in its detailed criticism of Proudhon and in the vitriolic tone in which it is written. Marx had clearly lost patience with Proudhon. More importantly, however, Marx had apparently seen the full challenge of Proudhon's position, as that position was put forward with great force in *The Philosophy of Poverty*. For this latter reason it is important to examine Marx's arguments in his response to Proudhon, for these arguments bear directly on the two thinkers' conflict concerning the state.

Marx's letter to P.V. Annenkov (dated December 28, 1846) gives a detailed sketch of Marx's reaction to Proudhon's work. On the whole, Marx found Proudhon's work "bad, and very bad."[110] In this letter, a reply to Annenkov's request for Marx's impression of Proudhon's work, Marx reiterates his criticism of Proudhon found in *The Holy Family*: Proudhon failed to understand the significance of the existing and historical economic conditions and their bearing on human relations and as a result Proudhon produced an ahistorical history of these relations. Rather than linking the form of society to the existing material conditions, Proudhon produces an abstract account of property and other economic "categories" which are changed not by action, but by other, different abstractions. "[E]very succeeding generation finds itself in possession of the productive forces acquired by the previous generation, which serve it as the raw material for new production, . . . [thus] a history of humanity takes shape which is all the more a history of humanity as the productive forces of man. . . . [Men's] material relations are the basis of all their relations."[111] Proudhon's error is in confusing this history with an abstract account of society:

> M. Proudhon, by establishing property as an independent relation, commits more than a mistake in method: he clearly shows that he has not grasped the bond which holds together all forms of *bourgeois* production, that he has not understood the *historical and transitory* character of the forms of production in a particular epoch. M. Proudhon, who does not regard our social institutions as historical products, who can understand neither their origin nor their development, can only produce dogmatic criticism of them.[112]

Because Proudhon did not (or would not) see the material and historical link between social (and political) products and the economic relationships of a given era, Marx held, the Proudhonian concept of change is merely one of the change of abstract categories.   This charge is not entirely fair. Proudhon denied the material and historical link of certain social concepts or categories, it is true, but this is a limited group of categories, including those of "justice," "labor," and "love." Proudhon was not blindly ahistorical. These few categories are enough for Marx's point, however. Proudhon denied the need for, as Marx put it, "public action" because "it is not necessary to change practical life in order to change the categories. Quite the contrary. One must change the categories and the consequence will be a change in the existing society."[113] Nothing could be further from Marx's own view. For Marx, fundamental change required not a change in "contradictory" categories but a change in the material conditions on which the social and economic categories rest. Proudhon, according to Marx could not even comprehend the origin and structure of existing society. Instead, he held to a *dualism* between life and ideas,"[114] one which incapacitated him when he attempted to give an account of social practice and change.

These are the criticisms Marx pursues in *The Poverty of Philosophy*. In the first chapter, Marx parodies Proudhon's claims to "science" while at the same time pointing to real weaknesses in Proudhon's account. As Marx notes, quite correctly, Proudhon's account of need presupposes the existence of the division of labor; since humans cannot provide for their own needs as individuals, labor is divided, as the Proudhonian account reads. Proudhon does not explain the origin of this division in the material conditions of life. Instead, Proudhon simply assumes the existence of such a division, thus inverting the order of explanation. This inversion leads to other errors, since Proudhon bases his account of exchange and exchange value on the presupposed division of labor. What Proudhon needs, Marx claims, is a historical explanation of how the single individual at the core of Proudhon's account, the solitary "Robinson" and his fellow "Robinsons," come to accept value and exchange. Proudhon's model is one of commerce developing from explicit "proposals" conveyed from one individual or group to another. Marx spends much of the rest of the initial parts of the book showing why Proudhon's account is untenable.

The central question for both Marx and Proudhon at this point is the nature of the relationship between use and exchange value. Marx claimed that Proudhon's account left out key aspects of the answer, including that of the role of demand. Proudhon's account apparently lacks "buyers," it has no explanation of the complex role played by the buyer, since demand is ignored. Marx detailed the reciprocal nature of supply and demand in order to show Proudhon's oversimplification. The nature of this basic economic relationship, according to Marx, is distorted by Proudhon's substitutions of abstract notions that do not explain the constraints inherent in exchange. Instead, Proudhon gives a "metaphysical" freedom to both producer and consumer, to seller and buyer, in order that each may deal as independent, conflicting powers. According to Proudhon's account, the opposition in this relationship is the result of opposing wills rather than material conditions and relations.[115] Marx is quick to point out that the division of labor necessitates selling by the producer and buying by the consumer. It is less a question of conflicting wills than it is a structurally mandated conflict.

> The producer, the moment he produces in a society founded on
> the division of labor and on exchange . . . is forced to
> sell. M. Proudhon makes the producer the master of the means
> of production; but he will agree with us that his means of
> production do not depend on *free will*. . . .

> The consumer is no freer than the producer. His judgment
> depends on his means and his needs. Both of these are determined by his social position, which itself depends on the
> whole social organization.[116]

Proudhon's inability or unwillingness to see this point is the result of the same fault Marx had noted in earlier criticisms: Proudhon deals with use and exchange value on a purely abstract level and so fails to elucidate the underlying structure of material conditions and relations. Marx is correct; he put his point quite well when he wrote that, in dealing with economic relations as mere abstractions, Proudhon makes of the producer and consumer *"knights of free will."*[117]

The same fault occurs in Proudhon's account of constituted value and labor value. Proudhon, in viewing labor in the abstract (as Proudhon certainly did), ignores the real character of the values generated by labor and the value of labor power. Marx traces the origin of Proudhon's theory to David Ricardo. Ricardo, however, more accurately describes the characteristics of value, according to Marx, whereas "M. Proudhon's theory of values is the utopian interpretation of Ricardo's theory."[118] Proudhon's "utopianism" stems from his failure to ground his theory of values in the real, existing economic conditions. Another result of this abstraction is that Proudhon fails to see that labor itself is a commodity and thus subject to the theory of value in so far as labor requires labor for its maintenance. On this basis Marx accuses Proudhon of advocating the exploitative status quo as "revolutionary": the workers are in fact "enslaved" not "emancipated" by the application of Proudhon's theory.

All of these criticisms of Proudhon's account of the values generated by labor and the value of labor power reflect a basic fault in Proudhon's view: Proudhon saw the labor time necessary to produce a commodity as the strict indicator of its value. Marx showed how Proudhon's subsequent analysis--that simple production historically and socially precedes complex production--fails to recognize the historical-dialectical conflict between the various groups or classes within a given society. It is these conflicts according to Marx, that have determined the modes of production and thus have determined the value of commodities. Again, this faulty explanation arises because Proudhon's account of value (especially labor value) is not grounded in the history of economic reality but in the abstraction of metaphysically free producers and consumers. As Marx states, "The use of products is determined by the social conditions in which the consumers find themselves placed, and these conditions themselves are based on class antagonism."[119]

This same charge is found throughout *The Poverty of Philosophy*. At one point, Marx criticizes Proudhon's account of money and its role in a theory of constituted value. Against Proudhon's claim that gold and silver as money is the result of certain properties of the metals, the difficulty of their production, and "above all, the intervention of public authority," that is, of the sovereign in fixing the metals as valuable by an act of will,[120] Marx shows that economic relations are the primary source of value. Even sovereigns are subject to the existing economic conditions. "Truly, one must be destitute of all historical knowledge not to know that it is the sovereigns who in all ages have been subject to economic conditions, but they have never dictated laws to them. Legislation, whether political or civil, never does more than proclaim, express in words, the will of economic relations."[121] Proudhon's abstract, "metaphysical" reasoning, where economic relations are dealt with as abstract categories, dooms Proudhonian dialectics to impotency. So long as Proudhon rests with the theoretical expressions of the relations of production, his method is backwards or, as Marx put it, Proudhon "hold[s] things upside-down like a true philosopher, see[ing] in actual relations nothing but the incarnation of these principles, these categories. . . ."[122]

One very important consequence of Proudhon's stance is that he makes "justice" a fixed, eternal idea, a principle, or category. Though Marx dealt largely with Proudhon's economic categories, the criticism of Proudhon's ahistoricality applies to his concept of justice as well. Just as Proudhon ignores the fact, if it is a fact, that economic relations are historical and transitory modes created by humans and just as Proudhon's "eternal ideas" concerning these economic relations are the historical and transitory reflections of these relations, so the social relations of a given society, which are "closely bound up with" and reflect the existing productive forces, are seen by Proudhon as fixed, eternal ideas.[123] In assuming that justice--and especially the tendency toward equality--is a fixed idea, an eternal idea or category, Marx claims that Proudhon illegitimately makes justice the goal of all historical movement and immanent in all economic contradiction. Thus the existing economic contradictions are seen by Proudhon as having their good and their bad sides, since they contain and move toward justice. Marx characterizes Proudhon's account of this tendency toward justice as "mystical," a "primordial intention," and a "providential aim" of "the social genius. . . ."[124]

In place of this "mystical" approach to justice and the tendency toward equality, Marx offers a historical and descriptive approach. This account details the history of material relations, describing changes in economic relations as proceeding from changes in productive forces, motivated by class antagonism. These changes in turn give rise to the form of social and political relations. Marx thus turns Proudhon on his head; rather than "justice" being immanent in and the goal of all history, the expressions of "justice" are the products of the movement of history and class conflict.

The result of Proudhon's approach is, as Marx stated, an opposition to the organization of workers in organized combinations and a virulent opposition to their participation in political activities. Proudhon's opposition is taken to task by Marx as both reactionary and the product of bad reasoning: Marx's historical dialectic does not appeal to an eternal standard of virtue or justice, as Proudhon's does. Rather, for Marx, the struggle between the classes is a necessary and progressive movement. The organization of the working class is an important step in this movement. The organization of the working class, its political activity, strikes, and the gains of such activity--including improved wages and working conditions--are important and legitimate movements in the transformation of society. Proudhon's principled opposition to such activities can be seen as essentially reactionary, since in supporting a personal, moral transformation based on an immutable standard of justice, Proudhon in effect cooperates with the existing dominant class and preserves the existing economic and social contradictions. According to Marx, the resolution of these contradictions, the emancipation of the working class and the creation of a new society, is possible only when the conditions preserving the class antagonisms are themselves transformed. This transformation requires the organization and political activity of the oppressed classes, working toward "an association which will exclude classes and their antagonism, and there will be no more political power properly so-called, since political power is precisely the official expression of antagonism in civil society."[125]

Thus, the elimination of the state--Proudhon's goal and the object of study in this work--proceeds not as a means of establishing the just order but as a consequence of the transformation of the antagonistic social and especially economic conditions of existing society. Until then, according to Marx, "Le combat ou la mort; la lutte sanguinaire ou le néant. C'est ainsi que la question est invinciblement posée."[126]

Much of Marx's criticism of Proudhon is justified. The central weakness of Proudhon's entire social theory is his faulty methodology, including his assumption that all existing economic relations are somehow the expressions of a completely free (if distorted) exchange of products. It is even unclear whether Proudhon held this view, or held it consistently, since he occasionally adopted a more historical stance. When Proudhon's methodology failed him, however, he assumed that a reformed notion of contract can correct the distorted exchange relationship while preserving the freedom of wills "inherent" in the exchange, all seemingly independent of the existing economic forces. Such a notion is clearly ahistorical and, as Proudhon found when he attempted to institute his principles in a "Peoples' Bank," naively unrealistic.

Another product of Proudhon's methodology is his view that labor and the value of labor somehow assume a primitive, near mystical, and moral force. Labor constitutes value as an independent economic (and moral) force, divorced from the alienating constraints imposed by capitalist modes of production. Such a view is tenable only as long as one ignores the real ground of labor in an existing mode of production.

There is some evidence that Proudhon accepted many of Marx's criticisms. The marginal notes in Proudhon's copy of Marx's book, as well as the tone of Proudhon's later works, reflect an acceptance of some of the Marxian critique while rejecting other parts. These marginal comments also indicate that Proudhon thought that Marx had misunderstood him.[127] Given all of the weaknesses in

Proudhon's vision and all of the criticisms he was willing to accept, there remain questions concerning some of Marx's basic criticisms and the starting-points of the two thinkers.

One of the main reasons for the harshness of Marx's attack
must have been Proudhon's attack on communism in *The Philosophy of
Poverty*. This Proudhonian attack is, for the most part, based on
the alleged violation of justice entailed by communist practice.
As an example, according to Proudhon, communist expropriation, the
revolutionary practice, always begins in promises of justice and
ends in "fire and the guillotine."[128] That is, in pursuit of their
ends, the ends of the classless society, the communists violate
individual liberty. What Proudhon does is make liberty an explicit
primary norm, the violation of which is never justified by the
goal of equality (or of the classless society). Just as Marx's
criticisms of Proudhon often rested on the denial of any such
transhistorical norms, Proudhon's defense is irremediably colored
by his fundamental moral judgment concerning the value of justice.
(It is, as he wrote, his alpha and omega.) It will not satisfy
Proudhonists to claim or even attempt to demonstrate the ideological origin or "reactionary" effects of such norms, since for Proudhon there remains a sphere of human thought and action relatively
free from such material and brute economic influence. It is in and
through this sphere, largely the sphere of individual labor (or at
least the attitude toward labor), the recognition of the demands
of justice, and the possibility of truly free exchange and mutualism that Proudhon hoped to effect social change. Violent revolutionary change is both unnecessary for this change and actually
counterproductive, since it entails the violation of a vital
aspect of justice.

For Marx, on the other hand, this sphere of freedom of which
Proudhon is an ephemeral sphere encompassing an illusory freedom.
Given the force of material conditions and the social relations so
closely bound to those conditions, Proudhon's postulation of
justice (as liberty and equality) could only seem fantastic. Moral
values like those advocated by Proudhon could never act as
vehicles of fundamental social change, nor could they help explain
such change, since their practical and historical ground was found

in the existing socio-economic conditions.

This contrast in the two thinkers' fundamental views is help-ful in assessing Marx's criticisms as put forward in *The Poverty of Philosophy* and elsewhere. One of the general thrusts of that work is the point that Proudhon uses abstract categories in "ex-plaining" concrete relations and change. Yet Proudhon does not claim to be giving a strictly historical account; when he does claim to be giving this, he is exaggerating. His real object is an account of the structure of the ideas and categories involved in the concept of justice and the "contradictions" inherent in the expressions of that concept. Thus, Marx's criticism, well put from a practical (or practical revolutionary) point of view, may be in-appropriate, since Proudhon does not pretend to give a historical account as given by Marx. When he is consistent, Proudhon must hold that an account as far-reaching as Marx's is (in intent) im-possible. Proudhon must hold that Marx's attempt to give a "scien-tific," that is, material and historical, account of the transfor-mation to a new society rests on unknowable premises, since for Proudhon the essence of the transformation to a just order is the moral conversion of the worker, a conversion beyond material and historical explanations.

Thus, in evaluating Proudhon's position in relation to Marx, a conclusion similar to that of the evaluation of Stirner and Marx found in the previous chapter must be drawn. Proudhon and Marx be-gan from fundamentally different points, one essentially moral and ahistorical, the other material and historical. Given these funda-mental differences, the two thinkers could not have agreed to any great extent. For Proudhon, the key to social change was to be found in the transformation of the existing, distorted expressions of morality, of justice, and in the self-development of workers guided by an undistorted justice within the sphere of moral and at least limited economic freedom. For Marx, the key was in the transformation of the existing economic conditions, of the materi-al conditions, in order to transform society from one of class-based antagonisms to a classless society, an emancipated society. Both thought the elimination of the state was an important part of such change. For Proudhon, though, the state was a primary cause of injustice; for Marx, it was an expression of the existing economic conditions. The resulting differences in emphasis on the state and its elimination therefore must be unsurprising.

NOTES

1. Pierre-Joseph Proudhon, letter to Marx, May 17, 1846, in *Selected Writings of Pierre-Joseph Proudhon*, ed. Steward Edwards, trans. Elizabeth Fraser (New York: Anchor Books, 1969), p. 150.

2. Karl Marx, letter to L. Kugelmann, October 9, 1866, in *Anarchism and Anarcho-Syndicalism*, (New York: International Publishers, 1972), p. 43.

3. The former comment is from a letter dated September 1847, the latter from Proudhon's diary entry of September 23, 1847, both in George Woodcock, *Pierre-Joseph Proudhon, His Life and Work* (New York: Schocken Books, 1972), p. 102. These two comments by Proudhon do not refer to the comments by Marx cited immediately above. Rather, Proudhon had finished reading Marx's *Poverty of Philosophy*, presumably the explanation of his strong reaction to Marx.

4. See, for example, Robert L. Hoffman, *Revolutionary Justice: The Social and Political Theory of P.-J. Proudhon* (Urbana, Ill.: University of Illinois Press, 1972), p. 11; and Alan Ritter, "The Anarchist Justification of Authority," in *Nomos XIX: Anarchism*, ed. J. Roland Pennock and John W. Chapman (New York: New York University Press, 1978), pp. 130-140, esp. p. 131. Ritter apparently thinks that, in many senses, Godwin is also basic to modern anarchist thought, a view shared by others, including George Woodcock and James Joll.

5. See Paul Eltzbacher, *Anarchism: Exponents of the Anarchist Philosophy* (New York: Libertarian Book Club, 1960), p. 56.

6. James Joll, *The Anarchists* 2d ed. (Cambridge, Mass.: Harvard University Press, 1980), p. 46.

7. Proudhon seemed to relish and even cultivate the image of the lonely voice of justice, especially in his letters and notebooks. In one letter to Maguet dated August 16, 1848, Proudhon declares: "I am like the salamander, I live in fire. Abandoned, be-

trayed,   proscribed,   execrated   by   everyone,   I   resist   everyone. . . ." (from *Correspondence de P.-J. Proudhon*, vol. II, in
HOF, p. 119). In another letter: "I am more convinced than ever
that there is no place for me in this world, and I regard myself
as in a state of perpetual insurrection against the order of
things." (Ibid., p. 197.)

8.   Proudhon, *System of Economic Contradictions or the
Philosophy of Poverty*, vol. II, p. 310, in Joll, p. 47.

9. Ibid., SEC, vol. II. p. 361, in Joll, p. 48.

10. Joll, p. 50.

11. See, for example, Marx's letter to Kugelmann (October 9,
1866): "Proudhon did enormous mischief. His sham criticism and
sham opposition to the utopians (he himself is only a petty-bourgeois utopian. . . .)," in *Anarchism and Anarcho-Syndicalism*, p.
43; and Engels's letter to Marx (August 21, 1851): in reference to
Proudhon's book, *The General Idea of the Revolution in the 19th
Century*, which he was then reading, Engels commented that "I have
the impression that the whole thing is a last attempt to defend
the *bourgeoisie* theoretically." Ibid., p. 39.

12. Henri Mouguin, "Avant-propos" to Karl Marx, *Misère de la
philosophie* (Paris, 1961), p. 15, in Alan Ritter, *The Political
Thought of Pierre-Joseph Proudhon* (Princeton: Princeton University
Press, 1969), p. 6. The long and curious history of Proudhon's
alleged support of class collaboration will receive some attention
below.   Whatever the results of acting on Proudhonian principles
might be, the intent clearly is not class collaboration. Paul
Thomas has seen this, especially in regard to political activity:
"Political activity is class collaboration, pure and simple; to
resort to electioneering is fatally to accept the rules of a game
that need to be changed, the game itself scrubbed out." TKM, p.
17. With the one caveat that nothing is "pure and simple" with
Proudhon, I agree with Thomas.

13. See, for example, J.S. Schapiro, "Pierre-Joseph Proudhon,
Harbinger of Fascism," in *American Historical Review*, L (1945),
pp. 714-737. As a response, see Nicola Chiaromonte, "Pierre-Joseph
Proudhon: An Uncomfortable Thinker," in *Politics*, III (January
1946), pp. 27-29.

14. Robert L. Hoffman has put this point well (in HOF):
Proudhon, no less than others on the left, recognized and attacked the reactionary elements in Bonapartism and its conservative supporters. Because of his antipathy toward authority he could find no other virtue in the imperial system than the possibility of its facilitating transition to a libertarian regime. For this reason it is foolish or disingenuous to put him in a class with fascist ideologues. (P. 204.)

15. The basis for claiming Rousseau as a forerunner of anarchism is, in part, his endorsement of human rational capacities and, even more importantly, his idea of humans being free in their "natural" state. Both Proudhon and Kropotkin were inspired by Rousseau's declaration that "Man is born free, and yet we see him everywhere in chains. Those who believe themselves the masters of others cease not to be even greater slaves than the people they govern." Jean-Jacques Rousseau, *The Social Contract*, ed. Charles Frankel (New York: Hefner, 1954), p. 5. The point remains that Rousseau favored political change not, as Proudhon advocated, the elimination of politics in the course of a broad-based economic transformation. In a note to his discussion of real property, Rousseau's remarks illustrate this difference. After remarking that the social compact establishes "a moral and legal equality" where natural physical inequality prevails, thus equalizing by "convention and legal right," Rousseau admits that "[u]nder bad governments this equality is but an illusive appearance, which only serves to keep the poor in misery, and support the rich in their usurpations." (Ibid., p. 22 and n. 1.) Proudhon's point, and the point of all social anarchists, is that all government is bad in this sense and that under any government equality is illusory. Proudhon's later, bitter criticisms of Rousseau reflect his growing conviction of the cogency of this point.

As William L. McBride has noted, "Many trace the ancestry of a kind of anarchism to Rousseau's *Discourse on the Origin [and Foundations] of Inequality*, sharply *distinguishing* that [anarchism] from *The Social Contract*." (Private communication.) Pursuit of this point would take us too far afield.

16. See K. Codell Carter's Introduction to William Godwin

Enquiry Concerning Political Justice (London: Oxford University Press, 1971), xii: "Through William Thompson and other early socialists Godwin's influence extended, faintly but perceptibly, to Owen and beyond to Proudhon and Marx." This seems more accurate than Hoffman's claim that "Godwin . . . had little or no influence on the [anarchist] movement when it developed." HOF, p. 11. This seems rather odd, especially when one considers that Malthus wrote his Essay on the *Principle of Population* (1798) in part as a response to Godwin's egalitarianism and Condorcet's progressivism. Hoffman admits that Proudhon's own extensive attacks on Malthusian doctrine are isolated from Malthus's level of argumentation because Proudhon insisted on "fundamental principle[s]" and "ideals" rather than the crude pragmatism of Malthus. (P. 36.) It is just this insistence, at least in part, which links Godwin to Proudhon.

17. Godwin, in Joll, p. 17.

18. Godwin, *Enquiry Concerning Political Justice*, p. 242. Godwin's point here is that the universality and secrecy of the ballot encourages the feebleminded and weak to make their prejudices permanent and hide their actions. This is both hypocritical and detrimental to the public spirit, according to Godwin.

19. Ibid., p. 291.

20. Ibid., p. 292; see also Godwin's comments on national assemblies, p. 219.

21. Ibid., p. 13.

22. James Joll has suggested that this theory of the possibilities for social change rests on "a profoundly optimistic view of human nature. . . ." *The Anarchists*, p. 17. He is correct in this and in his observation that it requires a Humean style rejection of innate ideas. Godwin states that if we

[a]pply these considerations to the subject of politics . . . they will authorize us to infer, that the excellencies and defects of the human character, are not derived from causes beyond the reach of ingenuity to modify and correct. If we entertain false views and be involved in pernicious mistakes, this disadvantage is not the offspring of an irresistable destiny. (*Enquiry*, p. 35.)

Proudhon began his career with an almost identical view of human

nature,   differing in that he postulated an immanent sense of justice   in   human   conscience.   Though his optimism was never extin-
guished,   it was diminished, concomitant with a loss of confidence
in the powers of reason and education.

23. Godwin, p. 25, 93.

24.   Thomas Malthus, *Essay on the Principle of Population*, 2d
ed. (London, 1803), p. 53; in HOF, p. 35.

25. Both Godwin and Proudhon would object to my separation of
the   moral and the practical. Granting that it is a somewhat artificial distinction, it remains a useful analytical tool.

26.   Proudhon,   SEC,   vol. I.,   trans. Benjamin R. Tucker (New
York: Arno Press, 1972; reprint of edition of 1888), p. 67.

27.   Proudhon, *Justice in the Revolution and the Church*, vol.
II, in SWP, p. 50.

28.   Proudhon, *De l'Utilite de la Celebration du Dimanche*, in
HOF, p. 35.

29. See Joll, p. 19.

30. See, for example, Peter Kropotkin, *The Great French Revolution* (New   York: Schocken Books, 1971). Kropotkin's (and Proudhon's)   emphasis   on   the   importance   of   the Revolution must be
tempered   by   the realization that the Revolution was completed by
and   for   the   supporters of mere political reform, mere political
equality;   economic   equality   was not their primary goal, nor was
property considered an obstacle to the Revolution. With the exception   of the *Enragés* and the impact of some of Marat's statements,
the   course of the Revolution was oriented toward the bourgeoisie.
Proudhon   recognized as much in his later criticisms of the French
Revolutionary   tradition,   especially   those statements concerning
Jacobinism and the influence of Rousseau.

31.   Pierre-Joseph   Proudhon, *The General Idea of the Revolution   in   the Nineteenth Century*, trans. J. B. Robinson (New York:
Haskell House Publishers, 1969), p. 292.

32.   George   Woodcock gives just such an interesting account.
See Woodcock, pp. 1-35. It is possible to overstate the importance
of   Proudhon's   childhood,   as James Joll does when he claims that
Proudhon's   writings   show   a   "nostalgia" for a vanished, simpler
society   peopled   by   "sturdy,   independent,   self-supporting

peasants." (Joll, p. 46.) Proudhon was influenced by his peasant origins, as he freely admitted, but not to the point of longing for an illusory rustic utopia. In fact, Proudhon claimed that no such society ever existed. See esp. Pierre-Joseph Proudhon, *What Is Property? An Inquiry into the Principle of Right and Government*, trans. Benjamin R. Tucker with a new introduction by George Woodcock (New York: Dover Publications, 1970; reprint of 1890 edition), pp. 254-256.

33. Proudhon, in Woodcock, p. 4.

34. Proudhon, letter to Just Muiron, ibid., p. 21. Hoffman states that the letter might be from 1832 (HOF, p. 28, note 8).

35. Woodcock, p. 27.

36. Proudhon criticized this essay in letters to Tissot (1842) and Bergman (1845); see HOF, p. 29, note 10.

37. Proudhon, in Woodcock, p. 30.

38. Proudhon, "Lettre de candidature à la Pension Suard," in HOF, p. 30.

39. HOF, p. 30.

40. Woodcock, p. 39.

41. Ibid. See also HOF, p. 37. Proudhon's claims against Malthus here and elsewhere (see note 15 above) are, in a curious fashion, also claims against Rousseau. Proudhon advocated the rule of moral law guided by reason rather than the rule of a monar-chical, democratic, or otherwise general will. Under the rule of will, basic human rights are often endangered by support for other rights, especially property rights (or so Proudhon held). In de-fense of Rousseau, Proudhon's claims show an incomplete under-standing of the nature and function of the general will. As Rousseau claimed, it is under bad governments that equalty is il-lusory. Presumably, under a good government, the expression of the general will would serve to promote genuine equality and the social good.

42. See, for example, Marx, "Communism and the Augsburg *Allgemeine Zeitung*," (first published October 16, 1842, in the *Rheinische Zeitung*), in *MECW* I, p. 220: "Such writings as the sharp-witted work by Proudhon [*What Is Property?*], cannot be criticized on the basis of superficial flashes of thought, but

only after long and profound study." In 1843 Engels hailed Proudhon as the most important French writer tending toward communism:
"[*What Is Property?*] is the most philosophical work, on the part
of the Communists, in the French language. . . ." "Progress of
Social Reform on the Continent," (first published in *The New Moral
World*, November 4 and 18, 1843), in *MECW* III, p. 399. Engels goes
on to praise Proudhon's anti-government remarks. Marx and Engels
gave qualified support to Proudhon's work as a first step, as "the
criticism of *political economy* from the standpoint of political
economy," in *The Holy Family*, in *MECW* IV, pp. 23-54, esp. p. 31.
What has not been generally recognized is that all of Marx's
favorable comments dealing with *What Is Property?* are qualified;
even in his early works Marx was quite critical of Proudhon's
unexamined assumptions. The one exception to this unqualified support is not Marx's: it is the support given by Engels in the passage cited above.

43. Jérome-Adolphe Blanqui, letter Proudhon (May 1, 1841), in
WIP, p. 7.

44. Ibid., p. 8.

45. Proudhon, Preface to WIP, p. 9. What Proudhon means by
"property" will become clear in the analysis of *What Is Property?*
One good example of Proudhon's sense of the abuse of property as
theft is found in John Steinbeck's novel, *East of Eden*. When one
of the sons (Cal) of the protagonist speculates on commodities fu-
tures during World War I and offers the profits to his father, his
father refuses the money: "'You'll have to give it back. . . .'
'Give it back? Give it back to who?' 'To the people you got it
from.' 'To the British Purchasing Agency? They can't take it
back. . . .' 'Then give it to the farmers you robbed.'" John
Steinbeck, *East of Eden* (New York: Viking Press, 1952), p. 543.
The abuse involved here was the manipulation of the farm price
through the power of accumulated capital.

46. Proudhon, WIP, p. 10.

47. Blaise Pascal, *The Thoughts of Blaise Pascal* (New York:
Dolphin Books, n.d.), *pensée* 295, p. 105.

48. Proudhon, WIP, p. 14.

49. Ibid.

50. Proudhon's faith in the power of enlightenment is based in part on his conception of this sense of justice he thought present in each person. He thought that

all men believe and repeat that equality of conditions is identical with equality of rights; that *property* and *robbery* are synonymous terms; that every social advantage accorded, or rather usurped, in the name of superior talent or service, is iniquity and extortion. All men in their hearts, I say, bear witness to these truths; they need only to be made to understand it. (WIP, p. 15.)

51. Ibid., p. 24.

52. Ibid., p. 26.

53. Ibid., p. 33. Proudhon concludes that the democratic "revolution" is no revolution at all; though democracy is progress, as it increases the chance that reason will take the place of will, the principle of sovereignty remains intact. Thus, "with the most perfect democracy, we cannot be free." (Ibid.) Proudhon did not, as Marx and others claimed, favor a Bonapartist style autocracy if the true social revolution was delayed or crippled. Though he later professed indifference as to the existing form of the state, these statements are tempered by his frequent affirmations that democracy is at least progress.

54. Ibid., p. 37.

55. Proudhon does mention Locke in WIP, in an obscure remark unrelated to the connection between property and labor. See p. 155.

56. Ibid., p. 103.

57. Proudhon exaggerates this point. What he comes close to showing is not that labor as the basis of property is a contradiction or even unworkable; what he should have said (and did in other places) is that a practical contradiction of the type he described exists in the capitalist economic system. It is possible to imagine, as was the case with Fourier's phalansterianism (and, to some extent, with the Saint-Simonians), a communal organization in which private property is preserved and labor is given its "due." As Proudhon (see WIP, pp. 121-128)--and Marx--showed, however, this is only an ideal.

58. WIP, p. 118.

59. Ibid., p. 45.

60. Ibid., p. 115.

61. Ibid., p. 149.

62. Ibid., p. 167. "Like the insect which spins its silk, the laborer never produces for himself alone. Property, demanding a double product and unable to obtain it, robs the laborer, and kills him." (P. 222.)

63. Ibid., p. 207.

64. Ibid., p. 221.

65. Ibid., p. 231 (emphases omitted).

66. Ibid., p. 243.

67. Ibid., pp. 260, 261.

68. See the passage cited in note 45 above.

60. WIP, p. 261.

70. Ibid., p. 271.

71. A comparison of the important themes of WIP with those of the posthumously published *Theory of Property* (1863-1864) reveals the consistency of Proudhon's moral vision. In the latter work he affirms the themes of WIP while emphasizing the need for mutualism, free contract, and the defense of equal possession. See SWP, pp. 125-143.

72. Professor Larry May has noted some of the similarities between Locke and Proudhon in "The Proudhonian Proviso: Scarcity and Property Rights," (unpublished manuscript), though he stresses the role of scarcity in Proudhon's critique of property rather than the moral demand for an egalitarian distribution of goods. See also Ritter, *The Political Thought*, pp. 17-23.

73. Alan Ritter (*The Political Thought*, pp. 30-33) overstates the change in Proudhon's conception of the efficacy of the sense of justice. Proudhon did not fully support the claim that humans are egoistic hedonists, though there are passages where he seems to imply this view. Had Proudhon fully supported the egoistic hedonist view, his moral vision--his basis for social change-- would have collapsed. Rather, Proudhon's emphasis on the power of egoism increased his moral fervor, since the need to strengthen the moral fiber of the worker had increased. Conscience could

still prevail, if only the rational basis of justice could be demonstrated to the individual.

74. Proudhon, SEC, vol. I., pp. 417, 429; translation amended slightly to that of SWP, p. 232.

75. Proudhon, *Carnets VII*, in Ritter, p. 51. In an earlier work, Proudhon makes a similar point (from *The Creation of Order in Humanity*, 1843): "Society is perpetually creating order. From the very first it traced a furrow which we cannot leave with impunity. Thus we must calculate its direction and its end if we are to continue successfully in the work which we began under God's very guidance." (SWP, p. 236.) This theme continued to dominate Proudhon's thought, especially in his later life. One of the last works published during his lifetime was an exposition of the theme of social progress in history, *The Philosophy of Progress* (1853). In this work and in *Justice in the Revolution and the Church* (1858), Proudhon remained optimistic about the course of history. Though Proudhon's optimism was shaken in his later years, charges that he became a pessimistic reactionary are unfounded, as is shown by a letter written near the end of his life:

> If everything only demonstrated to me that society has entered a crisis of regeneration, which will be long and perhaps terrible, I would believe in the irrevocable decadence and approaching end of civilization. But it is necessary to believe that we will emerge from it, precisely because our contemporaries are more dissolute and less intelligent than we were. The movement of history occurs by oscillations whose amplitude it is up to us to attenuate. (Letter to Millet, November 2, 1862, in HOF, p.281.

76. HOF, p. 280.

77. Proudhon, Letter to Millet, November 2, 1862, in HOF, p. 281.

78. See passage cited in note 52 above.

79. What Joll actually wrote was that "Proudhon, in fact, falls back on his early reading of Kant's moral philosophy, and his society rests on the categorical imperative. . . ." (P. 59.) Proudhon uses the primary norm of justice in much the same way that Kant used the categorical imperative, but the two principles

differ. Proudhon's principle of justice is more concrete than Kant's imperative; for Proudhon, justice as reciprocity entails certain particular obligations--it is more than just a test of possible maxims.

80. See Eltzbacher, p. 56.

81. See Plato, *Euthyphro* in *The Collected Dialogues of Plato*, ed. Edith Hamilton and Huntington Cairns (Princeton, N.J.: Princeton University Press, 1961); and Gregory Vlastos, ed., *The Philosophy of Socrates* (New York: Anchor Books, 1971), pp. 12-15.

82. On Hume's account "Every individual person must find himself a gainer, on balancing the account; since, without justice, society must immediately dissolve, and every one must fall into the savage and solitary condition, which is infinitely worse than the worst situation that can possibly be suppos'd in society." David Hume, *A Treatise of Human Nature*, ed. L.A. Selby-Bigge, rev. P.H. Nidditch (Oxford: Clarendon Press, 1978), p. 497. Though it cannot be argued here, I have argued elsewhere in support of Barry Stroud's rejoinder to Hume: "What reason is there to suppose that it [every individual finding himself a gainer] is so?" Barry Stroud, *Hume* (Boston: Routledge and Kegan Paul, 1977), p. 208. See Jeffrey H. Barker, "Hume on the Pre-Social State," *Auslegung* X:3 (Winter 1983), pp. 185-193. In any event, Proudhon's social psychology precluded this sort of explanation, since on Proudhon's account we are not completely egoistic.

83. Proudhon, *Justice in the Revolution and the Church*, vol. I, p. 325, in Alan Ritter, *The Political Thought*, p. 80.

84. Proudhon, SEC, vol. I, pp. 410-411, in SWP, p. 57.

85. Proudhon, *On the Political Capacity of the Working Classes*, in SWP, p. 60.

86. Proudhon, *General Idea of the Revolution in the Nineteenth Century*, p. 112.

87. Proudhon, *Justice in the Revolution and the Church*, vol. IV, in Alan Ritter, *The Political Thought*, p. 149. See also *Justice* IV, pp. 276-79 and p. 302, in SWP, pp. 254-257. At one point Proudhon states, "Man and woman together . . . form one organic whole composed to two persons. . . . The aim of this organism is to create Justice by stimulating consciousness, . . . by encourag-

ing the ideal that theologians call grace and poets love." (SWP, p. 254.)

88. Voline [Vsévolod Mikhailovtch Eichenbaum], *The Unknown Revolution, 1917-1921*, in Daniel Guérin, *Anarchism from Theory to Practice* (New York: Monthly Review Press, 1970), p. 26.

89. There is a sympathetic account of the essence of Proudhon's vision in Martin Buber, *Paths in Utopia*, trans. R.F.C. Hall (Boston: Beacon Press, 1958), pp. 24-37. Buber's account distorts only in its overemphasis on the importance of interpersonal relationships in Proudhon's thought.

90. TKM, p. 181.

91. Every account of Proudhon that I have read attempts to "solve" this "problem." A thorough listing of such articles can be found in HOF, pp. 86-91, esp., notes 5-27.

92. Ibid., p. 87.

93. See, for example, Karl Marx, "Letters from *Deutsch-Französische Jahrbücher*," (written in late 1843), in *MECW* III, p. 143; see also note 42 above.

94. See Peter N. Stearns, *Revolutionary Syndicalism and French Labor* (New Brunswick, N.J.: Rutgers University Press, 1971), pp. 9-13 and 100-102. Stearns comments: "Proudhon's thinking dominated French labor movements in the third quarter of the nineteenth century and syndicalism was in many ways the logical successor. (P. 11.)

95. Marx, *MECW* III p. 142.

96. Marx, *1844 Manuscripts*, in *MECW* III, p. 280.

97. Ibid.

98. Ibid.

99. Marx to Feuerbach, August 11, 1844, in *MECW* III, p. 356; in the text, Marx writes "σοφος ."

100. Ibid.

101. Marx-Engels, *The Holy Family*, in *MECW* IV, p. 33.

102. Ibid., p. 32.

103. Ibid., p. 42.

104. Ibid., p. 50.

105. Paul Thomas (TKM) has misunderstood Proudhon's idea of contract and so misunderstood the impact of Marx's criticism on

this point. Thomas--citing George Plekhanov's *Marxism and Anarchism*--claims that Proudhon's "solution" to the contradiction of a compelled "free" contract in capitalist society is "simply that of its [contract's] restitution, so that the freedom of the contracting parties, which had been revealed as a myth, would fulfill its promise by being made real." (P. 202.) As with most claims of simplicity in Proudhon's program, this is not accurate. Contract could only be free under certain specific conditions, as discussed in the previous section of this chapter. Both Thomas and Plekhanov fail to see the real impact of Marx's criticism of Proudhon's idea of contract: it is in the contractual relationship itself that the estrangement of man from man is expressed. Proudhon does not deal with this more basic problem, though he certainly did not support a simple restitution of contract.

106. Karl Marx, *Capital*, vol. I, trans. Samuel Moore and Edward Aveling, ed. Friedrich Engels (New York: International Publishers, 1967), p. 68, n. 1. See also p. 587, where Marx discusses the sale of labor-power as a commodity and the resulting development of capitalist production and appropriation.

107. The text of Marx's letter and Proudhon's reply are reprinted in SWP, pp. 147-154.

108. Marx to Proudhon, May 5, 1846, in SWP, p. 147.

109. Proudhon to Marx, May 17, 1846, ibid., pp. 150-152.

110. Marx to Annenkov, December 28, 1846, in *The Poverty of Philosophy* (Moscow: Progress Publishers, 1955), p. 155.

111. Ibid., p. 156.

112. Ibid., p. 160.

113. Ibid., p. 165.

114. Ibid., p. 166.

115. See Proudhon, SEC, vol. I, p. 80. See Proudhon's note on communism, p. 81.

116. Marx, *The Poverty of Philosophy*, p. 36.

117. Ibid., p. 37.

118. Ibid., p. 43.

119. Ibid., p. 54.

120. Proudhon, SEC, vol. I, pp. 109-110.

121. Marx, *The Poverty of Philosophy*, p. 72.

122. Ibid., p. 95.

123. Ibid.

124. Ibid., p. 104.

125. Ibid., p. 151.

126. Ibid., p. 152. Marx quotes George Sand's introduction to the novel *Jean Žiska. Episodé da la guerre des hussites. Introduction.* (Bruxelles, 1843): "Combat or death: bloody struggle or extinction. It is thus that the question is inexorably put." Trans. in text, n. 50, p. 201.

127. See HOF, p. 99.

128. Proudhon, SEC, vol. I, p. 62.

5
INDIVIDUALISM AND COMMUNITY: STATE, SOCIETY AND THE INDIVIDUAL

Finally, I choose liberty. For even if justice is not realized, liberty maintains the power of protest against injustice and keeps communication open. Justice in a silent world,
the justice of mute men, destroys complicity, negates revolt,
and restores consent, but in the lowest possible form.

Albert Camus[1]

LIBERTY AND AUTHORITY

Max Stirner's obscure, and in later years, pitiful life, an ob-
scurity broken only by the publication of *The Ego and Its Own*,
ended in 1856, reportedly due to the bite of a poisonous fly.
Stirner's funeral was as solitary as his life; Bruno Bauer and a
few others attended.[2] As the last step in the progression from
Hegelian idealism to an extreme individualism, Stirner's influence
ended long before his death. As the last of the "Young Hegelians"
(with the exception of Karl Schmidt), Stirner represents the isolation of Hegelian thought in a moment of abstract particularity,
an egoism no less abstract for its creator's claims to a "concrete" methodology and result.

The end of Stirner's immediate influence was not the end of
individualist anarchism, however. *The Ego and His Own* reemerged
late in the nineteenth century as an alleged forerunner of Fried-

rich Nietzsche and one of the precursors of modern individualism. Stirner was not a forerunner of Nietzsche or Nietzschean thought; the coincidence of terms and concerns found in the works of the two thinkers is less a harmony of views than the influence of the *Zeitgeist*.[3] The American individualist Benjamin R. Tucker published the first English language edition of Stirner's work in 1907, exposing Stirner's egoism to a much larger audience. Editions in several other languages spread Stirnerian doctrine throughout Europe. Stirner's ultimate influence can be traced through the early and mid-twentieth century as a powerful--even iconic--influence on the development of libertarianism. It is ironic that the extremism of Stirner should become the intellectual wellspring of such a socially, politically, and economically conservative movement, where private property is held as sacrosanct and political activism is seen as a legitimate avenue of change.

The period following Proudhon's 1865 death saw the fortunes of anarchism oscillate as charismatic leaders led splinter movements within the anarchist camp. The two most important of these leaders, Michael Bakunin and Peter Kropotkin, each carried the tradition of Stirner and especially Proudhon in vastly differing directions. Bakunin's collectivist theory incorporated many of Marx's more general notions but remained a fundamentally anti-authoritarian, anarchist doctrine, marked more by its emphasis on the direct action of "propaganda by the deed" than by a Marxian style scientific analysis of society. As distinctly social forms of anarchism, however, the specific doctrines of Bakunin and Kropotkin are beyond the scope of this work. It is enough to state that within the different currents of anarchism in the period following Proudhon's death, an opposition to Marx's developed communist theory as well as to the growing power of the industrial, capitalist state joined an otherwise disparate group of social theories and theorists. During this period anarchism had a broad back indeed.

Stirner and Proudhon serve as the two most important exponents of the philosophical doctrine of anarchism. From their ideas came the two main currents of anarchist thought, the individualist

or, to use more modern terminology, libertarian anarchism of
Stirner and the communitarian or social anarchism of Proudhon.
Despite Proudhon's emphasis on the social aspects of his theory,
however, he remains within the individualist tradition of anarchism (if not within the modern form of libertarianism) as a result of his consistent support of the essential concerns of individualist anarchism, especially his support of the primacy of individual liberty and individual moral change as the basis of
social change. Thus, while recognizing Proudhon's unique contributions to anarchist theory, his position and legacy in the conflict
between Marxian thought and anarchism is roughly comparable to
that of Stirner.

Both the egoism of Stirner and the more social anarchism of
Proudhon were represented in the post-1865 struggle between Marx
and anarchism and between Marxian thought and anarchism. The more
social anarchism of Proudhon and its syndicalist offshoots became
the focus of attention for Marx and most other anarchists, however, as Proudhonism was far more influential among many of the
workers in their early attempts at an organized solidarity.

Though this concluding chapter cannot deal with the entire
legacy of Stirner and Proudhon and the conflicts of their heirs
with Marx and Marxism, a brief review and discussion of the basic
principles and points of contact and conflict between anarchism
and Marxian thought will allow some general and preliminary conclusions concerning the role of state and society in the historical and philosophical conflict between Marx and early anarchism.
Such conclusions are preliminary in that they serve as a prelude
to a careful, critical, ongoing consideration of the post-Prou-
dhonian historical and philosophical conflict between anarchism
(libertarian and otherwise) and Marxism, a conflict still evident
in many of the principles underlying current ideological trends.

Stirner and Proudhon viewed the state as a relatively independent entity exercising an illegitimate and destructive power in
society. Where Proudhon saw the dismantling of the state and its
apparatus as a necessary but not sufficient step in transforming
society, Stirner held that the complete and immediate destruction
of state authority by autonomous egoists asserting their unique-

ness was necessary and sufficient for "radical" social change. For Proudhon as well radical change required the element of individually willed change, though that change was a personal moral transformation, the emergence of the natural sense of justice inherent in his optimistic view of human nature rather than an individualist auto-emancipation. Where Proudhon saw this as requiring and required by the "just order," Stirner opposed any such order as inimical to the unique ego. What joins the two views is the emphasis on the role of individual will and the power of that will to effect change. This emphasis could not help but bring them into conflict with Marx.

Marx did not and, given his specifically historical and materialist framework, could not grant such emphasis to the role and power of individually willed attempts at truly radical social change. Proudhon opposed any attempt to organize the working class and its revolution beyond the cooperative structure of workshops and factories joined in voluntary and non-coercive associations. He held that any centralized party attempting to organize and lead the working class toward social change inevitably dominates and contaminates the workers, since the leadership of such a party inevitably uses authoritarian means to maintain its control. In style similar to that used by Mohandas Gandhi in his struggles against the British Raj, the anarchists (especially Proudhon) emphasized the practical connection between the means used and the end achieved. As Gandhi stated in a reply to an inquiry concerning means and ends: "Your belief that there is no connection between the means and the end is a great mistake. Through that mistake even men who have been considered religious [Proudhon could have added, 'or revolutionary'] have committed grievous crimes. Your reasoning is the same as saying that we can get a rose through planting a noxious weed."[4]

Indeed, one could argue that the nature of social transformations is such that organized, widespread change requires authoritarian means and thus results, inevitably, in authoritarian ends. Engels conceded the premise of such an argument in his polemical works against the anarchists. At one point in his essay "On Authority" Engels declares that:

Whoever mentions combined action speaks of organization; now, is it possible to have organization without authority? . . . Have these gentlemen [the "anti-authoritarians"] ever seen a revolution? A revolution is certainly the most authoritarian thing there is; it is the act whereby one part of the population imposes its will upon the other part by means of rifles, bayonets, and cannon--authoritarian means, if such there be at all; and if the victorious party does not wish to have fought in vain, it must maintain this rule by means of the terror which its arms inspire in the reactionaries.[5]

Ignoring for the moment the simplistic character of Engels's analysis, his description of "the most authoritarian thing there is" grants the anarchists a significant point. Since any revolutionary "transitional state" uses centralized authority in order to establish and maintain the revolution, it is inherently flawed, according to the anarchists. Stirner, the most uncompromising of individualists, asserted that this was an inherent feature of any human organization beyond the level of a vaguely defined "association" of egoists. Proudhon's desire for justice and belief in an inherent sociality in individual humans allowed him to foresee a greater degree of self-organization of the workers. Still, Proudhon agreed with Stirner that any attempt at the type of organization characteristic of political states (and revolutions) could only lead to a solidified and more centralized permanent state, whether or not that state began life as a "transitory" phenomenon or device. All states are illegitimate, the anarchists held, since any use of authority in their organization--a necessary feature of states, as Engels noted--could only result in an authoritarian product.

On these issues--the issues of the concentration of power and authority necessary in revolutionary activity and the creation of the transitional organizations and the methodological coherence and practical efficacy of individually based change--Marx and the early anarchists were bound to clash. These issues played a significant role in the dispute between Marx and Bakunin and thus helped to destroy the first International Working Men's Association, though the role of the Marx-Bakunin clash has been overstated while the influence of the demise of the Paris Commune has been understated. The core of these disputes between Marx and the early anarchists can been seen in one of Marx's comments on Bakunin's role in the International Alliance of Social Democracy:

> Anarchy, then is the great war-horse of their master Bakunin, who has taken nothing from the socialist systems except a set of slogans. What all the socialists understand by anarchy is this: once the aim of the proletarian movement, the abolition of classes, has been attained, the power of the State, which serves to keep the great majority of producers under the yoke of a numerically small exploiting minority, disappears, and the functions of government are transformed into simple ad-ministrative functions. The Alliance puts matters the other way round. It proclaims anarchy in the proletarian ranks as the surest means of breaking the powerful concentration of social and political forces in the hands of the exploiters. Under this pretext it demands of the International, at the very moment when the old world is seeking to crush it, that it should replace its organization by anarchy. . . .[6]

This statement brings into sharp relief the source of a large part of the debate between Marx and the anarchists. For Marx, freedom is not something abstract possessed by an isolated self, needing only to be "unchained" by the realization of its unique nature (as in Stirner's view) or by a personal, moral transforma-tion (as in Proudhon's view). Marx's concept of freedom is far more complex, since the development of individual freedom for Marx is intimately connected to the transformations of the existing material conditions of life within capitalist society. For the an-archists, on the other hand, freedom or liberty is an absolute or near absolute, preexisting aspect of human nature, no matter how unfree the particular society in which humans live. This rather abstract concept of freedom results in the view, at least for Proudhon, that humans need only to be liberated from the coarser external constraints of the political state in order to develop their own free (and for Proudhon "just") natures. The new anar-chist world would be loosely federated, decentralized, and in all cases would avoid authoritarian institutions and practices which

might reintroduce the bondage of the political state in another
guise.

For Marx, Stirner and Proudhon had turned the social revolution on its head. The liberty that they proclaimed inherent in humans, needing only to be released from political (and for Stirner,
"moral") structures, in fact could be developed only in the absence of those material conditions engendered by the capitalist
economic system, the characteristic feature of which Marx had isolated as class society. For Marx, the truly radical revolution
aimed at transforming these material conditions so as to eliminate
the type of authority needed and created by them. Marx held that
the political state is the organized expression of those conditions, serving to perpetuate those conditions and eventually
disappearing with the transformation of those conditions. The type
of authority characteristic of political states in capitalist
society would be transformed as well, since such authority would
be both no longer needed and no longer created.

The specific conflicts between Marx, Stirner, and Proudhon
concerning authority in the political state illuminate the differences between early anarchism and Marxian thought on the
general issue of authority. For all anarchists and especially for
Stirner and Proudhon, authority is inherently destructive, its
exercise inherently alienating, and its institutionalization in
any political or economic structure a fatal blow to liberty. The
early anarchists thought that authoritarian means would produce
authoritarian needs because they saw authority as a uniform, homogeneous phenomenon, a deviation and (for Proudhon) a perversion of
the reign of liberty. These anarchists viewed the institutionalization of any authority as synonymous with the creation of an en-
trenched power base for the attempted domination of otherwise free
beings.

The only exceptions to the anarchist position on authority,
exceptions found in varying degrees in Godwin, Proudhon, Bakunin,
and Kropotkin (but conspicuously absent in Stirner) allow for the
use of public censure as a means of maintaining order and effi-
ciency. These anarchists held that, though each person should
decide important public issues on the basis of his or her own de-

liberation on the exercise of their own rational faculties, not all people are knowledgeable about all things and thus each should accept the expert advice of others in appropriate situations. Proudhon, in particular, accepted this compromise with authority. The "authority" of some should be accepted and backed by the threat of public censure not because of the personal power of any individual, not because of an individual's economic status, nor because of any threat of actual force. Rather, authority could be legitimate only in those cases where one person possesses a special competence which others lack, whether that competence be technical or intellectual. Even in these cases, however, the scope of authority is severely restricted and is never extended into the sphere of basic public policy decisions. In this sphere the anarchists held that no one person possesses a special competence. All rational, mature humans (with certain chauvinistic exceptions for some of the anarchists) are equally competent in this area. In the sphere of public policy, each is to have equal and reciprocal "authority" or "sovereignty," though these terms lose their ordinary significance in such a context.

For Marx and Engels, on the other hand, the fact of authority was less of a problem than was the exercise of authority in the existing authoritarian economic structures of capitalist society. For Marx, authority was not a uniform, homogeneous phenomenon but a multifaceted aspect of the existing structures of a given society. The structure of capitalist society, exhibited in its class nature, does utilize authority in a number of very different ways. Authority serves to maintain the rule of capital and to maintain the governmental structures necessary to a capitalist society. This use of authority Marx thought alienating and destructive. Still, he did not hold that any use of authority, in its many different manifestations, would be equally destructive. Rather, the destructiveness of authority results not from its inherent nature but from its particular form and use within the capitalist economic order. The use of authority within a revolution or revolutionary society Marx thought a practical necessity; the disorder of a "non-authoritarian" revolution would result in wasted effort. To abstain from authority in the revolution would be both wasteful and simplistic, Marx held, as such a view presupposes that all instances of "authority" are of the same type, with the same purpose, and of equal effect. Engels put this point quite well in a letter to Carlo Cafiero, where Engels criticized Bakunin's denunciation of authority and Bakunin's Proudhonist advocacy of abstention from politics: "In his opinion all political acts are 'authoritarian.' But how he hopes the present political oppression and the tyranny of capital will be broken . . . without 'authoritarian acts' he does not explain."[7] Engels later explains that the end of oppression demands the abolition of classes, and this in turn requires "the political dominion of the proletariat."[8] Marx made the same point in his letter to Friedrich Bolte: "The political movement of the working class has as its ultimate object . . . the conquest of political power for this class. . . ."[9] For Marx and Engels, anarchist denunciations of authority in general showed an ignorance of important distinctions in the types and uses of authority and an even more important ignorance of real economic conditions, especially ignorance of the need for authority of a non-alienating sort in large-scale economic activity. And, as the final irony, the anarchist general condemnation of authority within the revolutionary movement doomed that movement to impotence and ultimate failure, a fact Marx and Engels considered amply demonstrated in aspects of the collapse of the Paris Commune.[10]

In their conflicting positions on liberty and authority, Marx and the early anarchists brought together the elements of the conflict concerning the role of the state in the new society. In Marx's *Critique of the Gotha Programme*, his position on the role of the state and state authority in the revolution receives a thorough examination. A brief look at some of the more important points of Marx's *Critique* will aid in the evaluation of the conflict between Marx and the anarchists.

One of the more striking aspects of Marx's view of the state and state authority as put forward in the *Critique* is its similarity to and continuity with the accounts of the state, authority, and alienation found in his earlier works, especially in "On the Jewish Question" and the *1844 Manuscripts*. In the early works,

written more than thirty years prior to the *Critique*, Marx had emphasized the need for a complete, human emancipation rather than
mere political emancipation. This human emancipation would regain
control of the economic forces of society so that the alienation
resulting from capitalist economics and culture (as well as political life) could be eliminated; in place of the alienating forces
of capitalist society and its political expression, the state,
Marx advocated the assertion of a non-alienating control of or
authority over economic (and thus, at least initially, political)
life. In the *Critique*, Marx extended this point in such a way as
to explicate the differences between his program and that of other
socialists, including the programs of the social anarchists in the
tradition of Proudhon. The language of alienation and human emancipation is absent from the *Critique*, but the core of Marx's
theory is consistent. Though the *Critique* is directed at the fol-
lowers of Lassalle and their allies, much of it is applicable to
early anarchism generally and Proudhon in particular.

Marx's criticisms of the Lassallean Program are put forward
in order to develop some essential points Marx thought ignored by
the program. In its examination of the relationship between labor
and the development of wealth and poverty, the program ignored an
essential proposition: "In proportion as labor develops socially,
and becomes thereby a source of wealth and culture, poverty and
neglect develop among the workers, and wealth and culture among
the non-workers."[11]

What the Lassalleans ignored was the historical development
of the material and social conditions of life which resulted in
capitalist society and its failure to develop social labor as the
source of a truly human culture and wealth. This same development
(or lack of development) has made possible the transformation of
capitalist society, according to Marx, though only as the workers
themselves change the existing economic conditions. The Gotha Program, in treating "labor" and "society" abstractly, failed to give
a concrete, scientific statement of the existing social conditions
and thus could not give an accurate account of what needed to be
done--namely the transformation of the existing conditions of capitalism by the workers. This is the same type of criticism that

Marx advances against the anarchists, that they fail to deal with
in the real, material conditions of life and thus give only vague
and abstract accounts of social change.

This similarity between the Gotha Program and the position of
the anarchists becomes clearer in Marx's critique of the third
paragraph of the first section of the Gotha Program. In the third
paragraph, the program states that "The emancipation of labor demands the promotion of the instruments of labor to the common
property of society, and the co-operative regulation of the total
labor with equitable distribution of the proceeds of labor."[12]
The vagueness of the proposition becomes evident when the key
terms, the "proceeds of labor" and "equitable distribution," are
carefully examined. What Marx demanded was a concrete statement of
the nature of the proceeds of labor and what was meant by "equitable." In the case of "equitable distribution," Marx pointed out
that capitalists consider their distribution "equitable," given
the capitalist mode of production. What the Gotha Program's use of
"equitable distribution" ignores, according to Marx, is that,
rather than the legal concept of an equitable distibution being
able to govern or formulate economic relations, the "legal relations arise from economic ones."[13] It is misleading to treat legal
relations either as governing economic relations or as largely
separate from economic relations. For Marx, the economic relations
in fact give rise to the legal and political forms of society.
This is a point, according to Marx elsewhere, that the anarchists
fail to realize. In his attacks on Proudhon and Bakunin, Marx
criticizes this tendency to see legal, political, and cultural
relations as independent of economic relations or as governing
economic relations. This is not to claim that Marx saw the relationship between economic relations and legal, political, and cultural relations as one of unidirectional and unicausal determinism
of the "economic determination" of the latter set of relations.
It is this sort of simplistic explanation against which Marx
argued. For the early anarchists, the direction of the causal
chain of oppression moved from the political, legal, and social to
the economic--another unidirectional and unicausal explanation, a
"political determinism" of sorts. This historical and methodologi-

cal defect common to the Gotha Program and the anarchists is another aspect of differing perspectives on the state.

Marx then deals with the Gotha Program's abstract demand for the "proceeds of labor" to return, in undiminished form, to the laborer, a demand quite similar to Proudhon's position. The point of Marx's criticism is this: in the ideas of the Gotha Program, the vague demand for an "undiminished return" ignores the deductions from the "proceeds of labor" needed in order to maintain a society based on commodity exchange, as Marx noted earlier in his *Critique*. Even though the Gotha Program envisions a society based on the "instruments of production" being converted into common property, this society remains locked in the principles of commodity exchange, of "*equal right*," of "*bourgeois right*."[14] In the Lassallean conception, commodity exchange is retained and purified, as an "equal right" to a proportional amount of the proceeds of labor for consumption as one supplies labor. One gets, roughly, what one gives, according to an equal right or standard. The problem with this, as Marx saw it, was that such a standard recognizes and perpetuates the inequalities resulting from the inequality of endowments and talents: "*It is therefore a right of inequality in its content, like every right.*"[15]

Marx thought that the problems of "equal right" were inevitable in the first stage of the transformation to a communist society, though he did not see this stage as the eventual result of the transformation, as did the Gotha Program. In the *Critique*, Marx stresses the fact that a communist society arises out of a capitalist society; and thus the emerging communist society is marked by the economic, moral, and intellectual structures of the old capitalist order. In this "lower phase" of communism, the demand for equality (as a bourgeois right) remains an important part of society. As Lenin commented:

> If we are not to fall into utopianism, we must not think that having overthrown capitalism people will at once work for society *without any standard of right*; besides, the abolition of capitalism *does not immediately create* the economic prerequisites for *such* a change. And there is no other standard than that of "bourgeois right." To this extent, therefore,

there still remains the need for a state. . . .[16]
Marx comments succinctly: "Right can never be higher than the economic structure of society and the cultural development thereby
determined."[17]

In the higher phase of communism, according to Marx, these
limitations or "defects" would be overcome, since the alienating
effects (though Marx does not use the terminology of alienation in
the *Critique*) of the division of labor and other debilitating effects of capitalist society would be overcome. Once the economic
structure and the cultural development of capitalism is transcended, then "can the narrow horizon of bourgeois right be fully
left behind and society inscribe on its banners: from each according to his ability, to each according to his needs!"[18]

One of the errors of the early social anarchists, including
Proudhon, is in treating "equality" and the "undiminished proceeds
of labor" as abstract concepts, separated from the material conditions of the capitalist system. In doing so these anarchists made
the same mistake that Marx found in the Gotha Program. Marx's
point here--one of extreme importance in any consideration of the
state--is that using abstract concepts of this type and in this
fashion only detracts from the consideration of the actual needs
and problems of revolutionary social change. What is needed is
attention to the transformation of material and cultural conditions of the capitalist system, not the proclamation of an abstract right. As early as *The German Ideology*, Marx made this
point clear: only by "detaching" these abstract ideas from their
class origins and uses and attributing "to them an independent
existence"[19] can we speak of the "dominance" of an abstract concept such as freedom or equality. Detaching these concepts from
their real conditions only distorts them, however; it is only an
ideological use of "equality." Instead, according to Marx, the anarchists should have emphasized the origins, uses, and limitations
of any "right" within a given economic and cultural system.

Marx made a similar point in another context. In his critique
of Lassalle's view of wage labor, Marx criticized the Gotha Program's assertion that the German Workers' Party, in the course of
its struggle, should strive for "the removal of all social and

political inequality."[20] Marx's point is that this understanding
of the process of social change treats social and political inequality as abstract, that is, as having an independent existence,
determining the details of economic exploitation, rather than as
factors arising from and in a reciprocal relationship with the
economic conditions. According to Marx, "Instead of the indefinite
concluding phrase of the paragraph--'the removal of all social and
political [in]equality'--it ought to have been said that with the
abolition of class differences all the social and political inequality arising from them would disappear of itself."[21]

This, again, is Proudhon's mistake as well, according to
Marx. The abolition of the state for Proudhon and most anarchists
was identified with the abolition of all forms of exploitation and
injustice, or at least the two were causally linked, from the abolition of the state to the ending of all other forms of injustice.
The state, an independent and powerful entity dominating society
(including economic life), must be abolished, according to the
anarchists, in order to provide for a just and free life. In
another section of Marx's *Critique* important for this section,
Marx dealt directly with this conception of the state and with the
role of the state in communism.

In the fourth section of the Gotha Program, a call is made
for a state based on several principles, principles grouped under
"the free basis of the state," the "intellectual and moral basis
of the state," and the "economic basis of the state."[22] Marx immediately calls into question the notion of a "free state." In rejecting the Gotha Program's claim that the establishment of such a
free state is the goal of the workers, Marx characterizes freedom
as consisting not in a free state but in "converting the state
from an organ standing above society into one completely subordinated to it, and today also the forms of the state are more or less
free to the extent that they restrict the 'freedom of the
state.'"[23] The Gotha Program did not account for this sense of
freedom. Rather, in the program freedom consists in "freeing the
state," that is, in "liberating" the state so that the state, as
an independent entity, could foster change. According to Marx,
this brand of socialism is superficial in that, "instead of

treating existing society (and this holds good of any future one)
as the *basis* of the existing state (or of the future state in the
case of future society) it treats the state rather as an independent entity that possesses its own *intellectual, moral and free*
basis."[24]

This   position   criticized   by   Marx   was shared by the Gotha
Program and the anarchists. Stirner and Proudhon would agree with
Marx in rejecting the terminology of the "free [basis of the]
state," since for any anarchist this notion makes little sense.
Though the anarchists denied that the state could ever achieve a
truly moral and free basis, the key point--that the state is an
independent entity functioning or attempting to function as a determining force on society as a whole--is common to both types of
Marx's opponents. Marx denied this key point, holding instead that
the state (any given state) is the result of the economic conditions of its particular society. Where Stirner and Proudhon argue
that the state possesses an independent force and existence, Marx
attempts to show that the state's force is derived from (in capitalist society) the class structure of its society and that its
existence is perpetuated and circumscribed (though not determined)
by the economic conditions of that society. Where the anarchists
argue that the removal of the state would eliminate the destructive force of the state and thus liberate society, Marx instead
argues that society--particularly the economic conditions of
society--must itself be transformed in order to weaken any power
exercised by the state.

For the Gotha Program, the result of this fundamental error
was a call for what Marx termed "nothing beyond the old familiar
democratic litany. . . ."[25] What the Gotha Program and the anarchists had done was confuse the results of political emancipation
--the formation of a "free state," to some degree--with human
emancipation, though again Marx does not use such terminology in
the *Critique*. Had the Gotha Program's authors seen through the abstractions of the "present-day state" and "present-day society,"
they would have seen that, though all present-day societies were
in varying degrees of capitalist development, states take quite
differing forms. The "free state" exists, to a certain extent ac-

cording to Marx, alongside the capitalist society, in such coun-
tries as the United States and Switzerland.[26] Thus, the Lassallean
emphasis on political change, on political emancipation, blinded
them to what Marx sees as the real basis for change: the abolition
of bourgeois society, the transformation of the economic order
through class struggle. Marx does not propose abandoning political
struggle, as did the anarchists. Rather, he insists that political
struggle and its results, while important prerequisites, only pre-
sage the struggle for the complete transformation (what in his
earlier works he called the human emancipation) of society. It is
the role of the state in this revolutionary process that concerns
Marx near the end of the *Critique*. If Marx is correct and the anarchists mistaken, then the state poses no independent "danger,"
only a danger in so far as it serves and is supported by an exploitative economic system. Nor does any state hold any independent promise for the future, as the Gotha Program had implied.

Marx dealt with the question of the transformation of the
state in communist society in the *Critique*, though his treatment
of the issue is brief and must be considered in its polemical
context. Marx stresses that the form and function of a transitional "state" could only be determined "scientifically," and that
simply calling an institution a "people's state" will not yield
any relevant information.[27] As for Marx's conclusion concerning
the role of state authority in the transition, he holds: "Between
capitalist and communist society lies the period of the revolutionary transformation of the one into the other. There corresponds to this also a political transition period in which the
state can be nothing but *the revolutionary dictatorship of the
proletariat*."[28]

Thus, in the transitional period, the state--having been
transformed into an instrument of the working class--acts so as to
complete the revolution. This is the position taken by Marx in *The
Communist Manifesto* (see especially Chapter 2)[29] and in *The Poverty of Philosophy*. Marx's fully developed view, then, sees the
state as an instrument in the transitional period, moving from the
bourgeois state to the worker's "state" and, eventually, to the
abolition or rather the transcendence of the state as society

moved to that higher form of communism. In this higher form of communism which Marx has discussed in the *Critique*, the alienating, exploitative conditions of capitalism as a form of economic and cultural life have been overcome. Only at this point can the need for institutional authority be transcended, where class struggle has been supplanted by human emancipation.

This view of the state relies on Marx's assumption that the state as a political institution is not and does not become a completely autonomous entity before, during, or after the revolution nor an entity above and beyond the economic conditions of the revolutionary society. Marx's view results from his investigation of the economic basis of the political state and the dialectical interaction between the state and economic forces in capitalist society. Where the anarchists err, according to Marx, is in ignoring the role of economic forces or in relegating them to the realm of mere products of the actions of the political state. The important differences in approach result in the incompatibility of Marxian thought and that of the early anarchists.[30]

THE INCOMPATIBILITY OF MARXISM AND ANARCHISM

Despite attempts to bridge the theoretical gaps serious differences remain between Marx and the anarchists and between anarchism and socialism generally. The locus of these differences, as has become evident throughout this work, is the nature, role, and causal efficacy of the political state.

Both Marx and Proudhon stressed the importance of the development of individuality in community, contrary to the individualist egoism of Stirner and his successors. Both Marx and Proudhon agreed that the existing political state plays some significant role in the obstruction of what Alan Ritter has aptly called "communal individuality,"[31] while Marx and Stirner agreed that the political state in capitalism inhibits and alienates the individual. Where the positions differ radically is in their views of the nature and degree of the obstructive role played by the political state.

For Godwin, Proudhon, Stirner, Bakunin--for all anarchists--
the political state, whatever particular form it might take in a
historical period or geographical area, is inherently destructive,
impeding communal individuality in its inevitable constriction of
individual freedom. As was seen especially in the chapter dealing
with Stirner, anarchists view the state as a relatively independent entity standing against and to a certain extent apart
from the other social, economic, and cultural spheres of life. For
Proudhon, the state could only serve the interests of the non-producers, as its nature was that of a parasite on the working class,
oppressing the working class. Proudhon claimed, repeatedly, that
any worker who joined the state in an effort to effect social
change thereby ceased to be a worker and could only turn against
the interests of the workers in an attempt to consolidate and
stabilize the state's power.

Although Proudhon (and to a lesser extent, Stirner) recognized the influence of economic and other conditions on the role
and power of the state, this influence was held to not extend to
the nature of the state. The anarchists, viewing the state as the
ultimate source of alienating authority, argued from the state to
society, from the form of political authority to the economic and
cultural forms of any given society. This direction of argumentation and mode of explanation stems from the anarchists' explicit
normative commitment to an independent, ahistorical sphere of
freedom inherent in human beings. This sphere of freedom could be
affected by economic conditions, and in his more pessimistic
moments Proudhon came close to Marx's view that the form and practice of freedom (and authority) find their origins in the existing
economic conditions of capitalist society, thence to interact dialectically with those conditions. This pessimism is never permanent in the anarchists, however, and had it become permanent in
any of the anarchists, his position as an anarchist would have become untenable. Time and again, the anarchists return to the view
that the state is the source of all oppression, that it supports
and perpetuates economic oppression, and that as the institutionalization of political authority it is a more or less successful
attempt to subjugate otherwise free human beings.

Marx views the political state in capitalist society as the expression and instrument of the dominant economic forces of capitalist society, both the expression of an alienated humanity and the instrument of economic domination. As has been seen, especially in examinations of *The Poverty of Philosophy* and the *Critique of the Gotha Programme*, Marx does not attempt to write about the concept of the state per se; his materialist and historical methodology required him to examine the economic origins of particular states, especially the state-forms found in capitalist society. For Marx, the state "as such" holds no mystical power, in fact no inherently destructive characteristics at all, since the state "as such" is a philosophical abstraction. Similarly, the exercise of authority is not thought by Marx to be inherently destructive, as has been seen in the first section of this chapter. What has been destructive in past state-forms and what is destructive in the state-forms common to capitalism is the use of specifically political authority in the service of the dominant class. It is this use of authority that Marx sees as ending in the communist transformation of society. When class society is abolished, the need for an instrument of class domination will disappear. When what Marx had called in his earlier works "human emancipation" supersedes political emancipation, the need for an authority acting as a "government of persons" or a "special repressive force" will disappear.[32]

The contours of any residual authority are especially unclear in Marx's account and must remain so. Unless one interprets (with Engels and Lenin) Marx's theory as predicting a final state of society, an end-stage of communism, the exact dimensions of authority in emancipated society must (with the force of methodology) remain undetermined. This is so because of Marx's early stated and consistently held commitment to the free praxis of individuals in emancipated society, where the process of emancipation is intimately tied to the development of that free praxis. Presumably, such a society would emphasize the free self-determination of individuals at the expense of present authoritative institutions, but the character of any residuum of authority is unclear. As John Plamenatz noted,

>   Marx and Engels . . . really believed that, where there were
>   no classes in their sense of the word, there would be no need
>   for many of the institutions of what we ordinarily understand
>   by the State. I say *many* advisedly and not *all*. . . . Marx
>   and Engels, like Saint-Simon before them, made a distinction
>   between *government* and *administration*, predicting the disap-
>   pearance in the classless society of only the first. Though
>   they did not . . . make it clear just what this distinction
>   amounts to, they seem to have included in administration some
>   of the activities usually called governmental.[33]

Neither Marx nor Engels (nor Lenin, for that matter) considered the presence of authoritative administrative functions to be
an inherent danger since, unlike the anarchists, Marx's arguments
and explanations recognize the reciprocal interaction between the
economic conditions of a given society and the political and legal
institutions and practices of that society, with the former taking
precedence. Marxian arguments are specifically material, economic,
and especially historical; anarchist arguments are generally ahistorical, abstract, and "philosophical." The "nature" of the state
is explained by Marx in an examination of the attributes of the
society in which the state exists, not by the postulation of an
inherent and unchangeable state-nature. Ritter has shown how the
putative existence of just such a state-nature has linked anarchists from Godwin through Bakunin. For Godwin, "government is,
abstractly then, an evil, an usurpation upon the private judgment
and individual conscience of mankind." For Bakunin, "despotism
lies less in the *form* of the state or of power than in their very
principle."[34] For any anarchist, any organization functioning as a
centralized source of authority is inherently destructive; it precluded the freedom of the Unique, communal individuality, human
emancipation, or whatever name is given for such a social transformation. For Marx, no political state has such causal efficacy.

Given these two very different starting-points, the disagree-
ments concerning the nature, role, and causal efficacy of the
state--at heart a disagreement concerning the nature of philosophical explanation and argument--Marx and the anarchists remain fundamentally at odds. In the end Marx and the anarchists and Marxism

and anarchism reflect fundamentally incompatible views of human beings and their place in the world.

NOTES

1. Albert Camus, *Notebooks 1942-1951*, trans. Justin O'Brien (New York: Alfred A. Knopf, 1966), notebook IV, July 1945, p. 104.

2. Reported by John Henry MacKay, Stirner's biographer, in *Max Stirner, Sein Leben und sein Werk* (Berlin: Schuster und Loeffler, 1898), cited in C-EGO, p. 24.

3. See James J. Martin's Introduction to S-EGO, xvi.

4. Mohandas K. Gandhi, *Hind Swaraj or Indian Home Rule*, chap. xvi, reprinted in John Somerville and Ronald E. Santoni, eds., *Social and Political Philosophy* (New York: Anchor Books, 1963), p. 503.

5. Friedrich Engels, "On Authority," in *Anarchism and Anarcho-Syndicalism*, (New York: International Publishers, 1972), pp. 101, 103.

6. Ibid., p. 74.

7. Friedrich Engels, "Letter to Carlo Cafiero" (July 1[-3], 1871), in ibid., p. 47.

8. Engels, "On Political Action of the Working Class" (1871), in ibid., p. 51.

9. Marx, "Letter to F. Bolte" (November 23, 1871), in ibid., p. 57.

10. See especially Engels, "Letter to C. Terzaghi" (January 14[-15], 1872), in ibid., p. 67. See also Marx's *The Civil War in France*, in *The Marx-Engels Reader*, ed. Robert C. Tucker (New York: W.W. Norton, 1972), pp. 526-576.

11. Karl Marx, *Critique of the Gotha Programme*, ed. C.P. Dutt (New York: International Publishers, 1973), p. 5.

12. "Programme of the German Worker's Party," in ibid., pp. 6 and 89.

13. Marx, CGP, p. 6.

14. Ibid., p. 9.

15. Ibid. See also Friedrich Engels, *Herr Eugen Dühring's*

Revolution in Science (Anti-Dühring), trans. Emile Burns, ed. C.P. Dutt (New York: International Publishers, 1966):

> From the moment when the bourgeois demand for the abolition of class *privileges* was put forward, alongside of it appeared the proletarian demand for the abolition of the *classes themselves*. . . . The proletarians took the bourgeoisie at their word: equality must not be merely apparent, must not apply merely to the sphere of the state, but must also be real, must be extended to the social and economic sphere. . . . The real content of the proletarian demand for equality is the demand for the *abolition of classes*. Any demand for equality which goes beyond that, of necessity passes into absurdity. (Pp. 117, 118.)

Engels's last sentence in this quotation does not follow from his previous statements. It seems contrary to the emancipatory spirit of Marx's work.

16. V.I. Lenin, *The State and Revolution* (Peking: Foreign Language Press, 1976), p. 115. See also the quotation from Lenin's *Selected Works*, in the notes to Marx's CGP, p. 97, n. 11.

17. Marx, CGP, p. 10.

18. Ibid.

19. Marx and Engels, *The German Ideology*, I, in *MECW* V, p.60.

20. "Programme of the German Worker's Party," in CGP, pp. 14 and 89.

21. Marx, CGP, p. 15, reading "political equality" as an error.

22. "Programme of the German Worker's Party," in CGP, p. 90.

23. Marx, CGP, p. 17.

24. Ibid.

25. Ibid., p. 18.

26. Ibid.

27. Ibid.

28. Ibid.

29. Karl Marx and Friedrich Engels, *The Communist Manifesto*, trans. Samuel Moore, introduction A.J.P. Taylor (Harmonsworth: Penguin Books, 1967), esp. p. 105.

30. An important attempt at theoretical anarchism that at-

tempts to account for the dialectical relationship between political institutions and material, economic forces, while stressing
the constitutive role of the freedom of individual praxis is the
account of institutions, sovereignty, and the state in Jean-Paul
Sartre, *Critique of Dialectical Reason*, vol. I, trans. Alan
Sheridan-Smith, ed. Jonathan Ree (London: New Left Books; Atlantic
Highlands, N.J.: Humanities Press, 1976). Sartre's theoretical
social anarchism meets some of Marx's objections to the classical
anarchist stance. For a critical examination of Sartre's account,
see J. Barker, "Sartre's Dialectical Anarchism: Institution, Sovereignty, and the State," *Cogito* (II:2, June 1984), pp. 93-115.
Despite Sartre's advances, important difficulties remain for any
attempt to reconcile Marxism and anarchism.

31. See Alan Ritter, *Anarchism* (Cambridge: Cambridge University Press, 1980), pp. 2-5, 124.

32. Engels, "In Italy," and "The Workingmen of Europe in
1877," in *Anarchism and Anarcho-Syndicalism*, pp. 158, 160. See
also *Anti-Dühring*, p. 307.

33. John Plamenatz, *Man and Society*, vol. II (New York:
McGraw-Hill, 1963), p. 373. The distinction was also used by
Proudhon.

34. Godwin, *Enquiry Concerning Political Justice*, vol. II, p.
2; Bakunin, *Oeuvres*, vol. II, p. 327, in Ritter, p. 127.

BIBLIOGRAPHY

TEXTS CITED

Althusser, Louis. *For Marx*. Trans. Ben Brewster. New York: Vintage, 1970.

Aptheker, Herbert, ed. *Marxism and Democracy*. New York: Humanities Press, for American Institute of Marxist Studies, 1965.

Avineri, Shlomo. *Hegel's Theory of the Modern State*. Cambridge: Cambridge University Press, 1972.

---. *The Social and Political Thought of Karl Marx*. Cambridge: Cambridge University Press, 1968.

Buber, Martin. *Paths in Utopia*. Trans. R.F.C. Hull. Boston, Mass.: Beacon Press, 1958.

Camus, Albert. *The Myth of Sisyphus*. Trans. Justin O'Brien. New York: Vintage, 1955.

---. *Notebooks 1942-1951*. Trans. Justin O'Brien. New York: Alfred A. Knapf, 1966.

---. *The Rebel: An Essay on Man in Revolt*. Trans. Anthony Bower. New York: Vintage, 1956.

Carroll, John. *Break-out from the Crystal Palace: The Anarcho-Psychological Critique: Stirner, Nietzsche, Dostoevsky*. London, Boston: Routledge & Kegan Paul, 1974.

Chiaromonte, Nicola. "Pierre-Joseph Proudhon: An Uncomfortable Thinker." *Politics* III (January 1946): 2-29.

Christensen, Kit. "The Concept of 'Species-Being' in the Works of

Feuerbach and Marx." Unpublished Ph.D. diss. Purdue University, 1982.

Eltzbacher, Paul. *Anarchism: Exponents of the Anarchist Philosophy*. Trans. Steven T. Byington; ed. James J. Martin. New York: Libertarian Book Club, 1960.

Engels, Friedrich. *Herr Eugen Dühring's Revolution in Science (Anti-Dühring)*. Trans. Emile Burns; ed. C.P. Dutt. New York: International Publishers, 1966.

Feuerbach, Ludwig. *The Essence of Christianity*. Trans. George Eliot. New York: Harper and Row, 1957.

Godwin, William. *Enquiry Concerning Political Justice*. Ed. K. Codell Carter. London: Oxford University Press, 1971.

Goethe, Johann Wolfgang v. *Goethes Werke*. Band I, Weimer Ausgabe. Weimar: Hermann Bohlau, 1887.

Guérin, Daniel. *Anarchism from Theory to Practice*. Trans. Mary Klopper. New York: Monthly Review Press, 1970.

Hegel, G.W.F. *Berliner Schriften*, 1818-1831. Ed. J. Hoffmeister. Band XI. Hamburg: Verlag von Felix Meiner, 1956.

---. *The Phenomenology of Mind*. Trans. with notes and introduction J. B. Baillie; new introduction George Lichtheim. New York: Harper Colophon, 1967.

---. *The Philosophy of History*. Prefaces Charles Hegel and trans. J. Sibree; introduction C.J. Friedrich. New York: Dover Publications, 1956.

---. *The Philosophy of Right*. Trans. and notes T.M. Knox. London: Oxford University Press, 1967.

Hoffman, Robert L. *Revolutionary Justice: The Social and Political Theory of P.-J. Proudhon*. Urbana, Ill.: University of Illinois Press, 1972.

Hume, David. *A Treatise of Human Nature*. Ed. L.A. Selby-Bigge; rev. P.H. Nidditch. Oxford: Clarendon Press, 1978.

Joll, James. *The Anarchists*. Boston: Little, Brown/Atlantic Monthly Press, 1964 and 2d ed. Cambridge, Mass.: Harvard University Press, 1980.

Kemp, Jonathan, ed. *Diderot, Interpreter of Nature*. 2d ed. Trans. Jean Stuart and Jonathan Kemp. New York: International Publishers, 1963.

Kropotkin, Peter. *The Great French Revolution*. New York: Schocken Books, 1971; London: Orbach and Chambers, 1971.

Lenin, V.I. *The State and Revolution*. Peking: Foreign Language Press, 1976.

Lukes, Steven. *Individualism* (Key Concepts in the Social Sciences). New York: Harper and Row, 1973.

McLellan, David. *The Young Hegelians and Karl Marx*. London: Macmillan, 1969.

Marx, Karl. *Capital*. Vol. I. Trans. Samuel Moore and Edward Aveling. New York: International Publishers, 1967.

----. *Critique of Hegel's "Philosophy of Right."* Trans. Annette Jolin; ed. and introduction Joseph O'Malley. Cambridge: Cambridge University Press, 1970.

----. *Critique of the Gotha Programme*. Rev. trans., ed. C.P. Dutt. New York: International Publishers, 1973.

----. *The Economic and Philosophic Manuscripts of 1844*. Ed. and introduction Dirk J. Struik; trans. Martin Milligan. New York: International Publishers, 1964.

----. *The Poverty of Philosophy: Response to 'The Philosophy of Poverty' of M. Proudhon*. Moscow: Progress Publishers, 1955.

Marx, Karl, and Friedrich Engels. *The Communist Manifesto*. Trans. Samuel Moore; introduction A.J.P. Taylor. Harmondsworth: Penguin Books, 1967.

----. *The German Ideology*. Part 1. Ed. and introduction C.J. Arthur. New York: International Publishers, 1970.

----. *Marx-Engels Collected Works*. New York: International Publishers, 1975 *et seq.*

----. *Anarchism and Anarcho-Syndicalism: Selected Writings by Marx, Engels, Lenin*. New York: International Publishers, 1972.

Megill, Kenneth A. *The New Democratic Theory*. London: The Free Press, 1970.

Mézáros, István. *Marx's Theory of Alienation*. London: Merlin Press, 1970.

Moore, Stanley. *Marx on the Choice between Socialism and Communism*. Cambridge, Mass.: Harvard University Press, 1980.

Pascal, Blaise. *The Thoughts of Blaise Pascal*. New York: Dolphin Books, n.d.

Paterson, R.W.K. *The Nihilistic Egoist: Max Stirner*. London: Oxford University Press, 1971

Pennock, J. Roland, and John W. Chapman, eds. *Anarchism: Nomos XIX*. New York: New York University Press, 1978.

Plamenatz, John. *Man and Society*. 2 vols. New York: McGraw-Hill, 1963.

Plato. *Euthyphro*. Trans. Lane Cooper in *The Collected Dialogues of Plato*, ed. Edith Hamilton and Huntington Cairns. Princeton, N.J.: Princeton University Press, 1961.

Plekhanov, George. *Marxism and Anarchism*. Trans. Eleanor Marx Aveling. Chicago: Charles Kerr, 1918.

Proudhon, Pierre-Joseph. *The General Idea of the Revolution in the Nineteenth Century*. Trans. J.B. Robinson. New York: Vanguard Press, 1923; New York: Haskell House Publishers, 1969.

---. *Selected Writings of Pierre-Joseph Proudhon*. Ed. Stewart Edwards; trans. Elizabeth Fraser. New York: Anchor Books, 1969. London: Macmillan, 1970.

---. *System of Economic Contradictions, or the Philosophy of Misery*. 2 vols. Trans. Benjamin R. Tucker, from *Works of P.-J. Proudhon*. Boston: Benjamin R. Tucker, 1888.

---. *What Is Property? An Inquiry into the Principle of Right and Government*. Trans. Benjamin Tucker, with a new introduction George Woodcock. New York: Dover Publications, 1970.

Ritter, Alan. *Anarchism*. Cambridge: Cambridge University Press, 1980.

---. *The Political Thought of Pierre-Joseph Proudhon*. Princeton: Princeton University Press, 1969.

Rousseau, Jean-Jacques. *The Social Contract*. Ed. Charles Frankel. New York: Hefner, 1954.

Runkle, Gerald. *Anarchism: Old and New*. New York: Dell Publishing Co., Inc., 1972.

Sartre, Jean-Paul. *Critique of Dialectical Reason*. Trans. Alan Sheridan-Smith; ed. Jonathan Reé. London: New Left Books; Atlantic Highlands, N.J.: Humanities Press, 1976.

Schapiro, J.S. "Pierre-Joseph Proudhon, Harbinger of Fascism" in *American Historical Review*. Vol. L, no. 4 (July 1945); 714-737.

Stearns,   Peter N. *Revolutionary Syndicalism and French Labor.* New
Brunswick, N.J.: Rutgers University Press, 1971.

Steinbeck, John. *East of Eden.* New York: Viking Press, 1952.

Stepelevich, Lawrence S. *The Young Hegelians.* Cambridge: Cambridge
University Press, 1983.

Stirner, Max [pseud.]. *Der Einzige und sein Eigenthum.* 2d ed.
Leipzig: Wigand, 1882.

---. *The Ego and His Own.* Trans. Steven T. Byington. New York:
Libertarian Book Club, 1963.

---. *The Ego and His Own.* Trans. Steven T. Byington; ed., and
introduction, and trans. rev. John Carroll. New York: Harper
Torchbooks, 1974.

Stroud, Barry. *Hume.* Boston: Routledge & Kegan Paul, 1977.

Taylor,   Charles. *Hegel.* Cambridge: Cambridge University Press,
1975.

Thomas,   Paul. *Karl Marx and the Anarchists.* London: Routledge &
Kegan Paul, 1980.

Tucker,   D.F.B. *Marxism and Individualism.* New York: St. Martin's
Press, 1980.

Tucker,   Robert   C. *The Marx-Engels Reader.* Ed. and introduction
Robert C. Tucker. New York: W.W. Norton & Co., 1972.

Vlastos,   Gregory. *The Philosophy of Socrates.* New York: Anchor
Books, 1971.

Woodcock, George. *P.-J. Proudhon.* London: Macmillan, 1956.

GENERAL REFERENCES

Abad de Santillian, Diego. *After the Revolution.* New York: Green-
berg, 1937 (Translation of *El Organismo Economico de la
Revolucion.* Barcelona, 1937).

Aronson,   Ronald. *Jean-Paul Sartre--Philosophy in the World.* London: New Left Books; New York: Schocken Books, 1980.

Avrich,   Paul, ed. *The Anarchists in the Russian Revolution.* London: Thames and Hudson, 1973.

Bakunin,   Mikhail Aleksandrovich. *Bakunin on Anarchy: Selected
Works by the Activist-Founder of World Anarchism.* Ed.,

trans., and introduction Sam Dolgoff; preface Paul Avrich. New York: Alfred A. Knopf, 1971.

---. *Bakunin's Writings*. Ed. Guy A. Aldred. New York: Gordon Press, 1973.

---. *God and the State*. 1916. Reprint. New introduction Paul Avrich. New York: Dover Publications, 1970.

---. *The Knouto-Germanic Empire and the Social Revolution*. New York: Mother Earth Publishing Association, 1916.

---. *Michael Bakunin: Selected Writings*. Ed. Arthur Lehning. New York: Grove Press, 1975.

---. *The Political Philosophy of Bakunin: Scientific Anarchism*. Comp. and ed. G.P. Maximoff; introduction Rudolph Rocker; biographical sketch Max Nettlau. Glencoe, Ill.: Free Press, 1953.

---. *Selected Writings*. Trans. Steven Cox and Olive Stevens; introduction Arthur Lehning. London: Cape, 1976.

Baldelli, Giovanni. *Social Anarchism*. Chicago: Aldine, Atherton, 1971.

Berkman, Alexander. *The "Anti-Climax": The Concluding Chapter of My Russian Diary*. Berlin: Maurer and Demmick, 1925.

---. *The Bolshevik Myth (Diary, 1920-22)*. New York: Boni and Liveright, 1925.

Berlin, Isaiah. *Karl Marx: His Life and Environment*. 4th ed. London: Oxford University Press, 1978.

Bookchin, Murray. *The Spanish Anarchists: The Heroic Years 1868-1936*. New York: Free Life Editions, 1977.

Bottomore, T.B. *Karl Marx: Early Writings*. New York: McGraw-Hill, 1964.

Brenan, Gerald. *The Spanish Labyrinth*. London, 1943; Cambridge: Cambridge University Press, 1969.

Camus, Albert. *Resistance, Rebellion, and Death*. Trans. Justin O'Brien. New York: Vintage, 1974.

Carr, E.H. *Michael Bakunin*. London: Macmillan and Co., 1937.

Chiodi, Pietro. *Sartre and Marxism*. London: The Harvester Press, 1976.

Cohn-Bendit, Daniel and Gabriel Cohn-Bendit. *Obsolete Communism, The Left-Wing Alternative*. Trans. Arnold Pomerans. London:

Andre Deutsch Ltd., Penguin, 1968.

Dahl, Robert A. *After the Revolution? Authority in a Good Society*. New Haven: Yale University Press, 1970.

Dolgoff, Sam, ed. *The Anarchist Collective: Workers Self-Management in the Spanish Revolution 1936-1939*. New York: Free Life Editions, 1977.

Durant, Will. *Socialism and Anarchism*. New York: Albert and Charles Boni, 1914.

Ehrlich, Howard J., ed. *Reinventing Anarchy: What are Anarchists Thinking These Days?* London, Boston: Routledge & Kegan Paul, 1979.

Frei, Bruno. *Die anarchistische Utopie, Freiheit u. Ordnung*. Frankfurt a.M.: Verlag Marxistische Blatter, 1971.

Goldman, Emma. *Anarchism and Other Essays*. New York: Mother Earth Publishing Association, 1910 or 1911[?] (University Microfilms reprint).

---. *Living My Life*. Garden City, New York: Garden City Publishing Co., 1934.

---. *My Disillusionment in Russia*. Garden City, New York: Doubleday, Page, 1923.

Herzen, Alexander. *From the Other Shore*. Trans. Moura Budberg; introduction Isaiah Berlin. London: Weidenfeld and Nicolson, 1956.

Horowitz, Irving L., ed. *The Anarchists*. Introduction I.L. Horowitz. New York: Dell Publishing Co., 1964.

Krimerman, L., and L. Perry, eds. *Patterns of Anarchy*. Garden City, New York: Anchor Books, 1966.

Kropotkin, Peter. *The Conquest of Bread*. New York: Vanguard Press, 1927 (University Microfilms reprint).

---. *The Essential Kropotkin*. Ed. Emile Capouya and Keith Thompkins. New York: Liveright, 1976.

---. *Ethics*. New York: Tudor Publishing, 1947; New York: Benjamin Blom, 1968.

---. *Fields, Factories and Workshops [Tomorrow]*. London: Hutchinson, 1899; Boston: Houghton, Mifflin & Co., 1899. Under amended title, ed. Colin Ward: New York: Harper and Row, 1974.

---. *Kropotkin's Revolutionary Pamphlets: A Collection of Writings*. Ed. and introduction Roger N. Baldwin. New York: Benjamin Blom, 1968.

---. *Mutual Aid: A Factor of Evolution*. Ed. Ashley Montague. Boston: Extending Horizons, 1955; London: Allen Lane, 1972.

---. *Selected Writings on Anarchism and Revolution*. Ed. and introduction Martin A. Miller. Cambridge, Mass.: MIT Press, 1970.

---. *The State: Its Historic Role*. Trans. V. Richards. London: Freedom Press, 1969.

Lenin, V.I. *What is to be Done? Burning Questions of our Movement*. Moscow: Foreign Languages Publishing House, n.d.

Lévy, Bernard-Henri. *Barbarism with a Human Face*. Trans. George Holoch. New York: Harper and Row, 1979.

Lichtheim, George. *Marxism, an Historical and Critical Study*. New York: Prager, 1971.

McBride, William L. *Fundamental Change in Law and Society*. The Hague/Paris: Mouton, 1970.

---. *Social Theory at the Crossroads*. Pittsburgh: Duquesne University Press, 1980.

McLellan, David. *Karl Marx: His Life and Thought*. London: Macmillan, 1973.

Manicas, Peter T. *The Death of the State*. New York: Capricon Books/G. Putnam's Sons, 1974.

Marcuse, Herbert. *One-Dimensional Man: Studies in the Ideology of Advanced Industrial Society*. Boston: Beacon Press, 1966.

---. *Reason and Revolution, Hegel and the Rise of Social Theory*. Boston: Beacon Press, 1960.

Marković, Mihailo. *From Affluence to Praxis, Philosophy and Social Criticism*. Ann Arbor: University of Michigan Press, 1974.

Marx, Karl. *Grundrisse*. Trans. and introduction Martin Nicolaus. Harmondsworth: Penguin, 1973.

---. *Theories of Surplus Value*, 3 vols. Moscow: Foreign Languages Publishing House, 1972.

Marx, Karl and Friedrich Engels. *Marx-Engels Selected Correspondence*. Moscow: Foreign Languages Publishing House, 1965.

---. *Marx-Engels Werke*. Berlin: Dietz Verlag, 1956 *et seq*.

Masters, Anthony. *Bakunin, The Father of Anarchy*. New York: Saturday Review Press, 1974.

Miliband, Ralph. *Marxism and Politics*. London: Oxford University Press, 1977.

Nomad, Max [pseud.]. *Aspects of Revolt*. New York: Burns & Mac Eachern, 1959.

Nozick, Robert. *Anarchy, State, and Utopia*. New York: Basic Books, 1974.

Perlin, Terry M., ed. *Contemporary Anarchism*. New Brunswick, N.J.: Transaction Books, 1979.

Proudhon, Pierre-Joseph. *Solution of the Social Problem*. New York: Vanguard Press, 1927.

Pyziur, Eugene. *The Doctrine of Anarchism of Michael A. Bakunin*. Chicago: Gateway, 1968.

Read, Herbert. E., ed. *Anarchy and Order*. Introduction Howard Zinn. Boston: Beacon Press, 1971.

---. *Existentialism, Marxism, and Anarchism*. London: Freedom Press, 1949.

---. *Kropotkin: Selections from his Writings*. London: Freedom Press, 1942.

Reiman, Jeffrey H. *In Defense of Political Philosophy: A Reply to Robert Paul Wolff's in Defense of Anarchism*. New York: Harper and Row, 1972.

Schwarz, Frederick. *The Three Faces of Revolution: Communism, Radicalism, and Anarchism*. Washington, D.C.: Capitol Hill Press, 1972.

Stojanovic, Svetozar. *Between Ideals and Reality*. New York: Oxford University Press, 1971.

Tucker, Robert C. *Philosophy and Myth in Karl Marx*. Cambridge: Cambridge University Press, 1967.

Ward, Colin. *Anarchy in Action*. New York: Harper and Row, 1973.

Wolff, Robert Paul. *In Defense of Anarchism*. 2d ed. New York: Harper and Row, 1976.

Wolff, R.P., Barrington Moore, and Herbert Marcuse. *A Critique of Pure Tolerance*. Boston: Beacon Press, 1970.

Woodcock, George. *Anarchism*. Harmondsworth: Penguin, 1962.

INDEX

About the Author

JEFFREY H. BARKER is Assistant Professor of Philosophy at Albright College, Reading, Pennsylvania. His articles have appeared in *Cogito: An International Journal for Philosophy, Society, and Politics* and *Eros: Journal of Philosophy and the Literary Arts.*

T.S